D0876408

WINSTON CHURCHILL

By the same author:

HMS Hood: *Pride of the Royal Navy,* Stackpole Books, Mechanicsburg, PA, USA, 2001

By Swords Divided: Corfe Castle in the Civil War, Halsgrove, Tiverton, 2003

Thomas Hardy: Behind the Inscrutable Smile, Halsgrove, Tiverton, 2003

Tyneham: The Lost Village of Dorset, Halsgrove, Tiverton, 2003

T E Lawrence: Unravelling the Enigma, Halsgrove, Tiverton, 2003

Sir Francis Drake: Behind the Pirate's Mask, Halsgrove, Tiverton, 2004

Dunshay: Reflections on a Dorset Manor House, Halsgrove, Tiverton, 2004

Robert Mugabe and the Betrayal of Zimbabwe, McFarland & Company Inc., Jefferson, NC, USA, 2004

Enid Blyton and her Enchantment with Dorset, Halsgrove, Tiverton, 2005

Thomas Hardy: Christmas Carollings, Halsgrove, Tiverton, 2005

Adolf Hitler: The Final Analysis, Spellmount, Staplehurst, 2005

Agatha Christie: The Finished Portrait, Tempus Publishing, Stroud, 2007

Mugabe: Teacher, Revolutionary, Tyrant, The History Press, Stroud, 2008

The Story of George Loveless and the Tolpuddle Martyrs, Halsgrove, Tiverton, 2008

Agatha Christie: The Pitkin Guide, Pitkin Publishing, 2009

Purbeck Personalities, Halsgrove, Tiverton, 2009

Arthur Conan Doyle: The Man behind Sherlock Holmes, The History Press, Stroud, 2009

Father of the Blind: A Portrait of Sir Arthur Pearson, The History Press, Stroud, 2009

Jane Austen: An Unrequited Love, The History Press, Stroud, 2009

Bournemouth's Founders and Famous Visitors, The History Press, Stroud, 2010

Hitler: Dictator or Puppet?, Pen and Sword Books, Barnsley, 2011

WINSTON CHURCHILL

Portrait of an Unquiet Mind

Andrew Norman

Pen & Sword
MILITARY

First published in Great Britain in 2012
By Pen and Sword Military
an imprint of
Pen and Sword Books Ltd
47 Church Street
Barnsley
South Yorkshire S70 2AS

Copyright © Andrew Norman, 2012

ISBN 978 1 84884 677 7

The right of Andrew Norman to be identified
as the author of this work has been asserted by him in accordance
with the Copyright, Designs and Patents Act 1988.

A CIP record for this book is available from the British Library.

All rights reserved. No part of this book may be reproduced or transmitted
in any form or by any means, electronic or mechanical including photocopying,
recording or by any information storage and retrieval
system, without permission from the Publisher in writing.

Printed and bound in England by
CPI Group (UK) Ltd, Croydon, CR0 4YY

Typeset in Times New Roman by
Chic Media Ltd

Pen & Sword Books Ltd incorporates the imprints of
Pen & Sword Aviation, Pen & Sword Family History, Pen & Sword Maritime,
Pen & Sword Military, Pen & Sword Discovery, Wharncliffe Local History,
Wharncliffe True Crime, Wharncliffe Transport, Pen & Sword Select,
Pen & Sword Military Classics, Leo Cooper, Remember When,
The Praetorian Press, Seaforth Publishing and Frontline Publishing

For a complete list of Pen and Sword titles please contact
Pen and Sword Books Limited
47 Church Street, Barnsley, South Yorkshire, S70 2AS, England
E-mail: enquiries@pen-and-sword.co.uk
Website: www.pen-and-sword.co.uk

Contents

Acknowledgements

Lord Alexander, Rita M. Bosworth, David Cooper, Nicholas Dragffy, John Forster, John Gill, Irene Heath, Caroline Herbert, Dr Elbushra Herieka, Nicola Hilton, His Grace the Duke of Marlborough, Isabel McMann, Lord Moran, Katherine Thomson, Karen Wiseman.

Churchill Archives Centre, Churchill College, Cambridge, UK; City of London Cemetery and Crematorium; Elstree School, Woolhampton, Berkshire; Harrow School; Oxford University Archives, Bodleian Library, Oxford; Poole Central Library; Poole Hospital Library; Radcliffe Science Library, Oxford. I am most grateful to Tarka King for allowing me access to the Tara King Papers, and to Leonie and Luiz Monteiro de Barros for kindly transcribing them for me.

I am enormously indebted, as ever, to my beloved wife Rachel.

'I don't know why I get depressed as I do. Is much known about worry, Charles?'

Winston Churchill, in conversation with his doctor, Lord Moran, from Lord Moran, *Winston Churchill: The Struggle for Survival 1940-1965*, pp.600 & 167.

* * *

'I rack my brains, wondering what I can do. That I am so useless to him torments me.'

Lord Moran, writing in his diary about his patient, Winston Churchill, from Lord Moran, *Winston Churchill: The Struggle for Survival 1940-1965*, p.754.

Preface

The name Winston Churchill conjures up various images in the mind. A figure standing on the deck of a warship, in the dark days of the Second World War, holding onto the guard rail and staring grimly out onto a sombre sea; a figure with bowler hat, walking stick, and cigar, clambering over the rubble of what were once people's homes, following the attentions of the *Luftwaffe* in the London Blitz; and finally, a figure standing triumphantly on the balcony of Buckingham Palace, waving to the adoring throng below and giving them the 'Victory' sign. For, during the Second World War, Winston had provided a beacon of leadership and hope, around which the forces of the 'free world' could rally and direct their energies towards destroying Hitler's Nazi regime. Not for nothing was Winston regarded universally as the saviour of the 'free world'.

So much for the public face, epitomizing doggedness, courage, boundless energy, and the unshakeable belief that, in the end, Britain and her Allies would prevail. However, Winston's writings and correspondence, together with the testimonies of those closest to him, reveal a completely different side to Winston: a deeply insecure person who required continual reassurance; one who was prone to bouts of depression – which he called the 'Black Dog'. Perhaps what perplexed Winston's family, friends, colleagues, and acquaintances most of all was the seeming existence of three Winstons embodied in one and the same person: one who experienced extreme 'highs', alternating with extreme 'lows', and in between times, one who remained on a fairly even keel.

Winston had sufficient insight to realize that all was not as it should be as far as his make-up was concerned. He voiced his fears to his doctor, Lord Moran, who confessed that he did not know the answer either, and could only attribute it, vaguely, to what he called the 'Churchill melancholia'. To be fair, however, Moran was a physician and not a psychiatrist. So why did Winston's doctor not seek psychiatric help and advice for his patient? Perhaps for several reasons. He was afraid of what Winston's reaction might have been, and of any stigma and consequent damage to Winston's reputation; also of what treatment a psychiatrist might recommend, and if so what adverse side effects there might be. In the event, and probably because he felt protective towards his patient, Moran decided that he himself was capable of seeing Winston through the bad times.

Although the workings of Winston's mind were understood neither by Winston himself, nor by his doctor, Lord Moran, clues as to his character traits are discernable as his life unfolds. The challenge is to recognize these clues for what they are. Finally, when the various components are added together to complete the canvas – an analogy which Winston, as a painter, undoubtedly would have appreciated – then, and only then, does the complete picture emerge, enabling Winston's true nature finally to be revealed and understood.

CHAPTER 1

Formative Years

Winston Leonard Spencer Churchill was born on 30 November 1874 at Blenheim Palace, Oxfordshire, family seat of the Dukes of Marlborough and then the home of his paternal grandfather, John, the 7th Duke and his wife Frances, daughter of the 3rd Marquess of Londonderry. The palace, a country house with 320 rooms, built in the English baroque style and set in 2,700 acres of parkland, was designed by architect, Sir John Vanbrugh. It was presented to Winston's ancestor, John Churchill, 1st Duke of Marlborough, Queen Anne's commander-in-chief during the War of the Spanish Succession, by a grateful Parliament. This followed the Duke's victory over the French in the Battle of Blenheim, which took place on 13 August 1704.

*　*　*

Years later, Winston's granddaughter, Celia Sandys, declared:

My grandfather was born in one of the grandest places in England. He was pugnacious looking, with bright red hair. He was quite clearly a very curious [i.e. full of curiosity] child, and one of the subjects that fascinated him was history, and in particular, battles. He couldn't have failed to have been impressed by the sight of his ancestor on his horse [as depicted] in the tapestry in these huge rooms – they would have seemed huge to a little boy.[1]

Winston's father was Conservative (Tory) politician, Lord Randolph Henry Spencer Churchill. His mother, Jeanette (Lady Randolph) née Jerome, and known as Jennie, was the daughter of a New York financier whose ancestors had fought against Britain in the American War of Independence. The Churchill family home was 48 Charles Street, Mayfair, London. Money was not plentiful, Lord Randolph being the second son (and therefore not the heir to the Blenheim Estate), but it helped matters that on her marriage to Lord Randolph, his wife was able to provide a dowry of £50,000.

1

Winston's birth followed 'a rather imprudent and rough drive in a pony carriage'[2] by his mother, Lady Randolph, as she was returning to Blenheim Palace, where she was staying. This brought on labour pains and caused the infant to be born prematurely.

From January 1877 until spring 1880, the Churchills lived in Ireland in the capital city of Dublin, where Lord Randolph served as unofficial private secretary to his father, John, the 7th Duke, who had been appointed Lord-Lieutenant of that country by Conservative Prime Minister, Benjamin Disraeli. It was here, at the family home 'The Little Lodge', says Winston, that he was 'first menaced with education'.[3] Reading, writing, and, in particular, arithmetic, which he found difficult, taught to him by his governess (unidentified), 'cast a steadily gathering shadow over my daily life … [and] took away from [i.e. detracted from] all the interesting things one wanted to do in the nursery, or in the garden'.[4] However, when he did have the opportunity to retreat to the nursery, there were 'wonderful toys' to play with, which included 'a real steam engine, a magic lantern [apparatus for projecting pictures or slides onto a screen], and a collection of soldiers – already nearly a thousand strong'.[5]

Winston's brother, John Strange Spencer Churchill – known as Jack (who was his only sibling) – was born on 4 February 1880. Jack was, therefore, fully five years Winston's junior. However, the brothers were to develop an excellent relationship, despite the difference in their ages. As for their mother, Lady Randolph, she was popular in Ireland for the way she assisted her husband, Lord Randolph, in his role of secretary of a fund set up by the Duchess of Marlborough, the object of which was to combat the famine caused by repeated failures of the harvest from 1878 to 1880. In that same month of February 1880 the Churchills returned to England in preparation for the general election to be held in March/April. The outcome was that the Conservative Party, led by Benjamin Disraeli, was defeated by William Gladstone's Liberal Party. However, Lord Randolph retained his parliamentary seat as Member for Woodstock, Oxfordshire. The Churchills now took up residence at 29 St James's Place, Westminster.

To Winston, Lady Randolph, whom he idolized, seemed like 'a fairy princess: a radiant being possessed of limitless riches and power'.[6] In January 1882, and now aged seven, he wrote to her when she was absent from home, to thank her 'for the beautiful presents [of] those Soldiers and Flags and Castle'.[7] And in March, Winston wrote to his father, Lord Randolph, describing how, in the grounds of Blenheim Palace he had found 'a lot of primroses every day [and had] bought a basket to put them in'.[8]

In November 1882, Winston was sent as a boarder to St George's Preparatory School, Ascot, Surrey – an experience which he later described as 'penal servitude'.[9] Said the aggrieved Winston, 'I was no more consulted about leaving home than I had been about coming into the world. After all, I was only seven, and I had been so happy in my nursery with all my toys. How I hated this school, and what a life of anxiety I lived there for more than two years.'[10] 'Terror' might have been a more appropriate word than 'anxiety', for St George's was run by the Reverend Herbert William Sneyd-Kynnersley, a headmaster renowned for his sadistic attitude towards the boys in his charge. According to Roger Fry, once a pupil at the school, when boys were flogged by the headmaster with a birch rod, as was frequently the case,

> the swishing was given with the master's full strength and it took only two or three strokes for drops of blood to form everywhere and it continued for 15 or 20 strokes when the wretched boy's bottom was a mass of blood.[11]

At St George's, Winston was frequently in trouble with the power-that-be. Man of letters, Maurice Baring, who became a pupil there after Winston had left the school, for example, stated how the latter

> had been flogged for taking sugar from the pantry, and so far from being penitent, he had taken the headmaster's sacred straw hat from where it hung over the door and kicked it to pieces.[12]

With the sugar incident, Winston had taken a great risk, and been punished for it by perhaps the most cruel and sadistic headmaster in the land. Why then, did he take *another* risk by destroying his tormentor's hat, when he knew that the consequences would be equally, if not more, dire? Winston's propensity for living dangerously, regardless of the likely outcome, was a feature of his personality which will be further discussed later.

To add to his woes, Winston missed his parents greatly, as the numerous plaintive letters which he sent to them reveal. This is not to suggest that Winston was alone in thinking himself to be neglected, for his brother, Jack, when he was, in turn, sent to boarding school, wrote equally plaintive letters to his parents complaining that they did not visit him. What is more, said Winston, at this school, neither 'my reason, imagination or interest were … engaged'.[13] On 3 December 1882, Winston told his mother how, three days previously, he had 'spent a very happy birthday' and reminded her to 'come down' to visit him on the 9th of that month. 'With love and kisses I remain your loveing [sic] son, Winston xxx.'[14] At about this time the Churchills moved house, yet again, this time to 2 Connaught Place, Bayswater.

When, on 5 January 1883, Lord Randolph heard that Winston had recovered from yet another chest complaint – to which he was prone – he wrote to his wife to say, 'I am so glad to hear that Winnie is all right again. Give him a kiss from me.' Shortly afterwards, in another letter to Lady Randolph, he said, 'I suppose Winston will be going back to school in a few days. Give him a little money from me before he goes.'[15] (Winston's chest complaint was a legacy of the time when the family had lived in Ireland.)

In June 1883, Winston wrote to his mother imploring her to visit his school for 'the athletics', hopefully together with his brother, Jack, and his nanny, 'Mrs' Elizabeth Ann Everest.[16] ('Mrs' Everest was in fact a spinster whom Winston called 'Woom', or 'Woomany'. Born in Chatham, Kent, previously she had been governess to Ella, daughter of the Venerable Thompson Phillips, Archdeacon of Barrow-in-Furness, Cumberland). When Lord Randolph's father, John, 7th Duke of Marlborough died at his home, Blenheim Palace, aged sixty-one on 5 July, he was succeeded by his brother, George, as 8th Duke.

In October 1883, Winston informed Lady Randolph that he had visited a picture gallery at Hampton Court Palace.[17] Paintings, as will shortly be seen, were to play a significant part in his life, for not only did he enjoy viewing other people's works, but he would also create works of his own.

The following February, Winston wrote to his mother as follows:

I am wondering when you are coming to see me? I hope you are coming to see me soon, dear. How is Jack? You must send someone to see me. With love & kisses, I remain, Yours affet [sic] Winston.[18]

On 9 March, he tells his mother, only '30 day[s] more and the *Holidays* will be *Here*.'[19]

At St George's, Winston's school reports were indifferent, the one for May/June 1884 stating:

General Conduct	better but still troublesome
Headmaster's Remarks	He has no ambition – if he were really to exert himself he might yet be first at the end of the Term.

It was signed H. W. Sneyd-Kynnersley, Head Master.[20]

Years later, Winston confessed to his personal physician, Lord Moran, that at his preparatory school at Brighton, the boys threw cricket balls at him so that he was frightened and hid behind trees in a copse. He wished, he said, simply, to live down this humiliating memory. He was resolved that he would one day be as tough as any of them. And when he grew up he seized every chance of putting to the test his will to be tough.

But, said Moran, Winston:

was not cut out for the part [of 'tough guy', because he was] small in stature with thin, unmuscular limbs [and because] he spoke with a lisp and slight stutter.

Nevertheless, said Moran, 'he would not accept defeat'.[21]

And Winston himself confirmed that the experience of being bullied at school had only served to make him more resolute, for he later told his brother, Jack, that 'being in many ways a coward – particularly at school – there is no ambition I cherish so keenly as to gain a reputation for personal courage'.[22]

Nonetheless, preparatory school was not an entirely negative experience for Winston, who later declared,

I always loved cartoons. At my private school at Brighton there were three or four volumes of cartoons from *Punch* [magazine], and on Sundays we were allowed to study them.[23]

*　*　*

It is often stated, though without corroborative evidence, that it was Winston's nanny, Elizabeth Everest, who noticed the marks of a severe beating on Winston's buttocks, and brought this to the attention of his parents. However, as authors Celia and John Lee point out, 'The Nanny would have had no part in the undressing and putting to bed of a nine-year-old boy.'[24] However, a different explanation of how Winston's injuries came to light is provided by the unearthing, by Celia and John Lee, of a letter which they discovered amongst Peregrine Churchill's private papers (Henry Winston Spencer Peregrine Churchill being the son of Winston's brother, Jack), which was sent to Winston's father, Lord Randolph, by the Churchills' family physician, Dr Edward C. R. Roose. In the letter, Dr Roose (who practised in London and in Brighton) recommends to the Churchills that they transfer their son from St George's to a preparatory school in Brighton, which the doctor's own son, Bertie, was currently attending, and which did not employ corporal punishment.[25]

From this, and from the fact that Dr Roose had treated Winston on at least one occasion with 'stimulants [administered] by the mouth and rectum'[26] for a high temperature, Celia and John Lee deduce that it was probably the doctor who first noticed the evidence of the beatings. Furthermore, Peregrine Churchill declared that Winston's wounds 'had festered' (i.e. had become infected and were weeping pus).[27] However, the fact that Nanny Everest also had a hand in the proceedings is apparent from a subsequent conversation between Winston and author Anita Leslie, in which the former declared,

> If my mother hadn't listened to Mrs Everest and taken me away [from St George's] I would have broken down completely. Can you imagine a child being *broken down*? I can never forget that school. It was *horrible*.[28]

Winston's parents took their family doctor's advice and, in the autumn of 1884, Winston was duly transferred to the school in question, situated at 29/30 Brunswick Road, Hove near Brighton, and run by two elderly spinsters, Kate and Charlotte Thomson, who were joint headmistresses. Now, instead of being forced to learn Latin grammar, which he hated, Winston was 'allowed to learn things which interested me', such as French, poetry, and history, in addition to participating in horse-riding and swimming, which he loved.[29] At his new school, he declared that he was 'very happy', but nevertheless, kept imploring his mother to come and visit him, or at any rate, write to him. He laid great store by his mother's promises, and when she promised to send him a hamper he was aggrieved that it failed to materialize until several weeks later.[30]

A year later, in October 1885, Winston expressed his disappointment to his father that the latter did not visit him at Brighton. However, when Winston contracted pneumonia, his mother *did* travel to Brighton, where she remained with him for some time. Dr Roose and Brighton physician Dr Joseph Rutter were also in attendance.

When the Conservatives and others defeated Gladstone's Liberals in the election of November 1885, the new Conservative Prime Minister, Lord Salisbury, invited Lord Randolph to be Leader of the House of Commons – a post which he combined with that of Chancellor of the Exchequer. This made Winston's father the second most powerful politician in the land.

When Winston's pneumonia recurred in March 1886 and he became dangerously ill, both his parents 'hastened to his bedside'.[31] Later, Lord Randolph asked his wife to 'Give dear Winny my love when he is himself'.[32]

That November, Winston, putting on a brave face, wrote to his mother from school to say, 'It is superfluous to add that I am happy.'[33]

In December 1886, Lord Randolph resigned from the Government. Lord Salisbury described him as having 'a wayward and headstrong disposition' – qualities which, as will be seen, were also to be found in his son Winston's make-up!

In June 1887 Winston told his mother that, if she did not allow him to come home on the occasion of Queen Victoria's Golden Jubilee, 'I shall never trust your promises again'. However, he was confident that 'Mummy loves her Winny much too much' to let him down.[34] When there was no immediate reply to this letter, Winston became more and more desperate, even to the extent of drafting out a letter for his mother to send to Miss Thomson, pleading with the headmistress for him to be allowed to visit London for the Jubilee. 'Please, as you love me, do as I have begged you.'[35] Three months later, Winston's brother Jack, now aged seven, commenced as a boarder, not at the dreaded St George's, Ascot, but at Elstree Preparatory School in Hertfordshire.

Winston gives the impression that his mother was too preoccupied with her own life to give him the attention which he demanded. And one reason for this may have been that, from the early years of her marriage, Lady Randolph had taken a succession of lovers, one of whom was HRH The Prince of Wales who, doubtless, had first call upon her time. In later years Winston's son, Randolph, concurred with his father's opinion when he said of Winston that 'The neglect and lack of interest in him shown by his parents were remarkable, even judged by the standards of late Victorian and Edwardian days.'[36] But was Randolph's opinion based solely on what Winston had told him?

* * *

What may be deduced about Winston's character from his life so far? For his first five years, before the birth of his brother Jack, Winston was an only child. He became used to providing his own amusements, and was never happier than when playing in the nursery with his toys and, in particular, with his beloved collection of toy soldiers. (When Jack was old enough, he and Winston practised military manoeuvres with these soldiers.) In contrast to his war-like games, Winston was a sensitive child who appreciated the beauty of flowers.

He resented being sent away to school, where he discovered that much of the syllabus was not to his liking. And he particularly disliked St George's, whose headmaster was a sadist, renowned for his extreme brutality towards his pupils. It is, of course, not unusual for a young child to be unhappy after being separated from his or her parents; particularly from the mother but, in Winston's case, being separated from his mother was to him like an emotional bereavement, the pain of which failed to wane as the years went by. He was devoted to Lady Randolph; some might say obsessively so, and put her on a metaphorical pedestal. He also loved and had the greatest admiration for his father.

As time passed, it became more and more obvious that Winston regarded his home and family as his lifeline and, when his mother failed to visit him as often as he would have liked, his letters to her became more and more desperate and imploring. If he and Jack had been of similar ages, and had the brothers attended the same school at the same time, then Winston would, in all probability, not have felt as bereft as he did. Alas, this was not to be the case.

Being bullied at school made Winston both ashamed of his cowardice on the one hand, and all the more determined to be strong and courageous on the other. And the episode of the headmaster's straw hat showed that he *was* capable of displaying *great* courage, even when his opponent was his sadistic monster of a headmaster, the Reverend Sneyd-Kynnersley. Such qualities of strength and resilience, learned at school, would stand him in good stead in the years to come.

Notes

1. *Churchill: The Greatest Briton of All Time.*
2. Lord Randolph to Clara Jerome, Chartwell Trust Papers, Churchill College Archives, Cambridge, 30 November 1874.
3. Churchill, Winston S. *My Early Life*, p. 11.
4. Ibid.
5. Ibid, pp. 17-18.
6. Ibid, p. 12.
7. Churchill, Randolph S. *Winston S. Churchill, Youth, 1874-1900*. Companion Volume I, p. 78. Winston to Lady Randolph, 4 January 1882.
8. Ibid, p. 79. Winston to Lady Randolph, 20 March 1882.
9. Moran, *Winston Churchill: The Struggle for Survival*, p. 440.
10. Churchill, Winston S, op cit, p. 17.
11. From Woolf, Virginia *The Life of Roger Fry*, quoted in Churchill, Randolph S. *Winston S. Churchill*, Vol. I, *Youth, 1874-1900*, p. 55.

12. Baring, Maurice. 1922. *The Puppet Show of Memory*. Quoted in Churchill, Randolph S. *Winston S. Churchill*, Vol. I, *Youth, 1874-1900*, p. 53.
13. Churchill, Winston, op cit, p. 20.
14. Churchill, Randolph S., op cit, p. 82. Winston to Lady Randolph, 3 December 1882.
15. Lee, Celia and John. *The Churchills: A Family Portrait*, p. 31.
16. Churchill, Randolph S., op cit, p. 83. Winston to Lady Randolph, June 1883.
17. Churchill, Randolph S., op cit, p. 84. Winston to Lady Randolph, October 1883.
18. Churchill, Randolph S., op cit, p. 87. Winston to Lady Randolph, 24 February 1884.
19. Churchill, Randolph S., op cit, p. 88. Winston to Lady Randolph, 9 March 1884.
20. Churchill, Randolph S., op cit, p. 95.
21. Moran, op cit, p. 621.
22. Chartwell Papers, quoted in Birkenhead, Earl of, *Churchill*, p. 75.
23. Churchill, Winston S. *Thoughts and Adventures*, p. 9.
24. Lee, Celia and John. *Winston & Jack: The Churchill Brothers*, p. 53.
25. Ibid, p. 54.
26. Ibid, p. 53.
27. Ibid, p. 53.
28. Leslie, Anita. *Jennie: The Life of Lady Randolph Churchill*, p. 82.
29. Churchill, Winston S. *My Early Life*, p. 21.
30. Churchill, Randolph S., op cit, p. 109.
31. Churchill, Randolph S., op cit, p. 72.
32. Churchill, Randolph S., op cit, p. 118. Lord Randolph to Lady Randolph, 15 March 1886.
33. Churchill, Randolph S., op cit, p. 127. Winston to Lady Randolph, 23 November 1886.
34. Churchill, Randolph S., op cit, p. 134. Winston to Lady Randolph, 11 June 1887.
35. Churchill, Randolph S., op cit, p. 135.Winston to Lady Randolph, 12 June 1887.
36. Churchill, Randolph S. op cit, Companion Volume I, p. 45.

N.B. * denotes Film Documentary

CHAPTER 2

Harrow School

On 17 April 1888, Winston commenced at Harrow School (a type of school which is known, euphemistically, as a 'Public School' which was, in fact, for private, fee-paying pupils), Middlesex. Here, he joined the Army Class, which was designed to prepare pupils for entrance to the Royal Military Academy, Woolwich (a training college for artillerymen and engineers), and to the Royal Military College, Sandhurst (for the training of cavalry and infantry officers). As an army cadet he engaged in mock battles with cadets from other public schools, and learnt to use the Martini-Henry Rifle. (He excelled at rifle shooting and also at swimming and, in 1891, won the public schools' fencing championship.) Winston's housemaster, H. O. D. Davidson, however, initially was not pleased with him, on account of his 'forgetfulness, carelessness, unpunctuality, and irregularity in every way. Unless he mends his ways, he will really have to be heavily punished,' he said, which, of course, meant corporal punishment with the birch.[1] June 1888 found Winston memorizing a thousand lines of the poetry of English writer and politician Thomas Babington Macaulay for a school-prize competition which he was about to enter. Poetry was to become one of the great loves of his life.

At school, matters improved when, in April 1889, Harrow's headmaster, the Reverend J. E. C. Welldon, told Winston's father that his son 'has some great gifts and is, I think making progress in his work'.[2] And Winston justified his headmaster's faith in him by reciting 1,200 lines of Macaulay's narrative ballad, the *Lays of Ancient Rome*, 'without making a single mistake'.[3]

Winston received an excellent grounding in English grammar, which he was to put to good use, for, as he subsequently revealed, it was at Harrow that he first discovered that 'he could do what other boys could not do – he could write'. Not only that, but 'personal distinction' was his goal, and his dream was to become an orator, and thereby, as a Member of Parliament, to 'dominate the House of Commons'.[4]

Winston wrote yet another imploring letter to his mother in June 1889: 'I hope you will come my darling Mummy ... . Please come alone, when you come I like to have you all to myself.'[5] However, at Harrow, life proceeded just as it had done at Brighton, with Winston writing copious and plaintive letters to his mother asking her to come and visit him, and, as often as not, receiving in reply, either a belated letter, or none at all. This prompted him to write to her in the summer of 1889 to say, 'I should have imagined that as 300 Mamas & 300 Papas like to have their "offsprings" home You would like to have me. Please, Please do.'[6] In November of that year, he told Lady Randolph, 'I hope you don't imagine that I am happy here. Of course what I should like best would be to leave this place but I cannot expect that at present.' (Between 'this' and 'place', Winston had originally written the words 'hell of a' but he had crossed them out.[7])

In January 1890 Winston told his mother that he had begun taking drawing lessons.[8] That November he assured her that he was 'working my very best ... I cannot do anything more than try'.[9]

Winston, who was of a romantic disposition, became attracted to the appropriately named Mabel Love, a young actress from the Lyric Theatre, who signed some photographs that he sent to her – much to the envy of his schoolmates![10] Always short of money, Winston constantly appealed to his parents for more funds. However, the funds were not always for essentials. For example, in January 1891, the list of expenses which he sent to his mother included, '2 Pictures of Steeplechasing 7/-', together with '2 little tiny 2nd Hand Pictures & 2 Brackets 1/9'.[11] Horse racing was to become another of Winston's passions – if it was not already so!

Winston's father, who was visiting South Africa, wrote to him from Johannesburg in late June 1891 to bestow some rare praise. Said he, 'You cannot think how pleased I was to get your interesting & well written letter & to learn that you were getting on well.'[12] Winston, who longed to have a closer relationship with his father, subsequently declared that, instead of continuing at school, he

> would far rather have been apprenticed as a bricklayer's mate ... [as this] would have been real; it would have been natural; it would have taught me more; and I should have done much better. Also I should have got to know my father, which would have been a great joy to me.[13] [One day in the future, Winston would have the opportunity of building a brick wall of considerable proportions!]

In the autumn of 1891 Lady Randolph told her husband, 'Winston will be all right the moment he gets into Sandhurst [Royal Military College]. He is just at the "ugly" stage – slouchy and tiresome.'[14] Meanwhile, Winston's letters to his mother were becoming ever more desperate. 'I have been back [to school] 10 days & you have not sent me a single word. Please darling mummy do write to your Loving son. Winston S. Churchill'.[15] Whereupon Lady Randolph admitted that she had 'been very remiss about writing ... but [had been] too busy'.[16]

That autumn, Lord Randolph had occasion to speak sharply to Winston when the latter fired a shotgun at a rabbit 'which had appeared on the lawn beneath his [Lordship's] window'. Seeing that his show of anger had distressed Winston, his father then became more conciliatory and 'explained how old people were not always very considerate towards young people, that they were absorbed in their own affairs and might well speak roughly in sudden annoyance'. Then, having expressed pleasure in the fact that Winston liked shooting, Lord Randolph agreed for him to shoot partridges on his property from 1 September. Furthermore, recalled Winston, his father

> proceeded to talk to me in the most wonderful and captivating manner about school and going into the Army and the grown-up life which lay beyond. I listened spellbound to this sudden complete departure from his usual reserve, amazed at his intimate comprehension of all my affairs.

He then told Winston that he [Lord Randolph] was often misunderstood, and asked his son to 'make some allowances'. The fact that Winston remembered this conversation and recorded it in such great detail in his book, *My Early Life*, reveals just how much he loved his father, despite all, and just how important their relationship was to him.[17]

Years later Winston's son Randolph Churchill quoted his father, Winston, as saying,

> I remember once at the end of the long summer holidays – I should think I was 16 or 17 – I was going back to Eton [College, Buckinghamshire] and the last night we sat up late talking in his study at Chartwell [the Churchill family home, Chartwell Manor, in Kent], and we talked of many things, I should think till 1 or 1.30 in the morning, and then he said, 'You know dear boy, I think I've talked to you more these holidays than my father talked to me in the whole of his life' and there was no bitterness in it, but there was sadness.[18]

A serious disagreement broke out between Winston and his mother in December 1891 when the Reverend Welldon proposed that the former spend the forthcoming Christmas holidays in France, where he would be tutored by a Frenchman, Monsieur Elmering. For Winston, the thought of being denied a Christmas at home was too much. However, his mother told him that it was *she* who would decide 'what is best'.[19]

In that same month, his mother told Winston that she had refused to read more than one page of his most recent letter 'as its style does not please me'.[20] Whereupon, he replied to her in the strongest possible terms,

> I can't tell you how wretched you have made me feel – instead of doing everything to make me happy you go and cut the ground away from under my feet like that. Oh my Mummy! [And he ended the letter] I am more unhappy than I can possibly say. Your unkindness has relieved me however from all feelings of duty. Darling Mamma if you want me to do anything for you, especially so great a sacrifice don't be so cruel to Your loving son Winny.[21]

Shortly afterwards, he told his mother abjectly, 'Darling Mummy I despair. I am so wretched I don't know what to do.'[22]

From France, Winston wrote bitterly to his mother to say,

> It seems to me that with you 'out of sight is out of mind' indeed. Not a line from anybody. You promised to write 3 times a week – I have recd [received] 1 letter. It is not at all kind of you and, my darling Mummy, I am very unhappy about it. I wish you would try my mummy to fulfill your promise.[23]

However, by mid-January 1892, Winston's mother was in a more conciliatory mood. 'It will be very nice having you home,' she wrote.[24]

In March 1892 Winston's father admonished him for the fact that he had spent about £10 during that term:

> This cannot last, & if you are not more careful should you get into the Army six months of it will see you in the Bankruptcy Court. Do think this all over & moderate your ways & ideas. Ever y[ou]r most affte [affectionate] father Randolph S.C.[25]

On the academic side, the Reverend Welldon was pleased to report in May to Lord Randolph that 'Winston is working admirably so far …' .[26]

For reasons of economy, the Churchills sold their house at Connaught Place in September 1892 and moved in with the Dowager Duchess Frances, widow of the late John, 7th Duke of Marlborough, at her London mansion, No. 50 Grosvenor Square. Nanny Everest accompanied them and she now became the Duchess's housekeeper. In that same month Winston was joined at Harrow School by his younger brother, Jack, but for one term only when the brothers shared a room until, with the Christmas holiday, Winston's time at the school came to an end. (Incidentally, it is not to be supposed that Jack fared any better than Winston at boarding school, as far as his parents' attentiveness was concerned, for he too complained bitterly of their failure to visit him.)

Winston's introduction to the House of Commons came about at an early age and in a most unexpected way. Showing a tendency to that reckless bravado which would reveal itself at intervals throughout his life (the significance of which will be discussed in more detail shortly), on 10 January 1893 Winston made a daring leap from a bridge and was rendered unconscious for a period of three days, having sustained a serious head injury. It was while he was convalescing from his injuries, which included a ruptured kidney, that he first began to attend the House 'and listen to the great debates'.[27]

March 1893 found Winston being tutored for the Sandhurst entrance examinations by a Captain Walter H. James, who kept an 'establishment in the Cromwell Road', which Winston described as a 'crammer'. James felt confident that his pupil would pass the examinations that summer, provided that he had 'very firm handling'.[28]

When Winston did finally pass for Sandhurst (at his third attempt), Lilian (Lily), Duchess of Marlborough (whose husband George had become the 8th Duke on the death of his father, John, in 1883) sent him hearty congratulations and promised him the sum of £10 and help to buy a 'charger' [cavalry pony].[29] However, Winston's father, Lord Randolph, took a different view. He was annoyed that Winston had passed for the cavalry and not the infantry (which required higher grades in the examination), because this would cost him (Lord Randolph) an extra £200. Furthermore, he declared that the net result of Winston's education to date had been 'to prove his total worthlessness as a scholar or a conscientious worker'.[30] As for Lady Randolph, she pointed out to Winston, dryly, that his father was 'not as pleased over yr [sic] exploits as you seem to be!' But, nevertheless, she declared that she was 'glad of course that you have got into Sandhurst'.[31] In July 1893, Lord Randolph, whose health was deteriorating, consulted Dr Thomas Buzzard, MD, FRCP, specialist in diseases of the nervous system.

That summer, when he and his brother, Jack, were on a walking tour in Switzerland in company with a tutor from Eton College, Winston gave an early indication of how impressed he could be by a beautiful landscape. 'We climbed the Wetterhorn and Monte Rosa. The spectacle of the sunrise striking the peaks of the Bernese Oberland is a marvel of light and colour unsurpassed in my experience.'[32] The mountains of the Alps and the Alpine lakes inspired him, and he would revisit them again and again, as will be seen. Lord Randolph gave Winston the following warning on 9 August:

> I am certain that if you cannot prevent yourself from leading the idle useless unprofitable life you have had during your schooldays & later months, you will become a mere social wastrel one of the hundreds of the public school failures, and you will degenerate into a shabby unhappy & futile existence.[33]

That same month, Winston told his mother that he was aware that his father was 'very angry & dissatisfied' with him, but nevertheless 'I am also glad that I have a fresh chance to alter his bad opinion of me'.[34]

It was feared, at first, that Winston's modest grades in the Sandhurst Entrance Examination would preclude him from being accepted by the King's Royal Rifle Corps (known informally as the 60th Rifles). However, on 30 August 1893 he was able to tell his father that he had 'got an Infantry Cadetship and shall be able, after all, to enter the 60th'.[35] Lord Randolph expressed his pleasure at the news. 'It will save me £200 a year,' he said![36]

Having experienced first preparatory school and, subsequently, public school life, Winston made the comment, 'I am all for the Public Schools, but I do not want to go there again' which, in all the circumstances, was not surprising![37]

Notes

1. Churchill, Randolph S. *Winston S. Churchill, Youth, 1874-1900.* Companion Volume I, HOD Davidson to Lady Randolph, 12 July 1888, pp. 168-9.
2. Churchill, Randolph S., op cit, JEC Welldon to Lord Randolph, 2 April 1889, p. 182.
3. Churchill, Winston S. *My Early Life*, p. 26.
4. Moran, Lord. *Winston Churchill: The Struggle for Survival 1940-1965*, pp. 123-4.
5. Churchill, Randolph S., op cit, Winston to Lady Randolph, 11 June 1889, p. 184.
6. Ibid, Winston to Lady Randolph, Summer 1889, p. 188.
7. Ibid, Winston to Lady Randolph, 11 November 1889, pp. 193-4.
8. Ibid, Winston to Lady Randolph, January 1890, p. 197.
9. Ibid, Winston to Lady Randolph, ?November 1890, p. 214.
10. Ibid, Mabel Love to Winston, September 1894, p. 232.
11. Churchill, Randolph S., op cit, p. 223.

12. Ibid, Lord Randolph to Winston, 27 June 1891, p. 247.
13. Churchill, Winston S., op cit, p. 46.
14. Churchill, Randolph S., op cit, Lady Randolph to Lord Randolph, 25 September 1891, p. 268.
15. Ibid, Winston to Lady Randolph, September 1891, p. 273.
16. Ibid, Lady Randolph to Winston, 29 September 1891, p. 274.
17. Churchill, Winston S., op cit, pp. 39–40.
18. Randolph Churchill, interview, 1966.
19. Churchill, Randolph S., op cit, Lady Randolph to Winston, 8 December 1891, p. 291.
20. Ibid, Lady Randolph to Winston, 15 December 1891, p. 293.
21. Ibid, Winston to Lady Randolph, 16 December 1891, pp. 293-4.
22. Ibid, Winston to Lady Randolph,1891, p. 295.
23. Ibid, Winston to Lady Randolph, 29 December 1891, pp. 301-2.
24. Ibid, Lady Randolph to Winston, 15 January 1892, p. 307.
25. Ibid, Lord Randolph to Winston, 29 March 1892, pp. 328-9.
26. Ibid, J. E. C. Welldon to Lord Randolph, 12 May 1892, p. 331.
27. Churchill, Winston S., op cit, p. 42.
28. Churchill, Randolph S., op cit, Captain Walter H James to Lord Randolph, 7 March 1893, p. 371.
29. Ibid, Lily, Duchess of Marlborough to Winston, 3 August 1893, p. 383.
30. Ibid, Lord Randolph to Frances, Duchess of Marlborough, 5 July [August] 1893, p. 386.
31. Ibid, Lady Randolph to Winston, 7 August 1893, p. 388.
32. Churchill, Winston S., op cit, p. 44.
33. Churchill, Randolph S., op cit, Lord Randolph to Winston, 9 August 1893, p. 391.
34. Ibid, Winston to Lady Randolph, 14 August 1893, p. 395.
35. Ibid, Winston to Lord Randolph, 30 August 1893, p. 203.
36. Ibid, Lord Randolph to Frances, Duchess of Marlborough, 3 September 1893, p. 404.
37. Churchill, Winston S., op cit, p. 47.

CHAPTER 3

The Character of Lord Randolph: Winston's Relationship with his Father

There is an old saying, 'like father, like son', and whether this was indeed the case in respect of the characters of Lord Randolph and his son Winston will be discussed later. In the meantime, what sort of a person was His Lordship?

In his biography of his father, Winston declared that Lord Randolph, as a boy

> had an excellent memory, and was fond of reading books of history, biography, and adventure. But much more pronounced than any liking for study were his passion for sport and his love of animals. By the time he was nine years old he rode well, and even at that early age he showed decision and determination in his ways.[1]

Winston also describes how one of his father's contemporaries at the Reverend Robert S. Tabor's school at Cheam, Surrey, declared that Lord Randolph (who had commenced at that school at the age of eight) always spoke 'with a full voice and great rapidity of utterance, as if his thoughts came faster than his words could follow; the impression conveyed being that he was determined to overbear all opposition and gain the mastery of argument'.[2]

Winston also stated that both Lord Randolph and His Lordship's elder brother, George, the 8th Duke, 'throughout lives strongly marked by an attitude of challenge towards men and things, preserved at all times an old-world reverence for their father [John, the 7th Duke]'.[3]

Historian A. L. Rowse said of Winston's father:

> He was self-willed and impulsive, above all impatient. If he had only had patience all the rest would have come into line. But he had the

defect of the artistic temperament, what we in our day of psychological jargon diagnose as the manic-depressive alternation – tremendous high spirits and racing energy on the upward bound, depression and discouragement on the down.[4]

Archibald Philip Primrose, 5th Earl of Rosebery, was a British Liberal statesman who served as prime minister from March 1894–June 1895. He had known Winston's father since the time they were at school together at Eton College and, subsequently, at Oxford and in the world of politics. Said Roseberg of Lord Randolph:

> He was human, eminently human; full of faults, as he himself well knew, but not base or unpardonable thoughts; pugnacious, outrageous, fitful, petulant, but eminently lovable and winning.[5]

Lord Rosebery also spoke of Randolph's 'waywardness':

> He was always so from boyhood, but amiably and controllably so. From the first moments that I can remember him there was a tinge in him of the eccentric, the petulant, and the unexpected.[6]

And he describes how Lord Randolph would

> embrace the most preposterous propositions, and defend any extravagance that might happen to enter his head; if you were opposed [to him], he would carry it much further.[7]

The outcome was, said Rosebery, that Lord Randolph's political colleagues grew 'weary of his restless predominance' and became alienated from him by it.[8]

Lord Rosebery described Lord Randolph's resignation from the government in December 1886 as 'a striking catastrophe' which was

> largely to be explained by physical causes. Randolph's nervous system was always tense and highly strung; a condition which largely contributed to his oratorial success, but which was the principal cause of his political undoing. He would descend from the highest summit to a bottomless pit and up again, at the shortest notice; that is the liability of the temperament of genius. When he took office he worked unsparingly, which increased the strain on his nerves. He had, moreover, a morbid suspicion of intrigue .... That suspicion would enhance the stress, for he would be watching others and tormenting himself.[9]

This came about, said Rosebery, because of Lord Randolph's nature, which 'required a relief for its high-strung irritability in some sort of violence, and resignation was the only form that that violence could take'.[10]

In his biography of his father Winston also sheds light upon the character of Lord Randolph. Following a banquet in the hall of the Middle Temple, held on 10 July 1884, which was attended by the Prince of Wales, his Lordship received a terrific ovation on account of his current popularity. And yet, said Winston,

> in contrast with these signs of triumph, what inward misgivings darkened Lord Randolph Churchill's mind! In the presence of a trusted friend he dropped with relief his mask of unconcerned reserve and revealed himself plunged for a while in[to] one of those fits of despondency which so often followed or preceded the crisis and action of his life. 'I am very near the end of my tether,' he said to this friend who met him at the Turf Club in these anxious days. 'In the last five years I have lived twenty. I have fought Society. I have fought Mr. Gladstone at the head of a great majority. I have fought the Front Opposition Bench. Now I am fighting Lord Salisbury. I have said I will not join the government unless [Henry Stafford] Northcote [Conservative politician] leaves the House of Commons. Lord Salisbury will never give way. I'm done.'[11]

Following his resignation as Chancellor of the Exchequer and Leader of the House of Commons on 20 December 1886, Winston's father travelled to the Mediterranean. Said Winston:

> Although Lord Randolph's letters to his mother, [Frances, widow of the late John, 7th Duke of Marlborough] to give her pleasure, were written in a cheery and optimistic vein, there is no doubt that he felt very bitterly the sudden reversal of his fortunes and the arrest of his career. During this voyage, of which he gives so gay an account, he was afflicted by fits of profound depression and would often sit by himself for hours plunged in gloomy thought.[12]

Finally, said Lord Rosebery, by the time Lord Randolph went to South Africa (in the summer of 1891) 'the cruel disease which was to paralyse and kill him had begun to affect him'.[13]

WINSTON CHURCHILL

Notes

1.	Churchill, Winston S. *Lord Randolph Churchill*, p.17.
2.	Ibid, p. 19.
3.	Ibid, p. 23.
4.	Rowse, A.L. *The Churchills: The Story of a Family*, p. 373.
5.	Rosebery, Lord. *Lord Randolph Churchill*, p.81.
6.	Ibid, pp. 113-14.
7.	Ibid, p. 76.
8.	Ibid, p. 64.
9.	Ibid, pp. 51-2.
10.	Ibid, p. 56.
11.	Churchill, Winston S., op cit, p. 319.
12.	Ibid, p. 622.
13.	Rosebery, Lord, op cit, p. 71.

CHAPTER 4

Winston and 'Emotional Deprivation Disorder'

Duduring his time at boarding school (1882–1892) – which was almost a decade – Winston wrote home to his parents many times, principally to his mother. In his letters he did not say, explicitly, 'I feel abandoned, unloved, insecure, uncertain, frustrated, and restless', but, from them, it may be inferred that this is *exactly* how he felt. (Winston, however, largely exonerated his father, whom he knew was busy with affairs of state.)

However, Winston did go as far as to inform his mother that, in his opinion, she was unkind and unreliable, and most significantly, that as far as her attitude to him was concerned 'out of sight' was 'out of mind'. And as for the letters home in which he told his mother how happy he was, it should be borne in mind that these letters may have been written under duress, and censored by the teaching staff.

Winston subsequently told Frank Harris, editor of the *Fortnightly Review*, how he had strained every sinew to establish a good rapport with his father during the times when the two were together, but without success. 'He wouldn't listen to me or consider anything I said. There was no companionship with him possible and I tried so hard and so often. He was so self-centred that no one else existed for him.' 'You didn't like him?' enquired Harris. 'How could I? … He treated me as if I had been [i.e. was] a fool; barked at me whenever I questioned him. I owe everything to my mother; to my father nothing.'[1] From other, more conciliatory remarks made by Winston about his father, it seems that these words were written more in sorrow than in anger.

Whatever the rights and wrongs of the situation may be, all that mattered to Winston was that, during his schooldays, *he* considered himself to be emotionally deprived (though to what extent this was due to failures on the part of his parents on the one hand, or to him making excessive demands upon them on the other, will be discussed shortly). The Dutch psychiatrist Anna A. Terruwe, in her book *The Neurosis in the Light of Rational Psychology* (translated by Dutch-born US psychiatrist, Conrad W. Baars and published in 1960), gave the 'first brief description ... to appear in the English psychiatric literature ... of a newly crystallized neurotic disorder'. Originally called 'Deprivation Neurosis', this subsequently became known as 'Emotional Deprivation Disorder'.[2] In a subsequent book entitled *Healing the Unaffirmed* (the original, unabridged version of which was published in 1972 and entitled *Loving and Curing the Neurotic*), co-authors Anna A. Terruwe and Conrad W. Baars describe the needs of the normal child, and explain how emotional deprivation can come about in that child. According to the authors:

> The infant needs to experience genuine unselfish love from another human being if it is to attain the fullness of its human existence and authentic happiness; that is, the joy which is the fruit of loving and being loved. This love, of course, has nothing to do with sexuality ... .[3]

Both babies and children

> must be given the opportunity to receive the various emotional gratifications proper to his or her age. If not, the child's emotional life will show a gap, which prevents further harmonious emotional growth.[4]
>
> Through all their senses ... babies gather the experience that they are not alone, that others are dedicated to them and care for them. This is the affirmation of its being; the affirmation that complements the fulfilment of its physical needs. It provides the psychic harmony which is the basis for the feeling of inner security upon which their future growth and development becomes possible.[5]

And the authors go on to describe how both mother and father play a vital role in this process of 'affirmation':

> In the natural course of events, normal growth and development is brought about when the child feels the love of his or her parents. In the earliest years, this love will mainly be that of the mother, but when the child grows older, it will also include the dedicated and loving concern of the father. As a baby, the child can experience this love, this affirmation of its being, only by way of the sense of touch, for the other senses have not yet sufficiently developed. In later years the child must also be affirmed by the father. Here again affirmation must

be expressed in a tactile manner, although verbal affirmation by this time has assumed an even greater role. [In this way, children] come to *feel* that they are not alone, and that there is someone to whom they can entrust themselves, with whom they are really safe. [As for the person] who was deprived of motherly tenderness as a child and thus has a special need for it, everything depends on whether there is somebody who can and will give this motherly tenderness.[6]

One way in which an infant develops an emotional bond with its mother, and vice-versa, is by being breast-fed. Sadly, this opportunity was missed, and Winston was passed to a 'wet-nurse', rather than being breast-fed by his own mother.[7]

The authors describe the vital importance of

the tenderness with which a mother cradles her infant in her arms, cuddles and caresses it, and presses it to her [self] … It is through the tender *touch*, the tender look, the tender words and tone of voice that the child is affirmed in its own goodness, worth, and lovableness.[8]

Whether Lady Randolph was in the habit of cuddling her two sons is not known. However, a photograph, taken in about 1881, shows her with the infant, Jack, sitting on her knee, and Winston sitting beside her, in an intimate pose.

Affirmation by a 'father figure' is of particular importance, and especially so

in the case of male patients [who] often need this kind of affirmation more than motherly tenderness. They need to experience the firm support and steadfastness of the father through his words, understanding, and masculine cordiality.[9]

But what of the infant or child who receives none of these blessings? The authors use the terms 'unaffirmed', or 'inadequately affirmed' to describe a person who is suffering from Emotional Deprivation Disorder, a

syndrome [which] results from the frustration or deprivation of the natural sensitive need for affirmation in the infant, baby, or growing child by the mother, father, or both.[10]

When this affirmation as a baby or child is not forthcoming, the child remains in a dissatisfied, frustrated psychic state which involves his or her entire being and pervades the emotional life with deep-seated feelings of unrest, uncertainty, and insecurity. These feelings remain so deeply buried in their psychic life that they [the feelings] still continue to colour their entire emotional life when they become an adult. Without doubt, it is this non-affirmation which is the source of the feeling of uncertainty found in all people with emotional deprivation disorder.[11]

Terruwe and Baars stress how essential it is, if Emotional Deprivation Disorder is to be prevented, for the infant or child to receive 'mature, unselfish love' because of its 'affirming, creative effect on a human being':

> The nature of people as social beings absolutely demands the emotional *contact* with others; they cannot become open to others unless they have been affirmed by another's unselfish love. Without such affirmation they are doomed to a life of gnawing uncertainty about their own self-worth. No degree of professional or intellectual accomplishments, however outstanding and widely acclaimed, can make up for this emotional deficit. It can only be filled by the unselfish love of another person.[12]
>
> Only when unaffirmed people are unselfishly loved by another will they dare to lower their mask little by little, to play their role less rigidly in the realization that they are allowed to be who they really are; in this way they will find new strength and energy, will breathe more easily in the enlarging psychic sphere they share with the other, and will thus find *joy in living*.[13]

It may be said that, in their work, Anna Terruwe and Conrad Baars merely pointed out what all caring parents know by instinct. However, to them must go the credit for drawing the attention of the medical profession to the importance of 'affirmation' as an antidote to emotional deprivation, and for legitimizing these two syndromes as distinct clinical entities in their own right.

* * *

What did others think of Lady Randolph's attempts to bring up her children? Over a century later, Winston's daughter Mary Soames said that her mother, Clementine, 'believed Lady Randolph had been a bad mother ... it's no good pretending she did not feel that'.[14] Also, said Mary, 'I did once ask a very old cousin who had known Jennie whether Lord and Lady Randolph were really such awful parents', to which the reply was 'I think that even by the standards of their generation ... they were pretty awful.'[15] But is this the *entire* story?

By a piece of good fortune, Lady Randolph's diary for the year 1882 survives, and in the January of that year (when the family was resident at Blenheim Palace, prior to moving into 2 Connaught Place) 'she regularly recorded having given Winston his lessons, taking him for walks, and reading to the children [i.e. Jack, and the children of George Spencer-Churchill, 8th Duke of Marlborough – who included Charles, born 1871, who succeeded as 9th Duke in 1892]'.[16] Lady Randolph's 1882 diary was preserved by Jack's son, Peregrine. The diary is not available for public scrutiny, but the authors, Celia and John Lee, have had access to it via a member of the Churchill family. Celia and John Lee have also had access to other private documents belonging to the Churchill family, which indicate that when the Churchill boys were older, their mother took them out to restaurants to dine with her, and she also took them riding.[17]

It seems, therefore, that Lady Randolph may have been done a disservice in her role as mother, not only by Winston, but also by others, including members of the Churchill family. In other words, Winston may have 'over-egged the pudding' with his implied criticism of his mother, Lady Randolph, and in reality it was Winston who was equally at fault, through being over-demanding and attention-seeking.

Notes

1. Harris, Frank. *My Life and Loves*, p. 471.
2. Baars, Conrad W. and Terruwe, Anna A. *Healing the Unaffirmed: Recognizing Emotional Deprivation Disorder*, p. 203.
3. Ibid, p. 182.
4. Ibid, p. 5.
5. Ibid, p. 21.
6. Ibid, pp. 75-6 & 80.
7. Sebba, Anne. *Jennie Churchill: Winston's American Mother*, p. 74.
8. Baars, Conrad W. and Anna A. Terruwe, op. cit., p. 184.
9. Ibid, p. 99.
10. Ibid, p. xii.
11. Ibid, p. 21.
12. Ibid, pp. 181, 186.
13. Ibid, pp. 192-3.
14. Sebba, Anne. op cit, Mary Soames, interview with Anne Sebba, 16 November 2004, p. 289.
15. Meacham, Jon. *Franklin and Winston: A Portrait of a Friendship*, Jon Meacham, interview with Mary Soames, p. 11.
16. Lee, Celia and John. *Winston & Jack: The Churchill Brothers*, p. 36.
17. Lee, Celia and John. *The Churchills: A Family Portrait*, p. 59.

CHAPTER 5

The 'Affirmation' of Winston

Human beings are infinitely variable in their personalities, and clearly some require more 'affirmation' than others. Winston, it seems, was in the former category, probably because, deep down, he was a very insecure person. So given the fact that he considered himself to be largely 'unaffirmed' by his parents (despite evidence to the contrary), was it possible for him to affirm himself, i.e., to convince himself that he was lovable and valued? If not, then who else could give him the affirmation that he desired so desperately?

According to psychiatrists Terruwe and Baars:

> Self-affirmation is the unhealthy process of trying to convince yourself and others … that you are significant, worthwhile, important or special, when in reality you feel insignificant, worthless, and unimportant because you have not been loved for who you are.[1]

In other words, any attempt by a person to 'self-affirm' himself or herself, will of necessity be a futile exercise. On a more positive note, the authors state that

> If young men with emotional deprivation disorder are in need of motherly tenderness, it is sometimes possible that an older woman with maternal feelings toward them can help. Such a woman has to be older and must be absolutely emotionally mature.[2]

Winston was fortunate that there was, indeed, an 'older woman' who had 'maternal feelings' towards him – namely his nanny, 'Mrs' Everest.

Elizabeth Everest

Although the input of Winston's parents, as far as his 'affirmation' was concerned, was, to his way of thinking, inadequate for his needs, fortunately there were others who were able to fulfil this role in their stead. Principal amongst them was his nanny, (so-called 'Mrs') Elizabeth Everest, who, as soon as the family had returned home after Winston's baptism at Blenheim on 27 December 1874, was employed to look after him. Winston subsequently described his nanny as 'my confidante. Mrs Everest it was who looked after me and tended all my wants. It was to her I poured out my many troubles...'[3] (It has to be said that Elizabeth Everest displayed the same love and affection towards Jack as she did towards Winston, and referred to them as 'My Darling Precious Boys'.[4])

As the years spent by Winston at Harrow School went by, it was noticeable that the letters which he received from Elizabeth Everest were longer, more detailed and more compassionate than those from his mother. For example, on 11 June 1891, his nanny told him:

> Don't forget that I never cease to think of you [even] if I do not write my lamb [and she ended her letter] – Good bye dearest much love & heaps of kisses from Your loving Woom.[5]

Elizabeth Everest's love for Winston, however, was not of the gooey, sycophantic variety, and she was not slow to reproach him, should the need arise. For example, in November 1891, she admonished him for his extravagance, and pointed out how he had spent '15/- in a week [when] some familys [sic] of 6 or 7 people have to live upon 12/- a week. You squander it away & the more you have the more you want & spend.'[6] So highly did Winston rate Elizabeth Everest that on one occasion he did her the honour of inviting her to Harrow to be shown round the school, thereby incurring the ridicule of his fellow pupils. But perhaps the greatest compliment which he paid her was to immortalize her in his first and only novel, *Savrola*, set in the fictional country of 'Laurania' where the population is revolting against a dictatorial government. (Written in 1897, it was serialized in 1899 and published in 1900.) In *Savrola* Elizabeth Everest appears on several occasions – each time in the guise of an elderly nurse – one of the novel's minor characters, who had looked after Savrola, the hero

> from his birth up [onwards] with a devotion and care which knew no break. It is a strange thing, the love of these women. Perhaps it is the only disinterested affection in the world. The mother loves her child; that is maternal nature. The youth loves his sweetheart; that too may be explained. The dog loves his master; he feeds him; a man loves his friend; he has stood by him perhaps, at doubtful moments. In all there are reasons; but the love of the foster-mother for her charge appears absolutely irrational. It is one of the few proofs ... that the nature of mankind is superior to mere utilitarianism, and that his destinies are high.[7]

What finer tribute could there be from Winston, the author, to one who, for him, not only acted *in loco parentis* but offered unconditional love and absolute devotion and reliability?

Later in the novel Winston pays another tribute to the elderly nurse. 'The warm sheets, the cosy fire, the hot soup were the comforts she loved to prepare for others, enjoying them, as it were, by proxy.'[8] As to her attitude to the hero of the novel, 'Savrola' [who in reality is Winston],

> He was all she had in the world; others dissipate their affections on a husband, children, brothers, and sisters; all the love of her kind old heart was centred in the man she had fostered since he was a helpless baby. And he did not forget.[9]

Winston's relationship with Elizabeth Everest was fundamental to his wellbeing. He depended on her letters, her warmth, and her love. She was his rock of reliability. When his parents ignored him, failed to visit him, or chided him for his shortcomings, there was always Nanny Everest in the background to give love, praise and encouragement. The words, 'He was all she had in the world' might equally well have been reversed to say, 'She [Elizabeth Everest] was all he [Winston] had in the world'.

Finally, in *Savrola*, the author, Winston, comments regretfully, that 'of the old nurse, indeed, they [the people of 'Laurania'] will read no more, for history does not concern itself with such'.[10]

Frances, Duchess of Marlborough

Another female who took a lively interest in Winston was his paternal grandmother, Frances, Duchess of Marlborough (wife of John, the 7th Duke, and a widow since 1883) with whom he sometimes stayed at her London home in Grosvenor Square. Lady Frances was a compassionate woman who, in 1879, had founded the (non-sectarian) Irish Relief Fund, the purpose of which was to raise money for the victims of the famine that was ravaging that country. However, Lady Frances, like Elizabeth Everest, had no illusions about Winston, and she was not slow to recognize his faults, as well as his good qualities, and to offer words of advice if necessary. For example, in January 1888, she reported to his mother, Lady Randolph, that he was 'excitable' and 'goes out too much ... to late parties'.[11] Later that year, on 23 September, Lady Frances advised Winston to take care of himself, 'work well & keep out of scrapes & don't *flare* up so easily!!!' In other words, Winston must control his quick temper.[12] In July 1894 Lady Frances told Lady Randolph that she had granted Winston permission to attend a race meeting at Sandown Park and that he, in turn, had given her 'his word of Honour he will not be induced to bet. It is difficult to refuse him anything at his age. He is affectionate and pleasant but you know he is mercurial and plausible ....'[13] The significance of these remarks, made by Winston's perspicacious grandmother about Winston, will be discussed shortly.

Laura, Countess of Wilton

Sometimes, on the occasions when his parents pronounced it to be inconvenient for Winston to return home to them from Harrow in the holidays, he spent time with Laura Caroline, Countess of Wilton and wife of the 4th Earl. The Wiltons were friends of the Churchills and lived at 'The Hatch', Windsor, in Surrey. In January 1891 Laura sent Winston some oranges from the south of France, and ended her letter 'With your Deputy Mother's best love'.[14]

Consuelo (née Vanderbilt), wife of Charles, the 9th Duke of Marlborough

It is said that the camera never lies, and a photograph of Winston with Consuelo, taken in 1901, is most revealing. The two of them are sitting informally on the steps at Blenheim, like two pieces of flotsam washed up by an indifferent sea: Consuelo with a coy and loving look on her face, and Winston looking slightly anxious as if the photographer has interrupted a private conversation between the two of them. At the time Consuelo was aged twenty-four, and Winston twenty-six. Just as Winston's young life had been far from happy, so Consuelo's life as wife of the 9th Duke – whom she had married on 6 November 1895 – turned out to be not at all that she might have wished for.

Consuelo described herself and her husband as being 'people of different temperament [who were] condemned to live together ...'. She came to hate the formality of Blenheim, the extravagances of the guests who congregated there, and the endless political discussions.[15] Like Winston, she cared greatly for the 'underdog', and described her 'stricken feelings towards my housemaids, whose business it was [owing to the absence of bathrooms at Blenheim Palace] to prepare something like thirty baths a day'.[16] Said she,

> My duties ... consisted in visits to the poor, whose courtesy I found congenial. In almshouses founded and endowed by Caroline, Duchess of Marlborough [wife of the 4th Duke], there were old ladies whose complaints had to be heard and whose infirmities had to be cared for, and there were the blind to be read to. [Also] It was my duty to cram [surplus food from the dining table] into tins, which we then carried down to the poorest in the villages where Marlborough owned property.

Nonetheless, Consuelo took her duties seriously, and whereas previously 'Meat and vegetables and sweets had been mixed together in a horrid jumble in the same tin,' she took the trouble to sort 'the various viands into different tins, to the surprise and delight of the recipients'.[17]

Consuelo had liked Winston – 'a young, red-headed boy a few years older than I' – from the moment she first met him, which was in early 1896, after her return to Blenheim from her honeymoon. 'He struck me as ardent and vital and seemed to have every intention of getting the most out of life, whether in sport, in love, in adventure or in politics.'[18] Consuelo's affection for Winston and her unbridled admiration for him, were factors which undoubtedly assisted in his 'Affirmation'.

Notes

1. Baars, Conrad W. and Terruwe, Anna A. *Healing the Unaffirmed: Recognizing Emotional Deprivation Disorder*, p. 191.
2. Ibid, pp. 81 & 99.
3. Churchill, Winston S. *My Early Life*, p. 13.
4. Churchill, Randolph S. *Winston S. Churchill, Youth, 1874-1900*, Elizabeth Everest to Winston, 1 April 1895, p. 253.
5. Churchill, Randolph S., op cit, Elizabeth Everest to Winston, 11 June 1891, p. 242.
6. Ibid, Elizabeth Everest to Winston, 4 November 1891, p. 283.
7. Churchill, Winston S. *Savrola*, pp. 37-8.
8. Ibid, p. 113.
9. Ibid, p. 185.
10. Ibid, pp. 221-2.
11. Churchill, Randolph S., op cit, Frances, Duchess of Marlborough to Lady Randolph, 19 January 1888, p. 153.
12. Ibid, Frances, Duchess of Marlborough to Winston, 23 September 1890, p. 210.
13. Ibid, Frances, Duchess of Marlborough to Lady Randolph, 19 July 1894, pp. 507-8.
14. Ibid, Lady Wilton to Winston, January 1891, p. 219.
15. Balsan, Consuelo Vanderbilt. *The Glitter and the Gold*, pp. 104 & 148.
16. Ibid, p. 82.
17. Ibid, p. 68.
18. Ibid, p. 55.

CHAPTER 6

Sandhurst

Why did Winston choose to make his career in the Army? In his own words, 'This orientation was entirely due to my collection of [toy] soldiers.'[1] Said he,

From very early youth I had brooded about soldiers and war, and often I had imagined in dreams and day-dreams the sensations attendant upon being for the first time under fire. It seemed to my youthful mind that it must be a thrilling and immense experience to hear the whistle of bullets all round and to play at hazard from moment to moment with death and wounds.[2]

At first sight, such reckless bravado might be attributed to Winston's youth and to his family's military background, for he cannot fail to have been impressed by Blenheim Palace, the place of his birth and once the home of his soldier ancestor, John, 1st Duke of Marlborough. But did his words have a deeper significance? This will be discussed shortly.

The Battle of Blenheim (a village on the River Danube in Bavaria) was fought on 13 August 1704. In the battle, Marlborough was the supreme commander of the British and Dutch forces which, together with those of Prince Eugène of Savoy, defeated those of King Louis XIV. This battle put an end to the French king's ambition of dominating Europe. 'As a reward, Queen Anne granted Marlborough the Manor and Honour of Woodstock and the Hundred of Wootton, where a house would be built as a monument to his famous victory.'[3] The palace's architect was Sir John Vanbrugh, and its parkland – including the Grand Cascade at the western end of the lake – was landscaped by Lancelot 'Capability' Brown. Subsequently, between the years 1925 and 1930, Charles, the 9th Duke, commissioned French garden designer Achille Duchene to create the Water Terraces at the West Front.[4]

At Blenheim Palace images of John Churchill, hero of the Battle of Blenheim, were to be seen everywhere. For example, the 1st Duke appears on the ceiling of the Great Hall in a painting by Sir James Thornhill of 1716, where he kneels to Britannia and presents to her his 'plan of action at the Battle of Blenheim'; on the ceiling of the Saloon, in a painting by French artist Louis Laguerre, where he is shown 'in victorious progress but stayed by the hand of Peace'; in the Great Hall, in a painting by German artist John Closterman, in which he is depicted with the Duchess and their family; and in the Third State Room, where the Duke and his Chief Military Engineer, Colonel John Armstrong, are depicted in a painting by Polish artist Enoch Seeman.[5]

The 1st Duke is also depicted in the following tapestries: in the Green Writing Room – in the magnificent 'Blenheim tapestry, which shows Marlborough in his hour of triumph as he accepts Marshal Tallard's surrender after the Battle of Blenheim'; in the First Stateroom, where he is seen 'preparing to storm the hilltop fortress' of Donauwörth; in the Second Stateroom, where he has laid siege to Bouchain, 'including the penetration of Marshal Villar's vaunted *ne plus ultra* (meaning literally 'nothing more beyond', or 'unsurpassable') lines in 1711'; and in the Third State Room, where he is victorious at the Battle of Oudenarde (fought on 11 July 1708).[6]

In addition, in the Long Library is a bust of the 1st Duke by Flemish sculptor John Michael Rysbrack, and the Chapel is dominated by the dramatic monument to the 1st Duke (dressed as a Roman general) and Duchess and their two sons, both of whom died young. [It was] designed by William Kent and 'sculpted by Rysbrack at the Duchess's direction.'[7] Finally,

> the 41-metre (134-foot)-high Doric 'Column of Victory' stands at the entrance to the Great Avenue in the park. It is crowned by a lead statue of the 1st Duke by Robert Pit. The statue depicts the Duke dressed as a Roman general with eagles at his feet and a Winged Victory in his hand.[8]

As one who had always been interested in battles and military manoeuvres, the young Winston could not fail but have been inspired by the 1st Duke and his exploits, so vividly commemorated by these and other works of art at Blenheim. As for Winston's other military forebears, George, the 6th Duke of Marlborough, had commanded the Queen's Own Oxfordshire Hussars in 1845. Charles, the 9th Duke, had been commissioned into that same regiment in 1892, and fought in the Second South African (Boer) War as a staff captain. In the First World War he had served as a lieutenant colonel on the General Staff.

* * *

Winston entered the Royal Military College, Sandhurst, Surrey, in September 1893. There he was kept busy from morning until night, noting that 'I could count almost on my fingers the days when I had nothing to do.'[9] Raring for action, he bewailed the fact that 'the age of wars between civilized nations had come to an end forever'. Alas, how wrong this youthful statement of his would prove to be![10] The following month he told his mother that when he and Lord Randolph had met in London, 'Papa was very pleased to see me and talked to me for quite a long time about his speeches [political] & my prospects'.[11] Also in October Winston learned that, on the orders of his grandmother, Frances, the Dowager Duchess, his former nanny, Elizabeth Everest, had been sent away on holiday, and refused her 'board wages' (lodging and food in return for services rendered), and was now to be 'given her congé'(notice of dismissal from the Grosvenor Square household). He was appalled, and wrote indignantly to his mother as follows:

> I should be very sorry not to have her [Elizabeth Everest] at Grosvenor Square – because she is in my mind associated – more than anything else with *home*. She is an old woman – who has been your devoted servant for nearly 20 years – she is more fond of Jack and I than of any other people in the world & to be packed off in the way the Duchess suggests would possibly, if not probably break her down altogether. I am extremely fond of Everest & it [is] perhaps from this reason that I think such proceedings cruel & rather mean. She has for 3 months been boarding herself out of her own money and I have no doubt is not at all well off. ... when a good place has been secured for her she could leave and be given a pension [i.e. by the Churchills] – which would be sufficient to keep her from want – & which should continue during her life.[12]

Winston's appeal appears to have had some effect because, on 30 January 1894, he received a letter from Elizabeth Everest from lodgings which had been found for her at 5 Cranmer Road, Kennington, London. Furthermore, Lord Randolph had arranged for her to be paid a regular allowance. 'Mrs' Everest may or may not have guessed that Winston had played a part in this but, whatever the case may be, she ended her letter in her typically affectionate way, 'Goodbye my Darling best love to you From your affecte [sic] old Woom.'[13]

For most of the remainder of that year Elizabeth Everest resided with her former employer, the Venerable Thompson Phillips, Archdeacon of Barrow-in-Furness, Cumberland. By early July 1895, however, she had returned to

London and was living with her sister, Mrs Emma Richmond, at 15 Crouch Hill, Islington.

Now that Winston was a 'gentleman cadet' at Sandhurst, the tone of the letters which he received from his parents became more amenable and approving. In February 1894, for example, his mother told him:

> I felt so sorry you have to go [back to Sandhurst] – you poor thing – particularly when you are not feeling well [Winston was being troubled with boils at the time]. I don't know what I shld [sic] have done in G. [Grosvenor] Square without you. Make a little list of the things you want for your room & I will see if I have them.[14]

As for Lord Randolph, said Winston, 'Once I became a gentleman cadet I acquired a new status in my father's eyes. I was entitled when on leave to go about with him, if it was not inconvenient.'[15] On 21 February Winston's father wrote to say, 'I am glad to hear your riding has been so successful at Knightsbridge.'(This was a reference to Knightsbridge Barracks riding school, where Winston had undergone additional training with the Royal Horse Guards.) Lord Randolph also promised to send Winston some money and some books for him to read at weekends.[16]

In April 1894, a sterner letter arrived from Lord Randolph, telling Winston that his father was prepared to allow him to come home to London not more than once a month, and suggesting that he 'work on Sunday instead of loitering about ...'. The letter ended, 'This is all written in perfect kindness to you. If I did not care about you I should not trouble to write long letters to you.'[17] Shortly afterwards, Winston's father admonished him severely: firstly for carelessly dropping his watch onto a stone pavement and, subsequently, for dropping it into water, so much so that the workings became 'horribly rusty'.[18] Winston was at pains to respond to this by saying that he had 'borrowed 23 men from the Infantry Detachment, diverted the stream – obtained the fire engine and pumped out the pool [into which the watch had fallen] dry' in order to recover it. 'The labour of the men cost me over £3.'[19]

Winston had been warned by more than one member of the family about the dangers of gambling – which, of course, included betting on the horses! Nevertheless, in June 1894, he told his brother, Jack, that he had spent 'a very pleasant week at Ascot' where he 'saw all the races [and] backed a couple of winners'.[20] However, about this, Lord Randolph could hardly complain, for in His Lordship's later years he was elected a member of the Jockey Club, and, in partnership with Lord Dunraven, bred racehorses!

In September 1894 Winston ended a letter to his mother by saying,

'Excuse the badly written scrawl & accept only the love that it is meant to convey. I think of you always & long to kiss you again.'[21] Those who were ignorant of Winston's past life might regard this letter as immature, from one who was approaching his twentieth birthday. However, surely this is further evidence that Winston was still, even at his age, desperately seeking affirmation from his mother.

Notes

1. Churchill, Winston S. *My Early Life*, p. 27.
2. Ibid, p. 84.
3. *Blenheim Palace: World Heritage Site*, p. 4.
4. Ibid, p. 55.
5. Ibid, pp. 13, 26 & 31.
6. Ibid, pp. 26, 34 & 37-8.
7. Ibid, p. 46.
8. Ibid, p. 57.
9. Churchill, Winston S, op cit, p. 67.
10. Ibid, pp. 52-3.
11. Churchill, Randolph S. *Winston S. Churchill, Youth, 1874-1900*. Companion Volume I, Winston to Lady Randolph, 21 October 1893, p. 422.
12. Ibid, Winston to Lady Randolph, 20 October 1893 pp. 424-5.
13. Ibid, Elizabeth Everest to Winston, 30 January 1894, p. 435.
14. Ibid, Lady Randolph to Winston, 11 February 1894, p. 440.
15. Churchill, Winston S., op cit, p. 53.
16. Churchill, Randolph S., op cit, Lord Randolph to Winston, 21 February 1894, pp. 447-8.
17. Ibid, Lord Randolph to Winston, 13 April 1894, p. 465.
18. Ibid, Lord Randolph to Winston, 21 April 1894, p. 468.
19. Ibid, Winston to Lord Randolph, 22 April 1894, p. 470.
20. Ibid, Winston to Jack, 4 June 1894, p. 500.
21. Ibid, Winston to Lady Randolph, 15 September 1894, p. 521.

CHAPTER 7

The Decline and Death of Lord Randolph

Lord Randolph had written to Dr Thomas Buzzard on 8 June 1893 to complain about the 'most absurd rumours' which were circulating 'about my bad health'. His Lordship was also 'indignant' to learn that his wife, Lady Randolph, had consulted with both Dr Buzzard and Dr Roose on the matter.[1]

Dr Buzzard was a specialist in diseases of the nervous system and Consulting Physician to London's National Hospital for the Paralyzed and Epileptic. Dr Edward C. R. Roose was, as already stated, the Churchills' family physician.

Dr Buzzard believed that the first time he had been consulted by Lord Randolph was in October 1885, when Dr Roose had also been present. Said Buzzard:

> It was in the early summer of 1893 … if not before that I came to the conclusion that there was in all probability commencing G.P. [General Paralysis]. His articulation became slurred, and his tongue tremulous.[2]

The meaning and significance of the term 'General Paralysis' in this context will be discussed shortly. Meanwhile, Lord Randolph's health continued to deteriorate, to the extent that, in May 1894, Dr Roose recommended that he give up public life 'at least for a while'.[3]

Late in the following month of June 1894 Lord Randolph, accompanied by his wife and Dr George E. Keith, embarked on a world tour, commencing in North America. This was against the express advice of His Lordship's doctors.[4] Said Winston, when he and his brother, Jack, said goodbye to their parents at the railway station, Lord Randolph's 'face looked terribly haggard and worn with mental pain. He patted me on the knee in a gesture which however simple was perfectly informing.'[5] In other words, this was the affirmation which Winston so desperately needed that his father loved him . Continued Winston, 'I never saw him again, except as a swiftly fading shadow [i.e. of his father's former self].'

The advice of the doctors proved to be well founded, for there followed a series of ever more alarming bulletins from Dr Keith from abroad about Lord Randolph's deteriorating health. For example, on 4 August 1894, Dr Keith wrote to Dr Roose from Alberta, Canada, to say of Lord Randolph that:

On the day we arrived [2 August] the numbness came on very acutely [evidently in His Lordship's left arm], and though it quickly passed off, it was as bad as I have seen it. While the attack was on his talking was very bad, but there was no change in the reflexes or in the pupils.[6]

The mention of the words 'reflexes' and 'pupils' by Dr Keith suggests that Lord Randolph was suffering from a neurological condition, though precisely what this was is not specified.

Writing from Yokohama, Japan, on 3 October 1894, Dr Keith described in his report 'numbness and slight loss of power in the [Lord Randolph's] left hand [which] persisted for a day or two. His symptoms vary ... one hour quiet and good-tempered, the next hour violent and cross.'[7] Later in the month, on the 30th, Dr Keith reported from Malacca in Malaya:

Perhaps more loss of mental power .... There are no fixed delusions yet, but he has one or two fleeting ones daily. His speech is thicker, and he has a tendency to use wrong words.[8]

Winston must have suspected that something was amiss with his father for, on 2 November 1894, he wrote to Lady Randolph to say somewhat mysteriously, 'I asked Dr Roose and he told me everything and showed me the medical reports. I have told no one ....'[9]

On 4 November, Dr Keith reported from Government House, Singapore:

Lord Randolph has been violent and apathetic by turns since coming here. He is not sleeping well, is losing flesh, and I notice a peculiar condition of the lower part of his face at times. The lower lip and chin seem to be paralysed, and to move only with the jaw. His gait is staggering and uncertain. Altogether he is in a very bad way ....[10]

From these facts, Dr Buzzard concluded that Lord Randolph 'is well into the 2nd stage of G.P. [General Paralysis]'.[11] Winston wrote again to his mother on the 8th to say, 'You must not be cross with me for having persuaded Roose to keep me informed as I shall never tell anyone and it is only right I should know.'[12] In other words, it was imperative that the nature of Lord Randolph's illness be kept a secret. Fourteen days later, Dr Keith wrote from India (it is believed, to Lord Randolph's sister, Cornelia, Lady Wimborne)[13] to say:

> I would only cause you a great deal of grief if I told you what Lord Randolph does and says as it is too painful for words to see a man like Lord Randolph in the progress of this disease. I have had a doctor to see him here and he has confirmed me [i.e. my opinion] in every detail. We have no doubt what is the matter with Lord Randolph and none as to the inevitable end.[14]

On 24 November Dr Roose sent Dr Buzzard a copy of a telegram which he had received from Dr Keith in Madras, India, which read, 'Consultants confirm Diagnosis – time about six months tell Lady Wimborne'.[15] Again, what the diagnosis was is unstated but the clear implication is that Lord Randolph had only six months to live. Whereupon Dr Buzzard replied, 'I quite agree with you that we should telegraph the patient to come home at once.'[16] Finally, on 24 December 1894, Lord Randolph and his entourage arrived back in England.

In a letter to Sir Richard Quain (Physician Extraordinary to the Queen), dated New Year's Day 1895, Dr Buzzard wrote as follows, 'As you are aware Lord Randolph is affected with "General Paralysis" .... '[17] Buzzard's use of quotation marks in this context was quite deliberate, as will shortly be seen.

In two undated letters to Dr Buzzard, sent in January 1895, Dr Keith described how Lord Randolph had been 'bad all day having one delusion after another', and how His Lordship had 'had an attack of acute mania last night lasting twenty minutes and another this morning for two hours'.[18] On 24 January Dr Keith informed Dr Buzzard that the forty-five-year-old Lord Randolph had died 'very quietly this morning at 6.15'.[19] On His Lordship's death certificate the cause of death was stated as 'bronchial pneumonia from paralysis in the brain'.[20] But was there more to Lord Randolph's death than this?

From the above it is obvious, even to a layman, that the doctors who treated Lord Randolph were in no doubt as to the nature of his illness, what course it was likely to take, and what the outcome would be – even if, for reasons of discretion, they omitted, either in their notes or in their correspondence, to identify the condition by name.

When Dr Buzzard wrote 'General Paralysis' (or 'G.P.'), this was an abbreviation for 'General Paralysis of the Insane' (or G.P.I.), for the two expressions are synonymous, and refer to a condition which is the result of a subacute, progressive, meningo-encephalitis, caused by the disease syphilis, which occurs between three and twenty-five years after the primary infection.

Not only was Dr Buzzard in no doubt as to the correctness of the diagnosis, he also predicted its inevitable outcome, when he told Sir Richard Quain that just as His Lordship had experienced

> Successive assaults of paralysis on different parts [of the body] so he may at any time, experience others, & the occurrence of one in a vital situation might produce sudden death. Or it is possible that he may sink into a state of increasing dementia with its accompanying physical troubles – slowly ending in death.[21]

When a man becomes infected with syphilis through sexual intercourse, within a few weeks the disease invades the central nervous system (brain and spinal cord), and eventually causes behavioural changes and madness (to use an outdated term). The first sign that he has the disease is when, up to ten weeks later, but usually about three weeks later, a pimple, or ulceration (the clinical name for which is a primary chancre), occurs at the point of contact (primary syphilis). Within a few weeks, the chancre heals spontaneously, even in the absence of treatment. Six to twelve weeks after infection, a generalized rash appears temporarily (secondary syphilis). The disease then goes into a latent phase, when the patient is both asymptomatic and no longer infectious. This latent phase may last for several years, or even continue indefinitely.

Tertiary syphilis, which can occur between three and twenty-five years after infection,[22] may manifest itself in a variety of ways. Non-cancerous growths – 'gummas' – may form at almost any site in the body; there may be damage to the heart valves and aorta; neurosyphilis, with progressive brain damage and general paralysis, may occur, and, also, damage to the spinal cord (so-called 'tabes dorsalis'). Finally, death occurs, either from cachexia (weakness and wasting of the body), from a complication of syphilis, or from an epileptic seizure. With such a prospect in view, no wonder Lord Randolph was terrified! (It was not until the year 1905 that the causative agent for syphilis was discovered, namely the bacterium treponema pallidum. As for a cure for the disease, this had to wait until the discovery of penicillin in 1928.)

There being no cure for syphilis, all Lord Randolph's doctors could do was to record the progress of the disease, and apprise his family of the likely – some might say inevitable – outcome that was to be expected.

How had Lord Randolph contracted such a disease? In his book, *My Life and Loves*, published in 1925, Frank Harris recounts information, given to him by Louis Jennings (the former editor of the *New York Times* and Conservative politician who was elected Member of Parliament for Stockport, Cheshire, in 1885). Jennings, a mutual friend of both Lord Randolph and Harris (who, in 1889, had published *Speeches of the Right Honourable Lord Randolph Churchill, M.P., 1880-1888*), told the latter that whilst at Oxford University (where Lord Randulph was an undergraduate from the autumn of 1867 until December 1870). His Lordship was made a member of the exclusive Bullingdon Club. One evening, after dining at the club, Lord Randolph drank champagne and brandy, after which he remembered nothing until he awoke the following morning and found himself in bed with a prostitute.[23] Whereupon, panic-stricken and terrified that he may have contracted syphilis from the woman, he immediately consulted a doctor. And he was right to be frightened, for to be diagnosed with syphilis was usually the equivalent of being given a death sentence.

According to Lord Randolph (as reported by Harris), the doctor declared that he could 'find no sign of any abrasion [i.e. on the skin of Lord Randolph's genitalia, through which a venereal infection might have gained access], but he made up a strong disinfectant and I washed the parts with it ...'.[24]

Twenty-two days after the encounter with the prostitute, Lord Randolph returned to the doctor who examined him again and declared, 'Nothing, Lord Randolph, nothing! I congratulate you. You've got off, to all appearance, scot-free.'[25] However, the following evening, at dinner, Randolph 'felt a little tickling' and discovered a 'little, round, very red pimple ...'. (In syphilis, the primary sore – or 'chancre' – tends to cause irritation, rather than itching, so perhaps this is what Lord Randolph meant by 'tickling'.) He returned immediately to the doctor, who, to His Lordship's horror, declared, 'We have there a perfect example of a syphilitic sore!',[26] but added, 'Taken in time [i.e. if treated early enough] we can make it innocuous', and he prescribed mercury (which, when applied topically to the sore – 'chancre' – was believed to be efficacious), and assured His Lordship that if he persevered with the treatment, 'in a year you will be cured and have no ill effects'.[27]

A second, and independent, witness is American socialite and writer Julian Osgood Field, who stated of Lord Randolph as follows:

> The illness that first seized him during his Oxford days, began ere long to cause trouble, and although he was always willing, nay glad, to consult any specialist, he never would follow the treatment recommended.

This was the case when Field arranged for His Lordship to see 'a famous physician' in Paris, who 'prescribed for him, and warned him [i.e. that he must follow the doctor's instructions in respect of the medicines which he had been given]'. However, two days later, Lord Randolph informed Field that he had 'chucked the whole damned lot away'.[28]

The outcome was, said Field, that the 'Hound of Death' then followed him remorselessly, 'and then sprang on him in the first month of the new year [1895] and devoured him – destroyed him utterly'.[29]

Given the fact, as already mentioned, that General Paralysis (one of the possible manifestations of tertiary syphilis) commonly occurs between three and twenty-five years of infection, and that Lord Randolph is alleged to have contracted syphilis whilst at Oxford between 1867 and 1870, then one would expect the General Paralysis to have manifested itself, at latest, by the year 1895. Lord Randolph's General Paralysis had actually been present, according to Dr Buzzard's estimate, since about January 1892, which is well within the expected time-frame.

The classical 'textbook' features of General Paralysis (of the Insane) are as follows, the ones recorded by Lord Randolph's doctors in His Lordship's notes being marked by an asterisk – though the absence of an asterisk does not necessarily mean that the features were not present in his Lordship:

> Irritability*, forgetfulness*, headaches* ['He [Lord Randolph] had an attack last night like inflammation of the brain & groaned & screamed with pain...'],[30] weight loss, poor concentration* and work record*.
>
> Behaviour gradually deteriorates as memory, insight, and judgement are progressively impaired*.
>
> Dress, personal appearance, and social behaviour* become inappropriate.
>
> Alcohol excess, vagrancy, sexual aberration, and various psychotic delusions* may occur, although a simple dementia* is most often seen.
>
> Fits, sometimes with transient focal neurological deficits*, may accompany deterioration, or occasionally herald it.
>
> Motor signs gradually appear until the 'insane' patient becomes 'generally paralysed'* ['Lord Randolph is suffering from General Paralysis, and lies in a semi-comatose and very critical state'[31]], mute*, and incontinent.
>
> Physical signs usually appear after at least some degree of mental deterioration*.
>
> Commonly seen signs are a relaxed and expressionless face, tremor

of the face, tongue*, and lips, and often the whole body; a slurred and tremulous dysarthria* [defined as difficult or unclear articulation of speech, which is otherwise linguistically normal. An example of this in Lord Randolph is when, in May 1894, he told his friend, poet and writer Wilfred Blunt, 'I know what I want to say but damn it, I can't say it.'[32]; pupillary abnormalities....[33]

Given that, as a younger man, Lord Randolph suspected that he had contracted syphilis, why then did he not abstain from having sexual intercourse with his wife, Jennie? The fact that he did not is attested to by the birth of Winston, in 1874, and Jack, in 1880. Lord Randolph evidently contracted syphilis sometime between autumn 1867 and December 1870. However, His Lordship did not meet his wife-to-be until 12 August 1873 – by which time his syphilis would have progressed into a latent phase, in which it was no longer infectious through sexual contact, and in which the symptoms and clinical signs (including the chancre) would have long since healed. When did Lady Randolph first become aware that her husband had syphilis? Presumably from when she consulted with Dr Buzzard and Dr Roose, in the early summer of 1893.

Years later Winston confirmed that he knew the truth about the cause of his father's death when he told his secretary, Anthony Montague Browne, 'You know my father died of locomotor ataxia [inability to control one's body movements], the child of syphilis.'[34]

Did the fact that it was syphilis which caused Lord Randolph's death sully Winston's attitude towards his late father, he being only twenty years old? The answer is, no. Following Lord Randolph's death, Winston was distraught. He had loved his father dearly, even though, during His Lordship's lifetime, he had not been entirely able to attain the high standards which his father had set for him. Nonetheless, he had longed to show Lord Randolph that he could make a success of his life and that he was a son to be proud of, and he had also longed to join him in the political arena. Now, this would no longer be possible. Said Winston, 'All my dreams of comradeship with him, of entering Parliament at his side and in his support, were ended. There remained for me only to pursue his aims and vindicate his memory.' (This he did, by writing a biography of his father entitled *Lord Randolph Churchill*, which was published in 1905.)

Then came a remarkable transformation in the way in which Winston perceived his now-widowed mother, for, as he himself declared:

Indeed she soon became an ardent ally, furthering my plans and guarding my interests with all her influence and boundless energy.

We worked together on even terms, more like brother and sister than mother and son. At least so it seemed to me. And so it continued to the end [i.e. of her life]'.[35]

In particular, Lady Randolph read the books and articles which Winston wrote and attempted to place them with suitable publishers and obtain the best price. And he, in turn, persuaded her to record her recollections of her life with Lord Randolph from 1874 to 1880, which became Chapter 2 of *Lord Randolph Churchill*, Winston's biography of his father. And when she conceived the idea of founding a literary magazine, in order to produce some much-needed income, he was able to advise her. (The *Anglo-Saxon Review*, with Her Ladyship as editor, duly appeared in print in June 1899.)

Although Lord Randolph had, during his lifetime, opposed Winston's wish to transfer from the 60th Rifles to a cavalry regiment, his mother took the opposite view and she now supported her son.[36] The outcome was that, on 20 February 1895, Winston was commissioned as second lieutenant in the Queen's Own Oxfordshire Hussars. Jack would follow in his older brother's footsteps, and also come to hold a commission in the same regiment whose annual training camps were sometimes held in the grounds of Blenheim Palace. (Winston was promoted to captain in January 1902 and, in April 1905, to major in command of the Henley Squadron.)

Notes

1. Dr Thomas Buzzard: Correspondence, MS.B3626, RR: 13:1 Courtesy of Royal College of Physicians, of London. Randolph S. Churchill to Dr Thomas Buzzard, 8 July 1893.
2. Ibid, 25 December 1894.
3. Churchill, Randolph S. *Winston S. Churchill, Youth, 1874-1900*. Companion Volume I, Dr E.C.R. Roose to Dr Thomas Buzzard. 4 May 1894, p. 481.
4. Dr Thomas Buzzard: Correspondence, op cit, Dr Buzzard to Lord Randolph, 4 June 1894, and Dr Buzzard and Dr Roose to Lady Randolph, 25 June 1894.
5. Churchill, Winston S. *My Early Life*, p. 56.
6. Dr Thomas Buzzard: Correspondence, op cit, Dr Keith to Dr Roose, 4 August 1894.
7. Ibid, Dr Keith, Report No. 13, 3 October 1894.
8. Ibid, Dr Keith, Report No. 15, 30 October 1894.
9. Churchill, Randolph S., op cit, Winston to Lady Randolph, 2 November [1894], p. 237.
10. Dr Thomas Buzzard: Correspondence, op cit, Dr Keith, Report No. 16, 4 November 1894.
11. Ibid, Report by Dr Thomas Buzzard and Dr George E Keith, 25 December 1894.

12. Churchill, Randolph S., op cit, p. 238.
13. Cornelia, Lady Wimborne, eldest daughter of John, 7th Duke of Marlborough, and wife of Sir Ivor Bertie Guest, 1st Baron Wimborne.
14. Churchill, Randolph S., op cit, Dr G.E. Keith to Lady Wimborne, 22 November 1894, p. 536.
15. Dr Thomas Buzzard: Correspondence, op cit, Dr Roose to Dr Buzzard, 24.11.1894.
16. Ibid, Dr Buzzard to Dr Roose, 24 November 1894.
17. Churchill, Randolph S., op cit, Dr Thomas Buzzard to Sir Richard Quain, 1 January 1895, p. 544.
18. Dr Thomas Buzzard: Correspondence, op cit, Dr Keith to Dr Buzzard, undated.
19. Ibid, Dr Keith to Dr Buzzard, 23 January (1895).
20. Lee, Celia and John. *Winston & Jack: The Churchill Brothers*, p. 146.
21. Churchill, Randolph S., op cit, Dr Thomas Buzzard to Sir Richard Quain, 1 January 1895, p. 544.
22. Smith, Dr Tony (medical ed). *Complete Family Health Encyclopedia.*
23. Harris, Frank. *My Life and Loves*, p. 485.
24. Ibid, p. 483.
25. Ibid, p. 484.
26. Ibid, p. 484.
27. Ibid, p. 484.
28. Field, Julian Osgood. *Uncensored Recollections*, pp. 306-7.
29. Ibid, pp.314-15.
30. Churchill, Randolph S. *Winston S. Churchill, Youth, 1874-1900.* Companion Volume I, Mrs Moreton Frewen to Mrs John Leslie, January 1895.
31. Dr Thomas Buzzard: Correspondence, op cit, Report signed by Dr Thomas Buzzard and Dr George Keith, 25 December 1894.
32. Blunt, Wilfred S. My Diaries, p.175.
33. Quoted from Ledingham, John G.G. and Warrell, David A. *Concise Oxford Textbook of Medicine*, p. 1365.
34. Browne, Anthony Montague. *Long Sunset: Memoirs of Winston Churchill's Last Private Secretary*, p. 122.
35. Churchill, Winston S., op cit, p. 70.
36. Churchill, Randolph S., op. cit, p. 554.

CHAPTER 8

The Death of Elizabeth Everest: The 4th Hussars

When, at the beginning of July 1895, Winston heard that his former nanny, Elizabeth Everest, was terminally ill, he hurried to her bedside and arranged for 'a good specialist' from London to attend her. After her death, which occurred on 3 July, he declared that he 'felt very despondent and sad. It is indeed another link with the past gone'. He attended her funeral, which took place two days later, and when she was buried at Manor Park Cemetery, Forest Gate, he arranged for a suitable headstone to mark her grave. Its inscription reads as follows:

IN THE MEMORY
OF
ELIZABETH ANN EVEREST
WHO DIED 3rd JULY 1895
AGED 62 YEARS
BY
WINSTON SPENCER CHURCHILL
AND
JOHN SPENCER CHURCHILL

This gesture indicates clearly that Winston wished to preserve the memory of his nanny, and by adding his name and that of his brother, Jack, to the base of the plinth, this was an acknowledgement of the debt which they felt they owed her. 'Mrs' Everest, said Winston, was 'my dearest and most intimate friend during the whole of the twenty years I had lived.'[1]

It has been demonstrated that, during his formative years, Winston required a considerable degree of affirmation – a requirement which his nanny played a considerable role in fulfilling. The question now was, who would provide it for him, when his principal 'affirmer' had departed this life?

The day after the funeral Winston wrote to his mother from the 4th Hussars' barracks at Aldershot in Hampshire to say, 'I am longing for the day when you will be able to have a little house of your own [which was evidently Lady Randolph's ambition] and where I can really feel that there is such a place as home.' However, as far as the regiment was concerned, 'I always look forward to coming back to my friends and ponies here. I have a great many friends ....'[2] (Shortly afterwards, Lady Randolph relocated to 35A Great Cumberland Street, Marble Arch.) The statement by Winston – that he looked forward to seeing his friends – is one of great significance, and for the following reasons. Psychiatrists Terruwe and Baars state that

> Adults who have never grown beyond the childhood stage of emotional development ... *are and feel like children* in their contact with others. As far as their feelings are concerned they are unable to step outside themselves, but instead remain self-centred and egocentric. They can only establish emotional rapport with others when ... others direct themselves to them, precisely as parents orientate themselves to their children. They consider it a matter of course that adult relatives, friends, or acquaintances should ... adjust themselves to their feelings. As long as somebody does this, individuals with Emotional Deprivation Disorder feel at ease, safe, and happy; but in every other kind of contact they feel strange and uncertain. When adults do not orientate themselves to them, they experience this as a shortcoming in the other – they feel that the other is lacking in love. Reasoning this out for themselves, as they usually do, they feel more and more alone and isolated from others.[3]

'Physically and intellectually', state Terruwe and Baars, adults with Emotional Deprivation Disorder

> are grown up. They are regarded as adults and treated accordingly. People expect them to act and react in an adult fashion and do not realize that they are emotionally incapable of doing this. [Such adults may] find it most difficult to make decisions. As soon as they tend one way, they think of arguments that favour the opposite course of action. [They may be] overly sensitive to the opinions of others.
>
> When someone disagrees with them or thinks their actions could have been better, they may suddenly become depressed, downhearted, if not bewildered, and unable to carry on their activities. [They may often feel] helpless and ill at ease in company

because they are *self-conscious* … [They may also have] *a strong feeling of inferiority and inadequacy.*[4]

Had Winston been a severely emotionally deprived person, he would doubtless have exhibited all the above characteristics to the full. However, the fact that, as an adult, he was able to make friends indicates that, despite the trauma of his youth, he was now able to make friends. For, as Terruwe and Baars declare, the more a person develops emotionally 'the more the symptoms of their illness – the uncertainties, fears, and feelings of inferiority – disappear'.[5] And the credit for this must largely go to Winston's beloved nanny, Elizabeth Everest.

However, for Winston life was not all plain sailing, as he reveals in a letter sent from Aldershot to his mother on 24 August 1895 in which he states that, after the end of 'a very hard week', he had entered into a 'slough of Despond' (a quotation from *The Pilgrim's Progress* by John Bunyan), from which 'I try to raise myself by reading & re-reading Papa's speeches – many of which I know almost by heart'.[6]

* * *

Winston's passion for polo, said his godson and biographer Frederick Smith, 2nd Earl of Birkenhead, was 'beyond question'.[7] However, having dislocated his right shoulder at the age of twenty-one, Winston was thereafter obliged to play the game with the upper part of his right hitting-arm strapped to his chest. Winston also 'enjoyed hunting and an occasional day's shooting',[8] as well as a game of golf.

Frustrated by the 'want of a sufficient supply of active service', Winston obtained permission to spend the customary five months of winter leave (1895/96) allowed to him as a hussar officer, in Cuba, where Marshal Martinez Campos, Captain-General of Spain, had been sent to put down an insurrection in the Spanish colony by Cuban nationalists. Winston's companion for this visit would be a 'brother subaltern' named Reginald Barnes.[9] When he informed his mother of his plans, she replied,

You know I am always delighted if you can do anything which interests & amuses you – even if it be a sacrifice to me. I was rather looking forward to our being together & seeing something of you. Remember I only have you & Jack to love me.[10]

The boot was now on the other foot, and it was Lady Randolph who now looked to Winston for love and support!

In Cuba, in November 1895, Winston celebrated his twenty-first birthday, and it was here that he acquired his lifelong liking for Havana cigars. As for his desire for action, his wish was granted when, whilst travelling with a Spanish column of infantry, he was having his breakfast when he came under fire for the very first time, and the horse immediately adjacent to his own horse was struck by a bullet, from which the animal died.[11] He was therefore able to send to the *Daily Graphic* newspaper firsthand reports about the revolt – for a pre-arranged fee of five guineas a time.[12]

In October the following year, 1896, Winston sailed with his regiment to India, where, in his spare time, he read works (sent to him by his mother) by Greek philosopher Plato, Scottish economist and philosopher Adam Smith, English historian Edward Gibbon, English naturalist and evolutionist Charles Darwin and others, together with volumes of the *Annual Register* in which he 'annotated the summaries of old parliamentary debates with imaginary contributions of his own'.[13] (During his father's lifetime he had followed avidly the parliamentary debates in which Lord Randolph had taken part.) In his account of this period his artistic nature and eye for beauty is revealed by the following description of Bangalore:

> Flowers, flowering shrubs and creepers blossom in glorious profusion. Snipe abound in the marshes; brilliant butterflies dance in the sunshine, and *nautch*-girls [professional dancing women] by the light of the moon.[14]

The books that he read in India, said Winston, 'challenged the whole religious education I had received at Harrow'. They included *The Martyrdom of Man* by William Winwood Reade, and William E. H. Lecky's *Rise and Influence of Rationalism and History of European Morals*, and when he discovered that both of these authors, together with Edward Gibbon, took the view that, at the end of our lives 'we simply go out like candles', this, said Winston, 'established in my mind the predominantly secular view. For a time I was indignant at having been told so many untruths, as I then regarded them, by the schoolmasters and clergy who had guided my youth.'[15] Nonetheless, despite passing through what he described as this 'violent and anti-religious phase', Winston, in his own words, still 'did not hesitate to ask [Almighty God] for special protection when [he was] about to come under the fire of the enemy'.[16] In other words, in times of crisis, Winston continued to find comfort in a belief in God, and expressed surprise that the bishops and clergy made

> such heavy weather about reconciling the Bible story with modern scientific and historical knowledge. If you are the recipient of a

message which cheers your heart and fortifies your soul, which promises you reunion with those you have loved in a world of larger opportunity and wider sympathies ... then this was all that mattered.[17]

In December 1896 Winston told his brother, Jack, that he 'deprecated these missionary efforts' [by Christian missionaries in India] on the ground that 'they annoyed the heathen – without really benefiting him'.[18] In his view, 'too much religion of any kind ... was a bad thing. Among natives especially, fanaticism was highly dangerous and roused them to murder, mutiny or rebellion.'[19]

He continued to thirst for military action and procured attachments for himself to various units of the British Army which were involved in the thick of the fighting. To this end, he had no scruples about using his mother's social connections, or even those of his late father, including Prime Minister, Lord Salisbury, which made him unpopular in some circles.

Pashtun tribesmen of Afghanistan's Swat Valley, whose land was bisected by the Durand Line, established as the border between their country and British India, revolted on 26 July 1897 and laid siege to the British garrison in the tribal region of Malakand. One week later the siege was lifted by the Malakand Field Force, consisting of three brigades and commanded by Brigadier General Sir Bindon Blood. Sir Bindon promised that Winston might join him as war correspondent for the *Daily Telegraph* newspaper, prior to his rejoining the army.[20] Sir Bindon was as good as his word and, on Winston's arrival at the North-West Frontier, he was duly attached to Brigadier General P. D. Jeffreys' brigade, which was to mount a punitive expedition to the Mamund Valley. In Winston's words:

It is impossible for the British Government to be content with repelling an injury and it must be avenged. So we in our turn are to invade [the tribal lands of the] Afridis & Orakzais and [that of] others who have dared to violate the Pax Britannica.[21]

The notion of vengeance and retribution for perceived wrongs was one of Winston's core beliefs, as will be demonstrated further. The expedition lasted for seven weeks, and, despite the circumstances, provided Winston with an opportunity to admire the local scenery. Here, in Afghanistan, he said,

valley walls rise steeply, five or six thousand feet on every side. The columns [military] crawl through a maze of giant corridors down which snow-fed torrents foam under skies of brass.[22]

This episode in his life also gave Winston the opportunity to write *The Story of the Malakand Field Force* (1898). Further books would follow.

In his novel *Savrola*, Winston, in portraying the character of the eponymous hero, may equally well have been describing himself, in respect of his own motives and ambitions:

> Ambition was the motive force and he was powerless to resist it. He could appreciate the delights of an artist, a life devoted to the search for beauty, or of sport, the keenest pleasure that leaves no sting behind. To live in dreamy quiet and philosophic calm in some beautiful garden, far from the noise of men and with every diversion that art and intellect could suggest was, he felt, a more agreeable picture. And yet he knew that he could not endure it. 'Vehement, high, and daring' was his cast of mind. The life he lived was the only one he could ever live. [Such men as he] know rest only in action, contentment only in danger, and in confusion find their only peace.[23]

On 18 September 1897, Consuelo, wife of the 9th Duke of Marlborough, produced a son and heir, John Albert William Spencer-Churchill.

Writing from Peshawar in March 1898, Winston revealed his continuing sense of emotional insecurity when he expressed concern to his mother that, if she were to marry again – which she did – then this might be to 'some man I did not like – or did not get on with [in which case] troubles springing up … might lessen your affection for me'. Later in the letter he says how eager he is for a reply from Lady Randolph. 'After all at present there are only us three in the whole world' – in other words, himself, herself, and Jack.[24]

Writing from Bangalore to his Aunt Leonie (his mother, Lady Randolph's sister and the wife of Sir John Leslie) in May 1898, Winston complained he had received only

> two letters from Mamma in the last seven weeks which makes me furious as well as sad. I have never missed one mail although I have sometimes written under varied circumstances. Her silence always makes me pessimistic and forlorn. Indeed the future is very black.[25]

That summer found Winston in the Sudan, once again fulfilling his now familiar dual role of war correspondent – this time for the *Morning Post*, and 'Supernumerary Lieutenant' to the 21st Lancers. This was in the Sudan Campaign where Sir Herbert Kitchener, with his 20,000-strong British and Egyptian force, was engaged in destroying the power of Mohammed Ahmed (the Mahdi), who had revolted against the Egyptians (who had controlled the

Sudan since 1820). Here, once again, the young Winston's imagination was fired by the scenery. For exmple, he declared, in respect of the River Nile:

> From the rocky hills which here and there flank the great river the whole scene lay revealed in minute detail, curiously twisted, blurred and interspersed with phantom waters by the mirage. The finite and concrete presented itself in the most keenly-chiselled forms, and then dissolved in a shimmer of unreality and illusion.[26]

Winston wrote to his mother from Wadi Hebeshi, sixty-five miles west of Omdurman, on 24 August to say that he anticipated going into action 'within the next ten days. I can assure you I do not flinch – though I do not accept the Christian or any other form of religious belief.'[27] Here in the Sudan, Winston participated in the last great cavalry charge in British history (although there were cavalry charges after this, including during the Great War and at Chanak in Turkey after the war) at the Battle of Omdurman (2 September 1898), where he shot dead a Dervish (member of a Muslim tribe) who had suddenly appeared in the midst of his troop of cavalry and threatened him with a spear:

> I shot him at less than a yard. He fell on the sand, and lay there dead. How easy it is to kill a man! But I did not worry about it.[28]

Those inclined to call Winston 'bloodthirsty' would do well to ponder what he subsequently told his mother, that 'The victory of Omdurman was disgraced by the inhuman slaughter of the wounded and that Kitchener was responsible for this.'[29] Once again, out of this experience came another book by him, *The River War*.

On New Year's Day 1899 (the year in which *The River War* was published), Winston told his mother that the story was 'about the Mahdi [Mohammed Ahmed] who was left while still quite young an orphan', and he proceeded to quote from it as follows:

> Solitary trees, if they grow at all, grow strong: and a boy deprived of a father's care often develops, if he escape the perils of youth, an independence and vigour of thought which may restore in after life the heavy loss of early days.[30]

Here is Winston, almost four years after the event, still mourning the death of his late father, Lord Randolph. He now returned to India to complete his tour of duty.

Frances, Dowager Duchess of Marlborough, died at her home, 45 Portman Square, on 16 April 1899. That spring, Winston returned home, and in July, resigned his commission in the Army, albeit 'with many regrets'. His reasons for doing so, in his own words, were twofold: his 'allowance of £500 a year was not sufficient to meet the expenses of polo and the Hussars', and he was 'most anxious not to be a burden' upon his mother.[31] The proverbial boot was again now on the other foot and he urged Lady Randolph, 'I … beg you not to bet or play cards …'![32] In that same month, Winston contested a by-election, as Conservative candidate for the seat of Oldham, Lancashire, but he was defeated.

* * *

When the Second South African War broke out in the autumn of 1899, this gave Winston another opportunity to travel, and on 11 October he set sail for that continent in the capacity of Principal War Correspondent for the *Morning Post* – at a salary of £250 per month, with all expenses paid.

In Natal, on 15 November 1899, Winston found himself travelling in an armoured train which was ambushed and derailed by the Boers. Despite his civilian status he took charge of the situation and, showing great courage, managed to effect the freeing of the locomotive and its tender. According to Boer accounts, the British sustained in the action two killed, ten wounded and fifty-six captured; one of the prisoners was Winston.[33] As for Winston, he affirmed that 'upwards of forty [British] soldiers were carried to safety in the engine'.[34] (Winston subsequently learned that the 'mounted burgher [who] summoned me to surrender' was none other than General Louis Botha, Commander-in-Chief of the Boer forces, who later became Prime Minister of the Union of South Africa.)[35]

Winston was imprisoned at Pretoria but managed, after twenty-six days of captivity, to escape and, despite the Boers offering a price of £25 for him to be taken, 'dead or alive',[36] he made his way to Portuguese East Africa [now Mozambique] and from there to Durban.

At about this time, wealthy US citizen Bernard Nadel Baker, President of the Atlantic Transport Company, donated a former cattle-transporting ship, the *Maine*, to the British Government free of charge, for use as a hospital ship. Whereupon Lady Randolph, and other wealthy American women living in London, set up the US Hospital Ship Fund (of which she became chairman) the objective of which was to raise sufficient funds for the vessel to be fully equipped and staffed. By December all was ready and on the 23rd of that month the *Maine*, with Lady Randolph aboard, set sail from Portsmouth to Cape Town, and subsequently to Durban.[37]

In early-January 1900 Winston persuaded British Commander-in-Chief General Sir Redvers Buller to grant him a commission (unpaid) in the South

African Light Horse whilst at the same time permitting him to continue in his role of war correspondent. Meanwhile, on 5 January, his brother, Jack, sailed from England for South Africa, where he too became a lieutenant in the South African Light Horse. However, on 12 February, when Winston and Jack were fighting side by side at Hussar Hill in the vicinity of Colenso, the latter sustained a bullet wound to the leg. He was invalided out to Durban, to the hospital ship *Maine*, there to be received by his mother, Lady Randolph, where the two were joined by Winston, who had obtained a few days' leave. Winston subsequently participated in the Battle of Spion Kop (23/24 January 1900), in which the British were defeated, and in the relief of the town of Ladysmith, Natal, which took place on 28 February. The town had been besieged by the Boers for a period of almost four months.

In a subsequent action at Dewetsdorp, forty miles south of Bloemfontein in the Orange Free State, Winston had dismounted from his horse when he came under fire from the Boers. When he attempted to remount, the horse bolted. Fortunately, a passing scout gave Winston a lift on *his* horse, only to have it shot from under him by a Boer marksman. This time, however, Winston was able to make his escape. From these adventures, two more books followed, *London to Ladysmith via Pretoria* (1900), and *Ian Hamilton's March* (1900). Finally, in early May 1900, Winston joined Sir Ian Hamilton's column on its advance from Bloemfontein to Johannesburg and Pretoria in the Transvaal (which surrendered on 31 May and 4 June respectively).

Referring to an incident which had occurred in the South African War, Winston declared,

> I rode on my grey pony all along the skirmish line where everyone was lying down in cover. Foolish perhaps but I play for high stakes and given an audience there is no act too daring or too noble. Without the gallery things are different.[38]

In the South African War, Winston was Mentioned in Despatches, i.e. he had performed a deed so noteworthy as to be mentioned in an official report by a superior officer. Referring again to the South African War, Winston told his brother, Jack,

> I had no military command and only rode about trying to attract attention – when things looked a little dangerous.[39]

By 'attract attention', Winston presumably meant the attention of the Boers, whose first reaction on catching sight of him would be to open fire. Was this what he really wanted? To be fired upon by the enemy? And if so, why would any person in his right mind deliberately place himself in harm's way? Almost half a century later, in June 1944, whilst aboard a warship which was sailing off the coast of France, Winston was asked exactly the same question by his fellow passenger, Prime Minister of the Union of South Africa, Jan Christiaan Smuts. The significance of this will be discussed later.

* * *

Life in the Hussars suited Winston admirably, as long as there was action to be found, and although he sometimes incurred the opprobrium of his colleagues by using his family connections in his quest for that military action, he more than acquitted himself by the heroic deeds that he performed. And by writing articles for newspapers, he not only augmented his income but also proved that he could, if necessary, earn enough money to make a living in this field. His description, quoted earlier, of the scenery, flora and fauna of Bangalore, for example, is adequate testimony not only to his eloquence, but also to his eye for beauty and to his artistic temperament. Also, in India, he was able to compensate for the fact that he had not been to university, by reading extensively to improve his mind. But even now, whenever he was abroad, he depended on receiving letters from his mother, and all the more since the demise of Elizabeth Everest.

* * *

Already, various character traits in Winston have become apparent. For example, his exploits during the South African War indicate a willingness to engage in risky activities, despite the risk of painful consequences to himself.

Notes

1. Churchill, Winston S. *My Early Life (MEL)*, pp. 80-1.
2. Churchill, Randolph S. *Winston S. Churchill, Youth, 1874-1900.* Companion Volume I, (*YOUTH* CVI) Winston to Lady Randolph, 6 July 1895, pp. 579-80.
3. Baars, Conrad W. and Terruwe, Anna A. *Healing the Unaffirmed: Recognizing Emotional Deprivation Disorder*, pp. 8-9.
4. Ibid, pp. 22-4, 27 & 31.
5. Ibid, p. 113.
6. Churchill, Randolph S., *Winston S. Churchill, (YOUTH) 1874-1900.* Winston to Lady Randolph, 24 August 1895, p. 260.
7. Birkenhead, Earl of. *Churchill 1874-1922*, p. 60.

8.   Ibid, p. 115.
9.   Churchill, Winston S., *MEL* op cit, pp. 83-4.
10. Churchill, Randolph S., *YOUTH* CVI op cit, Lady Randolph to Winston, 11 October 1895, p. 590.
11. Churchill, Winston S., *MEL* op cit, p. 92.
12. Churchill, Randolph S., *YOUTH* op cit, p. 267.
13. Matthew, H.C.G., and Brian Harrison (editors). *Oxford Dictionary of National Biography*, Volume 11, p. 655.
14. Churchill, Winston S., *MEL* op cit, p. 111.
15. Ibid, p. 121.
16. Ibid, p. 121.
17. Ibid, p. 122.
18. Churchill, Randolph S., *YOUTH* CVI op cit, Winston to Jack, 16 December 1896, pp. 711-12.
19. Churchill, Winston S., *MEL* op cit, p. 121.
20. Churchill, Randolph S., *YOUTH* op cit, General Sir Bindon Blood to Winston, 22 August 1897, p. 349.
21. Churchill, Randolph S. *YOUTH* CVI op cit, Winston to Lady Randolph, 31 August 1897, p. 783.
22. Churchill, Winston S., *MEL* op cit, p. 141.
23. Churchill, Winston S. *Savrola*, p. 37.
24. Churchill, Randolph S. *Winston S. Churchill, Youth, 1874-1900*. Companion Volume II, (*YOUTH* CVII) Winston to Lady Randolph, 27 March 1898, p. 901.
25. Churchill, Randolph S., *YOUTH* CVII op cit, Winston to Mrs John Leslie, 3 May 1898, p. 925.
26. Churchill, Winston S., *MEL* op cit, p. 178.
27. Churchill, Randolph S., *YOUTH* CVII op cit, Winston to Lady Randolph, 24 August 1898, p. 969.
28. Churchill, Winston S, *MEL* op cit, p. 200.
29. Chartwell Papers, in Birkenhead, Earl of, *Churchill 1874-1922*, p. 84.
30. Churchill, Randolph S., *YOUTH* op cit, Winston to Lady Randolph, 1 January 1898, p. 428. Churchill, Winston Spencer. *The River War*, p. 17.
31. Churchill, Winston S., *MEL* op cit, pp. 204-05.
32. Churchill, Randolph S., *YOUTH* CVII op cit, Winston to Lady Randolph, 23 July 1899, p. 1039.
33. Ibid, P.J. Joubert to F.W. Reitz, 15 November 1899, p. 1062.
34. Ibid, Winston Spencer Churchill to the Editor, *The Spectator*, Undated, p. 1070.
35. Churchill, Winston S. *Thoughts and Adventures*, pp. 3–4.
36. Churchill, Winston S., *MEL* op cit, p. 298.
37. Ibid, p. 328.
38. Chartwell Papers, in Earl of Birkenhead, *Churchill 1874-1922*, pp. 74-5.
39. Ibid, p. 75.

CHAPTER 9

Politics

Winston described how

> The greatest and most powerful influence in my early life was of course, my father. Although I had talked with him so seldom and never for a moment on equal terms, I conceived an intense admiration and affection for him, and, after his early death, for his memory. I read industriously almost every word he had ever spoken, and learnt by heart large portions of his speeches. I took my politics almost unquestioningly from him.[1]

Winston also described how, when he became a gentleman cadet at Sandhurst, his father

> took me ... to important political parties [i.e. assemblies] at [London financier] Lord Rothschild's house at Tring [Hertfordshire], where most of the leaders and a selection of the rising men of the Conservative Party were often assembled. [However] If ever I began to show the slightest idea of comradeship, he was immediately offended; and when once I suggested that I might help his private secretary to write some of his letters, he froze me into stone.[2]

Nevertheless, this experience undoubtedly whetted Winston's appetite for politics. Of Winston's father, Lord Randolph, A. L. Rowse remarked,

> In his last years his views took an even more Radical turn ... He sensed the emergence of the working class as the foremost thing in the politics of the future. His views took on a collectivist tinge. He was anxious for the House of Commons to examine a demand for an eight-hour day [for workers including coalminers]. It is possible that had he lived, he would have moved over to the Liberal Party ... .[3]

Winston, in the years to come, would echo his late father's concern for the underprivileged, as will be seen.

It is clear that Winston was considering leaving the Army at least as early as 6 October 1898, when the Prince of Wales wrote to him to say,

> I can well understand that it must be very difficult for you to make up your mind what to do, but I cannot help feeling that Parliamentary & literary life is what would suit you best as the monotony of military life in an Indian [military] station can have no attraction for you … .[4]

However, in March 1899, in a letter to Frances, Duchess of Marlborough, Winston did not mention politics directly. He was about to leave the Army and declared that,

> had the army been a source of income to me instead of a channel of expenditure – I might have felt compelled to stick to it. But I can live cheaper & earn more as a writer, special correspondent or journalist, and this work is moreover more congenial and more likely to assist me in pursuing the larger ends of life.[5]

In the general election, held in October 1900, he stood again as Conservative candidate for Oldham, and, this time, not only was he successful but his Conservative Party was returned to power with a large majority.

Lady Consuelo, wife of the 9th Duke of Marlborough, wrote about Winston in glowing terms, describing him as

> the life and soul of the young and brilliant circle that gathered round him at Blenheim; the circle in which the women matched their beauty against more intellectual attractions of the men. Whether it was his American blood or his boyish enthusiasm and spontaneity, qualities sadly lacking in my husband, I delighted in his companionship. His conversation was invariably stimulating, and his views on life were not drawn and quartered, as were Marlborough's, by a sense of self-importance.[6]

Consuelo subsequently described how, at the dinner table at Blenheim 'at which we often lingered until midnight, [we were] carried away by Winston's eloquence …'.[7]

> I noted his frequent references to his father, Lord Randolph Churchill, and was struck by his evident admiration and respectful reverence for him; I had a presentiment that inspired with such memories he would seek to emulate him![8]

How right Consuelo was, for Winston would not only emulate the late Lord Randolph, he would eclipse him. Meanwhile, on 28 July 1900, Lady

Randolph, now aged forty-six, was remarried to British Army officer George Cornwallis-West, aged twenty-six.

Subsequently, following a highly profitable lecture tour of the USA and Canada, which 'netted him the handsome sum of £10,000',[9] Winston duly took his seat in the House of Commons in the government of Robert Cecil, Marquis of Salisbury (who had been Prime Minister since 1895) and, on 18 February 1901, he delivered his maiden speech to the House. Speechmaking, however, did not come easily to Winston, who described how, having made a speech in the House of Commons as a young Member of Parliament, he would become

> oppressed with the fear that he had committed an irreparable error which might prejudice his political future. He had to school himself not to think about things when they had gone wrong, for he found that he could not live with his mistakes and keep his balance. This urge to obliterate [his mistakes from his mind] had, in course of time, grown into a cast of mind in which he seemed incapable of seeing that he had been at fault.[10]

In December Liberal statesman, writer, and newspaper editor, John Morley, recommended to Winston that he read social reformer, Benjamin Seebohm Rowntree's book, *Poverty: A Study of Town Life*, which led Winston afterwards to say,

> I have been reading a book which has fairly made my hair stand on end, written by a Mr Rowntree who deals with poverty in the town of York. It is found that the poverty of the people of that city extends to nearly one-fifth of the population ... . That I call a terrible and shocking thing.

Winston went on to compare British labourers with their 'stronger, larger, healthier [and] better fed' American counterparts, 'and this is surely a fact which our unbridled Imperialists, who have no thought but to pile up armaments, taxation, and territory, should not lose sight of'.[11]

When Lord Salisbury was succeeded as Prime Minister by his nephew, Arthur Balfour in May 1902, Winston was not offered a place in the government. Meanwhile, he made some influential friends, among them the financiers, Sir Ernest Cassel and Baron Maurice de Forest, who invited him to cruise with them on their yachts in the Mediterranean. A year later Joseph Chamberlain, Leader of the Opposition Liberal Unionists and Secretary for the Colonies (in the Conservative/Liberal Unionist coalition government) began pressing for protection and tariff reform (the protection of British industry from 'unfair' foreign imports) – a concept which Winston, who was in favour of free trade, strongly opposed. The party became divided and, on 31 May 1904, Winston crossed the floor of the House to join the opposition Liberal Party. Said he, with a heavy heart,

> it is a lamentable thing to leave the party which you have been brought up in from a child, and where nearly all your friends and kinsmen are.[12]

Meanwhile, in the previous month of April, there was drama when Winston addressed the House of Commons during the debate on the Trade Union and Trades Disputes Bill. Years later Winston's grandson and namesake stated as follows: he

> had been speaking for 45 minutes when his memory failed him. There was a long, embarrassed silence. He sat down and covered his head with his hands in despair and humiliation. Thereafter he always had a text as a back up. I think he was frightened that he might be headed the way his father was, who by the age of 40 was losing his marbles. He must have a horror fear that this might be his fate, too. It gave him a terrific compulsion to make his mark before it was too late.[13]

The irony of the situation was that this was the same Winston, whose avowed intention was to dominate the House of Commons. He would not make this mistake again.

When, in December 1905, Conservative Prime Minister Arthur Balfour resigned, Liberal Sir Henry Campbell-Bannerman succeeded him as Prime Minister of a minority government. Campbell-Bannerman now offered Winston his first post as a government minister – that of Under-Secretary of State at the Colonial Office. Whereupon, Winston immediately appointed Edward Marsh, a collector of paintings, patron of contemporary artists, and scholar, as his private secretary.[14]

In the general election, held from 12 January to 8 February 1906, the Liberal Party won by a landslide. This time, Winston stood for North-west Manchester and was elected Liberal MP for that constituency.

Violet Asquith (later Violet Bonham Carter) first met Winston in the early summer of 1906. At the time her father, Herbert Henry Asquith, was Chancellor of the Exchequer in Campbell-Bannerman's Liberal government. (Asquith subsequently became Liberal Prime Minister, 1908-1916.) Violet commented on how industrious and assiduous Winston was at that time. Said she, he

> indulged in very little 'play'. He was entirely absorbed in his work

and thought of little else. [Much as] pleasure might beckon, and the sirens [winged creatures from Greek mythology, who sang to lure unwary sailors onto the rocks] sing in vain, it could not coax his nose from the grindstone. Even at week-end parties ... he arrived accompanied by his work and often spent the whole morning toiling at it in his bedroom, appearing at luncheon still in its grip. At balls as elsewhere he was impervious to his surroundings, blind and deaf to the gyrating couples, the band, the jostling, sparkling throng.[15]

Violet Asquith's comments on Winston's obsessive focus, or what today would be described as 'goal-directed activity' gives yet another valuable insight into his character.

In that year, 1906, Winston visited France, Switzerland, Silesia and Venice. In September, he was invited to Germany as the guest of German emperor Kaiser Wilhelm II, to observe military manoeuvres by the army of that country. In the autumn of 1907, Winston went on a hunting expedition to East Africa. However, always anxious to combine pleasure with business, he soon turned this into a fact-finding mission. The outcome was that he wrote a series of articles for the *Pall Mall Gazette*, later published as *My African Journey* (1908).

When, in March 1908, Campbell-Bannerman was succeeded by Herbert H. Asquith, Winston, then aged thirty-three, joined Asquith's Cabinet as President of the Board of Trade. Convention dictated that Winston was now obliged to re-contest his North-west Manchester parliamentary seat.

As a Tory, Winston had opposed Irish Home Rule. However, as a Liberal, he wrote to his Prime Minister, asking the following rhetorical question, 'Is Mr Churchill in favour of Home Rule, meaning an Irish Parliament for the management of purely Irish affairs ... ? Yes,' and he continued, 'I am encouraged by the striking success of a bold and generous policy in South Africa to approach Irish difficulties in a similar spirit ... .'[16]

Winston's defeat, on 24 April 1908 in the North-west Manchester by-election, came as a shock, and three days later he wrote to Clementine Hozier (whom he was to marry shortly) as follows,

I was under the dull clouds of reaction on Saturday after all the effort & excitement of that tiresome election, and my pen did not run smoothly or easily. This morning however, I am again buoyant ... . Write to me again – I am a solitary creature in the midst of crowds. Be kind to me.[17]

However, in the following month of May Winston contested a by-election in

Dundee, Scotland, this time successfully. (He retained his Dundee seat until 1922.) That summer he compared himself with 'Sunny' (his cousin Charles, 9th Duke of Marlborough) who, he said, was 'absolutely dependent upon feminine influence of some kind for the peace & harmony of his soul'. In contrast, said Winston, he himself was 'naturally quite self-reliant & self-contained. Yet by such [very] different paths we both arrive at loneliness!'[18] And yet, in the very same month, Winston told Clementine 'I do long for you so much – I wonder how I have lived 23 years without you.'[19]

Notes

1. Churchill, Winston S. *Thoughts and Adventures*, [*TA*] p. 31-2.
2. Churchill, Winston S. *My Early Life*, pp. 53-4.
3. Rowse, AL. *The Churchills: The Story of a Family*, pp. 402-03.
4. Churchill, Randolph S., *Winston S. Churchill, Youth, 1874-1900*, (*YOUTH*) Prince of Wales to Winston, 6 October 1898, p. 420.
5. Churchill, Randolph S., *YOUTH* op cit, Winston to Frances, Duchess of Marlborough, 26 March 1899, p. 442.
6. Balsan, Consuelo Vanderbilt. *The Glitter and the Gold*, p. 103.
7. Ibid, p. 114.
8. Ibid, p. 103.
9. Matthew, H.C.G., and Harrison, Brian (editors). *Oxford Dictionary of National Biography*, Volume 11, p. 656.
10. Moran, Lord., *Winston Churchill: The Struggle for Survival 1940-1965*, pp. 181-2.
11. Churchill, Randolph S., *Winston S. Churchill, Young Statesman*, (*YS*) 1900-1914, pp. 31-2.
12. Churchill, Winston S., *TA* op cit, p. 6.
13. Winston's grandson, Winston Churchill, in *Churchill: The Greatest Briton of All Time*, 2002, A TW1/Carlton Production.
14. Edward Howard Marsh who was knighted in 1937; served as Winston's Private Secretary from 1905-1915; 1916-1922, and 1924-1929.
15. Bonham Carter, Violet. *Winston Churchill an Intimate Portrait*, pp. 113-15.
16. Churchill, Randolph S., *YS* op cit, Winston to HH Asquith, 18 April 1908, pp. 447-48. (On 31 May 1910 the Union of South Africa came into being as a self-governing dominion of the British Empire. In May 1921, following the enactment of the Government of Ireland Act of 1920 and the ratification of the Anglo-Irish Treaty of 1921, Ireland was partitioned into the Irish Free State (Saorstát Éireann) and Northern Ireland – Ulster – the population of which had opted to remain part of the United Kingdom.)
17. Soames, Mary (editor). *Speaking for Themselves: The Personal Letters of Winston and Clementine Churchill*, Winston to Clementine, 27 April 1908, p. 9.
18. Ibid, Winston to Clementine, 8 August 1908, p. 13.
19. Ibid, Winston to Clementine, probably August 1908, p. 16.

CHAPTER 10

Romance: Marriage

Violet Bonham Carter (née Asquith) commented on the fact that Winston's 'inner circle of friends contained no women. His approach to women was essentially romantic.' In other words, Winston saw women purely from a romanticized viewpoint. But, nevertheless, she affirmed that he did have female friends.[1] In fact, Winston previously had been attracted to Pamela Plowden, whose father was Resident (i.e. Governor) at Hyderabad, India, American actress Ethel Barrymore, and Muriel Wilson, society beauty and daughter of a shipping magnate. But none of these relationships had come to fruition. However, for him, romance was just around the corner.

Winston had first met his wife-to-be, Clementine Ogilvy Hozier, daughter of Sir Henry Hozier and Lady Blanche Ogilvy (who in turn was daughter of the 10th Earl of Airlie), in the summer of 1904 at a ball at Crewe House – home of Liberal politician the Marquess of Crewe. Winston was then aged twenty-nine and Clementine nineteen. The couple did not meet again for four years.

Winston proposed to Clementine on 11 August 1908 at the ornamental Temple of Diana – situated in the grounds of Blenheim Palace overlooking the lake – and the couple were married at St Margaret's, Westminster, on 12 September that year. At the wedding the address was given by Winston's former headmaster from Harrow, James Welldon – now Bishop and Dean of Manchester, who declared,

> There must be in the statesman's life many times when he depends upon the love, the insight, the penetrating sympathy, and the devotion of his wife.[2]

How prophetic and insightful these words would turn out to be.

The couple spent the first few days of their honeymoon at Blenheim before proceeding to Italy. On their return they commenced their married life together at Winston's home – 12 Bolton Street, Westminster, London. Winston, as already mentioned, was a person who needed 'affirmation' in his life more than most. The question now was, would Clementine be able to provide him with this 'affirmation'?

* * *

At this time, Winston was working closely with David Lloyd George, Chancellor of the Exchequer in Herbert Asquith's Liberal Government. The two men had a warm relationship and Winston was 'always welcome' at, and 'a frequent visitor' to, Lloyd George's house at Cobham in Surrey. This was an honour which Lloyd George reserved for specially selected friends only.[3] The two men now worked together on various social projects designed to give those employed in the 'sweated trades' (those whose workers were obliged to work excessively long hours in poor conditions) a statutory minimum wage; to provide state-run employment exchanges whose purpose was to assist the unemployed in their search for work; and to make unemployment insurance compulsory.[4]

Winston and Clementine acquired 33 Eccleston Square, which they made their home, in March 1909. In May Winston was to be found at 'Camp Goring' (presumably in Goring-by-Sea in Sussex), performing military manoeuvres with the Queen's Own Oxfordshire Hussars, in which both he and his brother Jack held commissions.

From here he wrote to Clementine in the terms of greatest affection, beginning his letter 'My darling sweet', and ending it 'Goodbye my beloved Clemmie I would so much like to kiss your dear lips & to curl up snugly in your arms ... .'[5] On 11 July the couple's first child, Diana, was born.

Clementine's pet names for Winston included 'Pug', 'Puggie Wow', 'Amber Pug', or 'Pig', whereas his pet names for her included 'Cat', or 'Kat', 'Clem Pussy Bird', and 'Clemmie-cat'. When Clementine became pregnant the couple nicknamed the unborn child 'PK', short for 'Puppy Kitten'. When the child was duly born on 11 July 1909, she was christened Diana.[6]

When he was at boarding school Winston had set great store on receiving letters on a frequent and regular basis from his nanny and from his parents. Now, when he and she were separated, the same applied in respect of his new wife. For instance, on 31 August 1909, Winston wrote to Clementine to say, 'I have had no letter from you today .... Do send me a telegram in the morning – in case you have not written.'[7] Many such plaintive letters to Clementine were to follow, reflecting Winston's dependency upon her as his new 'affirmer'. And Clementine duly obliged in her characteristically loving and supportive way.

In a letter to Winston, dated 11 September 1909, Clementine enclosed a drawing of two cats: the larger, designated 'Kat', representing herself, and the smaller, designated 'Kitten', representing the infant Diana. The following day, Winston wrote as follows,

> My precious & beloved Clemmie my earnest desire is to enter still more completely into your dear heart & nature & to curl myself up in your darling arms. I feel so safe with you ... .[8]

Four days later Winston wrote to his wife again, including in his letter a drawing of 'the galloping Pug'.[9] Such amusing sketches were a feature of the couple's correspondence over many years. Four days later, writing to Clementine from Würzburg, Germany, Winston ended his letter 'Sweet cat – I kiss your vision as it rises before my mind. Your dear heart throbs often in my own. God bless you darling & keep you safe & sound.'[10]

What was the significance of Winston and Clementine's 'Pug' and 'Cat' conversations, and of his letters to her in which he includes such amusing sketches as 'the galloping Pug', 'a tranquil Pug', and a 'wistful but unashamed Pug', and of her letters to him in which she includes sketches such as 'The Kat', whose 'tail is gradually getting its curl back'?

In his book *Games People Play: The Psychology of Human Relationships*, Canadian-born psychiatrist Eric Berne states that 'The most gratifying forms of social contact ... are games and intimacy.'[11] He then goes on to describe how an individual, in the course of his or her daily life, has a tendency to shift from one 'ego state' to another. For example, at one time he may find himself in the mindset of a child, in another in that of an adult, and in a third, in that of a parent.[12] When Winston and Clementine indulge in 'Pug Speak' this represents an ego state which is clearly more reminiscent of that of a child rather than an adult. However, says Berne reassuringly, varying ego states within one individual can be regarded as 'normal physiological phenomena', and 'each type of ego state has its own vital value for the human organism'.[13]

In Germany, on 15 September 1909, Winston, again the guest of the Kaiser, watched 'great manoeuvres' performed by the German Army, and remarked,

> I think another 50 years will see a wiser & a gentler world. But we shall not be spectators of it. Much as war attracts me & fascinates my mind with its tremendous situations – I feel more deeply every year – & can measure the feeling here in the midst of arms – what vile and wicked folly & barbarism it all is.[14]

A few days later Winston visited the battlefield of Blenheim in Bavaria,

Germany, where his ancestor, the 1st Duke of Marlborough, and Prince Eugène of Savoy had defeated the French on 13 August 1704.[15]

In October 1909 Winston spoke of the 'good and comforting influence' which Clementine had brought into his life. 'It is a much better life now.'[16] Writing from the Board of Trade in late October 1909 Winston told Clementine, 'My Sweet I felt [very] lonely in my bed last night & thought often of you.'[17] Clementine wrote to Winston in her usual loving and supportive way on 3 November to tell him 'how much I think of my Pug all day & of all the struggles, difficulties & complications he is encountering just now ... '.[18] Winston was then preparing to contest the parliamentary seat of Dundee in the general election of January 1910. A week later Winston wrote to Clementine from the Board of Trade to give reassurance to her about some misunderstanding which had arisen between the two of them. He spoke of

absolutely wild suspicions [which] are so dishonouring to all the love & loyalty I bear you & will please god bear you while I breathe. I could not conceive myself forming any other attachment than that to which I have fastened the happiness of my life here below. And it offends my best nature that you should ... indulge small emotions & wounding doubts. You ought to trust me for I do not love & will never love any woman in the world but you and my chief desire is to link myself to you week by week by bonds which shall ever become more intimate & profound.[19]

In the General Election of January 1910, the Liberals lost their overall majority and the result was a hung parliament, led by Prime Minister Herbert Asquith, who appointed Winston to the post of Home Secretary. Two of the burning issues of the day were prison reform (of which Winston was in favour) and women's suffrage – to which, said Mary Soames, Prime Minister H. H. Asquith 'was resolutely opposed'. Winston, however, was in favour of votes for women in principle, but he deplored the violent tactics employed by the suffragettes, which included attacking members of parliament, amongst them himself and the Prime Minister, damaging paintings in the National Gallery, disrupting political meetings, and arson.[20] Many of the suffragettes were arrested and imprisoned, including Mrs Emmeline Pankhurst, who, in 1905, had launched the Militant Suffrage Movement. It was probably for this reason that Winston opposed the Suffrage Bill of 1910.

Writer James Pope-Hennessy describes how the 'emotional and impatient' new young Home Secretary, Winston, threw himself into his work with gusto, as he proceeded to bombard the new head of the Colonial Office [Lord Crewe, Secretary of State for the Colonies – from 1910-15] with a shower of suggestions, uninvited hints and scraps of unsolicited advice.[21]

When, on 7/8 November 1910, rioting broke out in the South Wales coalfield in a dispute over wages, (the so-called Tonypandy riots), Winston despatched both troops and police with instructions that the police act as a buffer between the strikers and the troops. This was in order to avoid unnecessary bloodshed.[22] However, on 16 December, during the 'Siege of Sydney Street', Winston met violence with violence, by sending troops to assist the police in a gunfight with immigrant burglars from Latvia who were attempting a robbery.

The general election of December 1910 resulted once again in a hung parliament led by Asquith. On the 20th of that month, Clementine commented to Winston, 'Dearest you work so hard & have so little fun in your life ... .'[23]

The Churchills' second child, Randolph – nicknamed 'Chum Bolly' or 'Rabbit', was born on 28 May 1911. On 23 October, Asquith appointed Winston First Lord of the Admiralty, where, with the help and inspiration of retired First Sea Lord John 'Jackie' Fisher, he instituted a programme of reform. With characteristic thoroughness, but also a disregard for protocol, Winston

inspected ships, dockyards, and naval installations with a vigilant eye ... he sometimes bypassed senior naval officers and sought information directly from junior officers or ordinary seamen.

As he presided over the development of 'a fast division of battleships, the Queen Elizabeth Class, equipped with the new 15-inch gun', foremost in his mind was that Britain 'should retain a clear margin of naval supremacy over Germany'.[24] He also became involved in the vexed question of home rule for Ireland.

Winston played a round of golf with Louis Botha, South African statesman and commander-in-chief of Boer forces during the South African War, and the very man who had captured Winston during that campaign, who was visiting England in June 1911. 'We are all thoroughly friendly now and these fierce memories scorch no longer,' said Winston.[25] The following month he told Clementine he had purchased 'some toys for the P.K. [Diana]' – some painted 'Noah's Ark animals'.[26]

There was, however a cloud on the horizon, what Winston described as the 'Black Dog' – his term for the episodes of depression to which he was prone. For example, in a letter to Clementine, dated 11 July 1911, he referred to Lady Alice (née Grosvenor, wife of his cousin Sir Ivor Churchill Guest), as follows:

Alice interested me a great deal in her talk about her doctor in Germany, who completely cured her depression. I think this man might be useful to me – if my Black Dog returns. [However] He [the 'Black Dog'] seems quite far away from me now – It is such a relief. All the colours came back into the picture. Brightest of all your dear face – My darling.[27]

(The circumstances in which the 'Black Dog' had previously affected Winston, who was now aged thirty-six, are not specified, but from the above it is clear that he had experienced it prior to July 1911.) Mary Soames said of her father, Winston,

Although 'Black dog' had haunted him as a younger man, the beast had never undermined his power of action...[28]

However the truth was that, for Winston, the Black Dog would prove to be an enduring affliction.

On 9 February 1912 Winston declared,

The purposes of British naval power are essentially defensive. We have no thoughts of aggression ... and we attribute no such thoughts to other great Powers. There is, however, this difference between the British naval power and the naval power of the great and friendly Empire ... of Germany. The British Navy is to us a necessity and, from some points of view, the German Navy is to them more in the nature of a luxury. Our naval power involves British existence. It is existence to us; it is expansion to them.[29]

In April Winston told Clementine who was visiting Paris with friends, that 'both the chicks [children] are well and truculent. Diana & I went through the Peter Rabbit picture book together & Randolph gurgled ... He looks vy [sic] strong & prosperous.'[30]

In July Winston sent the British First Fleet secretly through the Straits of Dover into the North Sea and assembled the Second Fleet at Portland, Dorset, on a 'preparatory and precautionary basis'.[31] Nine months later, Kitchener paid this compliment to Winston, when he told him, 'Well, there is one thing at any rate they cannot take from you. The Fleet was ready.'[32]

In a letter to Clementine of January 1913, sent from HMS *Enchantress*, a *Bittern*-class sloop, Winston revealed his underlying sense of insecurity. There had evidently been another misunderstanding between them, for which he apologized, saying,

I was stupid last night – but you know what a prey I am to nerves & prepossessions. It is a great comfort to me to feel *absolute* confidence in your love & cherishment of your poor P.D. [Pug-Dog] Don't be disloyal to me in thought. I have no one but you to break the loneliness of a bustling and bustled existence.[33]

On 6 April 1913 Winston expressed satisfaction to Clementine that 'three creatures are in their pens [i.e. in prison]'.[34] This was a reference to three suffragettes, one of whom was Emmeline Pankhurst, who had been sentenced to three years' imprisonment 'for inciting her supporters to place explosives in the house of the Chancellor of the Exchequer – David Lloyd George'.[35]

In late April Winston asked his mother, Lady Randolph, if she would care to join himself and Clementine on a Mediterranean cruise.[36] That October he encouraged Clementine to accept an invitation from his Aunt Cornelia (Lady Wimborne), saying, 'I have a great regard for her – & we have not too many friends.'[37] Meanwhile, Clementine delivered political speeches on Winston's behalf, counselled him against mixing with the wrong type of politicians, and was solicitous for his welfare – for example, by urging him, in October 1913, to abandon his flying lessons.[38] Shortly afterwards, on 3 November, Winston told Clementine, 'Alas I have no [very] good opinion of myself. At times, I think I [could] conquer everything – & then again I know I am only a weak vain fool.' He went on to describe Clementine's love for him as his 'greatest glory. I only wish I were more worthy of you, & more able to meet the inner needs of your soul … .'[39] However, on 29 November, he confessed that he had 'been naughty today about flying',[40] i.e. he had once more taken to the skies.

On 8 February 1914, having had to fight hard in order to persuade the Cabinet to provide more ships for the Royal Navy, Winston wrote, 'I am becoming more & more a fatalist', and proceeded to quote from the *Holy Bible*'s Book of Revelations, 'He that overcometh shall inherit all things … .' However, he declared '"overcometh" means "overcometh oneself" – [which] is a hard job when so many others are at it too.'[41]

Lady Randolph and George Cornwallis-West were divorced in April 1914. The following month Winston wrote to Clementine to request that she 'Kiss … with care and earnestness Diana & Randolph on my behalf. Did you buy him a birthday toy from me & what was it? I am hoping much to come & see them next week … .'[42] On 28 July Winston wrote to her again from the Admiralty, and declared,

Everything trends towards catastrophe & collapse. [But nevertheless] I am interested, geared-up & happy. Is it not horrible to be built like that? The preparations have a hideous fascination for me. I pray to God to forgive me for such fearful moods of levity – Yet I [would] do my best for peace, & nothing [would] induce me wrongfully to strike the blow – I cannot feel that we in this island are in any serious degree responsible for the wave of madness wh [which] has swept the mind of Christendom. No one can measure the consequences.[43]

He ended the letter, 'Kiss those kittens [Diana and Randolph] & be loved forever only by me Your own W.'[44] On 2 August he told Clementine, 'I miss you much – Your influence when guiding & not contrary is of the utmost use to me.'[45] On the same day he told her, 'It is all up. Germany has quenched the last hopes of peace by declaring war on Russia … .'[46]

Britain and France declared war on Germany on 4 August, that country having declared war on both Russia and France, and invaded Belgium.

Notes

1. Bonham Carter, Violet. *Winston Churchill an Intimate Portrait*, pp. 117-18.
2. Churchill, Randolph S. *Winston S. Churchill, Young Statesman, 1900-1914*, [*YS*] p. 274.
3. Thompson, Walter H. *I was Churchill's Shadow*, p. 193.
4. Matthew, H.C.G. and Harrison, Brian (editors). *Oxford Dictionary of National Biography*, Volume 11, p. 658. (These plans came to fruition with the passing of the 'Trade Boards Act' of 1909.)
5. Churchill, Randolph S. *Winston S. Churchill, Young Statesman, 1900-1914*. Companion Volume II, [*YS* CVII] Winston to Clementine, 30 May 1909, p. 894.
6. Soames, Mary (editor). *Speaking for Themselves: The Personal Letters of Winston and Clementine Churchill*, p. 19.
7. Ibid, *SP* Winston to Clementine, 31 August 1909, p. 26.
8. Ibid, Winston to Clementine, 12 September 1909, p. 29.
9. Ibid, pp. 27-8 & 30.
10. Churchill, Randolph S., *YS* CVII op cit, Winston to Clementine, 15 September 1909, p. 912.
11. Berne, Eric. *Games People Play: The Psychology of Human Relationships*, p. 18.
12. Ibid, p. 23.
13. Ibid, p. 26.
14. Soames, Mary, *SP* op cit, Winston to Clementine, 15 September 1909, p. 30.
15. Ibid, p. 31.
16. Ibid, Winston to Clementine, 18 October 1909, p. 33.
17. Ibid, Winston to Clementine, 26 October 1909, p. 35.
18. Ibid, Clementine to Winston, 3 November 1909, p. 36.
19. Churchill, Randolph S., *YS* op cit, Winston to Clementine, 10 November 1909, p. 295.

20. Soames, Mary, *SP* op cit, p. 32.
21. Pope-Hennessy, James, *Lord Crewe: the Likeness of a Liberal*, in Churchill, Randolph S. *Winston S. Churchill, Young Statesman*, p. 246.
22. Matthew, H.C.G. and Harrison, Brian, op cit, Volume 11, p. 659.
23. Soames, Mary *SP* op cit, Clementine to Winston, 20 December 1910, p. 42.
24. Matthew, H.C.G., and Harrison, Brian, op cit, Volume 11, p. 659.
25. Soames, Mary, *SP* op cit, Winston to Clementine, 18 June 1911, p. 47.
26. Ibid, Winston to Clementine, 11 July 1911, p. 53.
27. Ibid, Winston to Clementine, 11 July 1911, p. 53.
28. Soames, Mary, *Clementine Churchill*, p. 254.
29. Churchill, Randolph S., *YS* op cit, p. 563.
30. Soames, Mary, *SP* op cit, Winston to Clementine, 18 April 1912, p. 63.
31. Churchill, Randolph S.,*YS* op cit, p. 708.
32. Gilbert, Martin. *Churchill*, p. 43.
33. Soames, Mary, *SP* op cit, Winston to Clementine, 30 January 1913, p. 69.
34. Ibid, Winston to Clementine, 6 April 1913, p. 72.
35. Ibid, Winston to Clementine, p. 73, note 1.
36. Churchill, Randolph S., *Winston S. Churchill, Young Statesman, 1900-1914,* Companion Volume III, Winston to Lady Randolph, 24 April 1913, p. 1379.
37. Soames, Mary, *SP* op cit, Winston to Clementine, 19 October 1913, p. 77.
38. Ibid, Clementine to Winston, 23 October 1913, p. 80.
39. Ibid, Winston to Clementine, 3 November 1913, p. 81.
40. Ibid, Winston to Clementine, 29 November 1913, p. 82.
41. Ibid, Winston to Clementine, 8 February 1914, p. 84.
42. Ibid, Winston to Clementine, 29 May 1914, p. 88.
43. Ibid, Winston to Clementine, 28 July 1914, p. 96.
44. Churchill, Randolph S., *YS* op cit, Winston to Clementine, 28 July 1914, p. 711.
45. Soames, Mary, *SP* op cit, Winston to Clementine, 2 August 1914, p. 98.
46. Ibid, Winston to Clementine, 2 August 1914, p. 98.

CHAPTER 11

War: First Lord of the Admiralty;
The Dardanelles Campaign

A s First Lord of the Admiralty, Winston would now become embroiled in a campaign which would be disastrous, both for the Allied cause and for his own standing as a politician. The Allied Fleet was about to steam, full ahead, into a minefield. The minefield which Winston was now to enter was of a political nature.

Meanwhile, Clementine continued to give her husband her loyal support but, nevertheless, was quite capable of criticizing or reproving him when she felt that the occasion demanded it. For example, on 4 August 1914, the day Britain declared war on Germany, she warned Winston, in respect of two senior naval officers who had been replaced by others considered to be more suitable to perform the tasks in hand, of the possible resentments that this might cause:

> Don't underrate the power of women to do mischief. I don't want Lady Callaghan & Lady Bridgeman[*] to form a league of retired Officers' Cats, to abuse you.[1]

And, on 12 August 1914, Winston's wife advised him never to miss his morning horse ride, to go to bed 'well *before* midnight' and to avoid smoking 'too much'.[2]

At the onset of the First World War relations between Britain and Turkey were good. In fact, British Rear Admiral Arthur Limpus, for the previous two years, had been naval advisor to the Turkish government, and the Turks had agreed to purchase two battleships from Britain: the *Reshadieh* and the *Sultan*

---

[*] Lady Callaghan was the wife of Sir George Callaghan, Supreme Commander of the Home Fleet, until the outbreak of war when he was replaced by Sir John Jellicoe. Lady Bridgeman was the wife of Admiral Sir Francis Bridgeman, who had retired prematurely as First Sea Lord in 1912, to make way for Prince Louis of Battenberg.

Osman I. (In the event, neither ship was delivered to the Turks.) Ironically, as it transpired, it was Admiral Limpus who, in July 1914, advised the Turks to strengthen their defences in the Dardanelles. The Dardanelles strait, which was of great strategic significance, was situated in north-western Turkey, and connected the Mediterranean Sea with the Sea of Marmara and the Black Sea.

Turkish leader Enver Pasha, however, was pro-German, and, on 2 August, two days before Britain declared war on Germany, he signed a secret treaty with the Germans whereby, in the event of war between Turkey and Russia, Germany and Turkey would become allies. Turkey proceeded to put its fleet, its army and its capital, Constantinople (today's Istanbul), under the control of the Germans, and German Admiral Wilhelm Souchon was made commander-in-chief of the Turkish navy, which was reinforced by the German battlecruiser *Goeben* and the light cruiser *Breslau.*

On 8 August the Russian Ambassador to London, Count Benkendorff, expressed concern to the Foreign Secretary, Sir Edward Grey, that, 'with the connivance of Turkey', the Austrian Fleet might mount an attack on Russian ports by being allowed passage from the Adriatic to the Black Sea, Austria-Hungary being Germany's ally. When, on 11 August, Winston learnt that the two aforementioned German warships had entered the Dardanelles strait, he ordered Admiral Sir Archibald Milne, Commander of Britain's Mediterranean Fleet, to blockade this waterway.

On 27 August, Major Frederick Cunliffe-Owen, British Attaché to Turkey, declared that

> It may be advisable to consider [the] question of our fleet entering the Straits. In respect of this, if mines can be negotiated, there should be little apprehension of difficulty in running past the shore defences and once off Stamboul [Constantinople], [our] position would be a commanding one, completely paralysing all military movements between [the] European and Asiatic shore.

Having issued the above caveat in respect of the mines, Cunliffe-Owen added another. Said he, 'I should be against a fleet enterprise only.'[3] In other words, he felt that land forces would be required to support the fleet.

Meanwhile, Lady Randolph was anxious to make a contribution to the war effort, just as she had done in the South African War. Now, she was instrumental in persuading Paris Singer, son of Isaac Merritt Singer – founder of the Singer Sewing Machine Company – to permit his residence, Oldway Mansion, Paignton, Devonshire, to be used as a military hospital. Also, Lady Randolph became chairman of the American Women's War Relief Fund's

Executive Committee which financed the provision of ambulances for the Front, and clothing for refugees, etc.[4]

On 1 September 1914 Winston, with Kitchener's approval and with Cunliffe-Owen's suggestion in mind, asked the Chief of the Imperial General Staff, General Sir Charles Douglas, 'to examine and work out a plan for the seizure, by means of a Greek army of adequate strength, of the Gallipoli Peninsula, with a view to admitting the British Fleet to the Sea of Marmara'.[5] Such an action would force Turkey out of the war and allow the Allies to continue sending supplies to the Russians via the Black Sea. However, such a plan depended on the Allies being able to persuade Greece, a neutral country, to enter the war on their side. The plan came to nought (and it was not until 2 July 1917 that Greece entered the war on the Allied side). Nevertheless, matters progressed, as the memorandum of a meeting between Major General Charles Callwell, Director of Military Operations and Intelligence (DMO) at the War Office, and Colonel Milo Talbot, General Staff Officer at the War Office, held that same day, 1 September, at the Admiralty, indicates:

> The representatives of the Admiralty stated that with 6 weeks' warning they could collect sufficient military transport to convey 40,000 to 50,000 men to the selected landing places. Ships of war could also be provided to cover the landing with their fire. [However] The DMO stated that, considering the strength of the Turkish Garrison & the large force already mobilized in European Turkey [i.e. by the Turks], he did not regard it as a feasible military operation & that he believed this to be the War Office view.[6]

Following another meeting at the Admiralty, held on 3 September, between Winston, Callwell, Captain Cecil Lambert (Fourth Sea Lord), Captain Herbert W. Richmond (Assistant Director of Operations at the Admiralty) and Prince Louis of Battenberg (formerly First Sea Lord), Callwell reported to Kitchener as follows. Although an attack on Gallipoli was

> 'likely to prove an extremely difficult operation of war', he nevertheless now considered that with a force of sixty thousand men such an attack would be justifiable.[7]

The implication is, therefore, that Callwell changed his mind, albeit reluctantly, because he was 'leaned upon', presumably by Winston and others.

On 5 September 1914 the Belgian Government asked Britain to assist in the defence of the fortress of Antwerp. Winston responded by despatching one marine and two naval brigades, the latter drawn from the Royal Naval Division, a formation which he himself had created only as recently as 16 August 1914. The exercise was a failure and, on 10 October, Antwerp surrendered to the Germans.

On 27 September 1914 the squadron commanded by British Vice Admiral Sackville Carden, which was patrolling off Cape Helles at the southern extremity of the Dardanelles, intercepted a Turkish torpedo boat. Finding German sailors aboard, Carden ordered it to turn back whereupon Colonel Erich Weber, the German officer commanding the Turkish defences, closed the strait and mined its waters, the minefield stretching for a distance of about eight miles either side of the Narrows, where the waterway was less than one mile wide. Meanwhile, on 7 October 1914, Sarah, nicknamed 'Bumble Bee', the Churchills' third child, was born.

In late October 1914, when the First Sea Lord, Prince Louis of Battenberg, was forced to resign on account of anti-German sentiment, Winston recalled seventy-three-year-old Admiral of the Fleet, Lord John 'Jackie' Fisher, to come out of retirement and fill his post.

On 30 October 1914 the *Goeben* and the *Breslau* bombarded the Russian Black Sea ports of Odessa, Nikolaev, and Sevastapol, which – the Dardanelles being closed – they could do with impunity. Whereupon the British sent an ultimatum to the Turks demanding that the German military and naval missions to Turkey be withdrawn, and also the two warships, within twelve hours. When this warning was ignored, Vice Admiral Carden was ordered to bombard the Dardanelles forts, which he did on 3 November. Meanwhile, on 2 November, Russia declared war on Turkey and three days later, on 5 November, Britain and France also declared war on Turkey. That winter the Turks launched an offensive against Russia in the Caucasus.

On 22 December 1914 Winston told Fisher, 'The Baltic is the only theatre in [which] naval action can appreciably shorten the war.'[8] Fisher responded by stating that any attack on Turkey must be 'IMMEDIATE'. Fisher also stated that such an attack must be a combined naval and military operation, involving in excess of, at least, 75,000 troops.[9]

On 30 December Grand Duke Nicholas II, the Russian Tsar, advised Sir John Hanbury-Williams, Chief of the British Military Mission to the Russian Army, that the Turks

> were seriously threatening the Russians in the Caucasus, and asked
> for British help in reducing the Turkish pressure which endangered
> the Russian military effort against the Germans.[10]

As a result, Kitchener asked Winston, 'Could we not ... make a demonstration at the Dardanelles?'[11] However, when Winston pressed him to supply troops for the enterprise, Kitchener, whilst acknowledging that the Turks were probably sending their troops via the Black Sea to reinforce their army which was fighting the Russians, declared, 'We have no troops to land anywhere' and that even if he had, 'We shall not be ready for anything big for some months.'[12]

On 3 January 1915 Winston enquired of Vice Admiral Carden, 'Do you consider the forcing of the Dardanelles by ships alone a practicable operation?' To this Carden replied two days later, 'They [the Dardanelles] might be forced by extended operations with large numbers of ships.'[13]

On 13 January, at a meeting of the British Government's (Cabinet) War Council (presided over by the Prime Minister, and composed of senior ministers and their advisors who met to formulate and instruct war policy), both Lloyd George and Kitchener declared that they were in favour of a naval operation to capture the Dardanelles strait.[14] On 15 January, Winston informed Carden that the War Council had 'authorized plans to go ahead and that he [Carden] would be in command of the attack'.[15]

On 18 January 1915 Winston sent a telegram to the French Minister of Marine, Victor Augagneur, seeking France's support for a proposed naval attack on the Dardanelles forts. The draft of this telegram was approved by Asquith, Kitchener, Fisher, and Foreign Secretary Sir Edward Grey.[16] However, on 21 January, Fisher (a member of the War Council) broke ranks and reverted to his original position, telling Admiral of the Fleet, Sir John Jellicoe, 'I just abominate the Dardanelles operation, unless a great change is made and it is settled to be made a military operation, with 200,000 men in conjunction with the Fleet.'[17]

On 3 February 1915 a Turkish attack on Egypt was repulsed. On 14 February 1915 Captain Herbert Richmond, Assistant Director of Operations at the Admiralty, came in on the side of Fisher when he declared in a memorandum that 'the bombardment of the Dardanelles, even if all the forts are destroyed, can be nothing but a local success, which without an army to carry it on can have no further effect'. Maurice Hankey, Secretary to the War Council, entirely concurred with Richmond's sentiments and duly forwarded the latter's memorandum – which he declared to be 'absolutely A.1' – to Fisher. Fisher told Richmond, 'Your paper is excellent.'[18]

On 15 February Admiral Sir Henry Jackson, of the Admiralty War Staff, added his weight to the proceedings by declaring in a memorandum that 'The naval bombardment is not recommended as a sound military operation, unless a strong military force is ready to assist in the operation, or, at least, follow it up immediately the forts are silenced.'[19]

A combined land and sea attack on the Dardanelles was therefore agreed to, for which, on 16 February 1915, at an emergency meeting of the War Council, Kitchener consented to make the 29th Division, of 19,000 troops, available. (This was a division of the Regular Army, formed in 1915 of units recalled from garrison duties throughout the Empire.) Furthermore, it was agreed that a large contingent of Australian and New Zealand troops – already stationed in Egypt – together with a battalion of Royal Marines, should be made ready 'in case of necessity to support the naval attack of the Dardanelles'.[20] The strength of the combined force would be about 50,000 men.[21] However, by the time the War Council met on 19 February, Kitchener had changed his mind. Citing recent Russian reversals in East Prussia, he now declared that the 29th Division was required to be held in reserve for possible reinforcement of the Western Front.

On 10 March 1915 Kitchener informed the War Council that his position in regard to the 29th Division had altered yet again, and that he now felt sufficiently confident that the situation on the Western Front had been stabilized, and therefore 29th Division was available for the Dardanelles operation. However, the Division would not be able to reach the Dardanelles in less than a month.[22] Despite this fact, the Anglo-French naval attack on the Dardanelles commenced at 10.45am on 18 March 1915, when ten battleships – six British and four French – entered the strait and bombarded the Turkish forts covering the minefields in Kephez Bay. However, a combination of poor weather and the fact that not all of the Turkish land batteries had been put out of action meant that the British minesweepers were unable to clear the minefields. This was to have disastrous consequences, there being in excess of 400 mines to contend with, together with others which the Turks floated down on the current towards the Allied ships. Shortly after 2.00pm the French battleship *Bouvet* struck a mine and was sunk. Subsequently, four more battleships were also put out of action by the Turks. These were Britain's *Inflexible* (disabled by a mine); *Irresistible* and *Ocean* (both sunk by mines) and France's *Gaulois* (disabled by gunfire). To add to the difficulties, on 16 March, Carden was obliged to relinquish his command on medical grounds. He was succeeded by his second-in-command, Rear Admiral John de Robeck.

By the time of the subsequent land campaign the Turks had, of course, been alerted thoroughly. The plan for the campaign was, in de Robeck's words, to effect a decisive and overwhelming attack on the Narrows, in which Navy and Army can mutually assist each other to the utmost, the first duty of the Navy being to cover landing and advance of Army; second, to attack the Narrows in conjunction with the Army.[23]

The attack commenced on 25 April 1915 when an expeditionary force consisting of British (including the 29th Division), Australian, New Zealand, Indian and French forces was landed at various points on the Gallipoli peninsula. (During the campaign, Winston's brother, Jack, served at Gallipoli as major on the staff of the army commander, Major General Sir Ian Hamilton.) Meanwhile, the Turks had used the intervening time to reinforce their positions and, over the next nine months, 46,000 Allied troops would be killed in action, with virtually no progress having been made.

On 11 May 1915 Fisher and Hankey were of one mind – that military success was a prerequisite before any further naval attempt on the Dardanelles was made. This is reflected in a memorandum, prepared by Hankey for Fisher, and sent to Winston, which read,

> I cannot, under any circumstances, be a party to any order to Admiral de Robeck to make an attempt to pass [force] the Dardanelles until the shores have been effectively occupied.[24]

On 12 May, the British battleship *Goliath* was sunk by a Turkish torpedo boat. On 13 May Winston telegrammed de Robeck to say, 'We think the moment for an independent naval attempt to force the Narrows has passed and will not arise again under present conditions.' On that same day, Fisher told Asquith's wife, Margot, 'I was always as you know against this mad expedition.'[25]

Two days later, on 15 May, Fisher resigned his post, and, the next day, the exasperated former First Sea Lord told Winston, 'YOU ARE BENT ON FORCING THE DARDANELLES AND NOTHING WILL TURN YOU FROM IT – NOTHING – I know you so well!' In other words, Fisher was convinced that Winston was obsessively focused on this particular 'goal', and would pursue it come what may and at whatever cost.[26]

Also on the 16th, Violet Asquith, at her home, the Wharf, situated on the bank of the River Thames at Sutton Courtenay, Oxfordshire, observed Winston

> standing at the bottom of the lawn by the river's brink looking like Napoleon at St Helena. He was very low I thought poor dear. I asked him if he knew he was on the edge of a volcano in his relations with

Fisher – he said no – they had always got on perfectly well – differed on no principle – he had always supposed him perfectly loyal etc. *Poor* Winston – there is a very naïve disarming trustfulness about him – he is quite insensitive to climatic conditions.[27]

On 18 May 1915 Sir Max Aitken (created 1st Baron Beaverbrook in 1917) declared, 'What a creature of strange moods he is – always at the top of the wheel of confidence or at the bottom of an intense depression … .'[28] The following day, said Violet, Winston

sat down on a chair – as I have never seen him – really despairing for the moment – with no rebellion or anger even left. He never even abused Fisher – simply said, 'I'm finished … I'm done. What I want above all things is to take some active part in beating the Germans. But I can't – it's being taken from me.[29]

The question now was, what future, if any, did Winston have at the Admiralty? Before his fate was decided, Clementine interceded loyally with Asquith on his behalf, but to no avail,[30] and, on 21 May, the Prime Minister wrote to Winston to say, 'You must take it as settled that you are not to remain at the Admiralty.'[31] On that same day Winston told Asquith, 'My responsibility is terrible. I did not believe it was possible to endure such anxiety.'[32]

On the weekend of 22/23 May, Asquith offered Winston the Chancellorship of the Duchy of Lancaster – a minor Cabinet position, which he accepted. He would, however, be permitted to retain his place on the War Council.[33] On 26 May, Asquith announced the formation of a Liberal/Conservative coalition government but, in exchange for their cooperation, the Conservatives had made it a condition that Winston was removed, both from the Admiralty and from the War Council.

On that same day, 26 May, having resigned from the Admiralty, Winston and his family vacated the First Lord's official residence – Admiralty House. (He was replaced as First Lord of the Admiralty by Arthur Balfour.) As the Churchills had let their home – 33 Eccleston Square – Winston's brother, Jack, and his wife, Gwendeline (nicknamed 'Goonie'), invited them to share their abode at 41 Cromwell Road, South Kensington with themselves and their two sons. Meanwhile, Clementine had not been idle, for throughout the course of the war she had organized canteens (premises where refreshments were served) for munitions workers on behalf of the Young Men's Christian Association.

WAR: FIRST LORD OF THE ADMIRALTY

Notes

1. Soames, Mary (ed.). *Speaking for Themselves: The Personal Letters of Winston and Clementine Churchill*, Clementine to Winston, 4 August 1914, p. 99.
2. Ibid, Clementine to Winston, 12 August 1914, p.102.
3. Gilbert, Martin. *The Challenge of War: Winston S. Churchill 1914-1916*, p. 199.
4. Lee, Celia and John. *The Churchills: A Family Portrait*, p. 178.
5. Gilbert, Martin, op cit, p. 202.
6. Ibid, Colonel Charles Milo Talbot, Memorandum prepared 5 September 1914, p. 203.
7. Ibid, p. 203.
8. Ibid, p. 225.
9. Ibid, p. 234.
10. Ibid, p. 231.
11. Ibid, p. 232.
12. Ibid, pp. 232-3.
13. Ibid, pp. 234 & 237.
14. Ibid, p. 252.
15. Ibid, p. 254.
16. Ibid, p. 256.
17. Ibid, p. 260.
18. Ibid, pp. 286-7.
19. Ibid, p. 287.
20. Ibid, p. 288.
21. Ibid, p. 288.
22. PRO.ADM, 1437b.q.1251. In Birkenhead, Earl of. *Churchill 1874-1922*, p. 362.
23. Gilbert, Martin, op cit, p. 382.
24. Ibid, p. 420.
25. Ibid, p. 426.
26. Ibid, p. 441.
27. Pottle, Mark (ed.). *Champion Redoubtable: the Diaries and Letters of Violet Bonham Carter 1914-1945*, p. 52.
28. Beaverbrook, Lord. *Politicians and the War, 1914-1916*, p. 385.
29. Pottle, Mark, op cit, p. 53.
30. Ibid, p. 57.
31. Gilbert, Martin, op cit, Churchill Papers 13/52, p. 464.
32. Ibid, Winston to H.H. Asquith, 21 May 1915, pp. 463-4.
33. Ibid, p. 468.

CHAPTER 12

Winston Resigns from the Government: Aftermath; A Painter is Born

O n 5 December 1914 Asquith had said of Winston,

His volatile mind is at present set on Turkey & Bulgaria, & he wants to organize a heroic adventure against Gallipoli and the Dardanelles: to [which] I am altogether opposed ... .[1]

Asquith's words imply that it was solely at Winston's instigation that the Dardanelles campaign was launched, and ignore the fact that the question arose as the result of the Russian Tsar asking Britain for help, and from Major Frederick Cunliffe-Owen, British Attaché to Turkey's notion of 'our fleet entering the Straits'. Furthermore, the decision for action was agreed unanimously by the members of the War Council, each and every one of whom – including Asquith – must take their share of the blame.

Also, to be fair to Winston, he had always envisaged a combined naval *and* military operation – and not simply a naval one. Of this fact he subsequently reminded the Dardanelles Commission, which was established in 1916 to enquire into the Dardanelles campaign. Refusing to blame Kitchener for the debacle, he said, in regard to the build-up to the campaign,

At this time I must make it clear that I was pressing for the collection of an army in the Eastern Mediterranean for contingencies, among which helping the Fleet through [the Dardanelles strait] was one, reaping the fruits if they got through was another, and general action in support of our diplomacy to bring in [neutral] Greece was a third.[2]

And to be fair to Kitchener, the latter would have given his support more readily, and more quickly, had his hands not been tied by the uncertain situation of the Western Front.

WINSTON RESIGNS FROM THE GOVERNMENT

The following statement by Winston indicates that he accepted full responsibility in the Dardanelles campaign, for his failure to coordinate the land and sea attacks so that they occurred simultaneously. Nevertheless, he considered it to be unfair that he should be made scapegoat for the failure of the operation:

It seems clear now that when Lord Kitchener went back upon his undertaking to send the 29th Division to reinforce the army gathering in Egypt for the Dardanelles expedition and [thereby] delayed it for nearly three weeks, I should have been prudent then to have broken off the naval attack. I did not do it, and from that moment I became accountable for an operation, the vital control of which had passed to other hands. The fortunes of the great enterprise which I had set on foot were henceforward to be decided by other people. But I was to bear the whole burden in the event of miscarriage.[3]

Violet Bonham Carter wrote poignantly of

the unfair attacks [made] upon him [Winston] for the failure at Gallipoli, of his desire for a public enquiry, in which he could have the chance of vindicating himself, of the Government's duty to lay the relevant papers before parliament; of his sense of unjust exclusion from the great world struggle in which he knew that he could play an essential part, of all the ideas he could pour into it – now running to waste in the sand.[4]

But it was perhaps Lloyd George who gave the fairest summing up of Winston's role in the Dardanelles campaign, when he wrote,

It is true that the conception of a one-sided Naval operation without simultaneous military action was due to Mr Churchill's impetuosity, but both the Prime Minister and Lord Kitchener were equally convinced that it was the right course to pursue.[5]

In June 1915 Winston, who was champing at the proverbial bit, told his brother, Jack,

I find it [very] painful to be deprived of direct means of action, but I bear the pangs ... . I do not think the present arrangement will last forever and I hope to regain a fuller measure of control [over government policies] before the end of the year.[6]

Said Clementine of Winston,

The Dardanelles haunted him for the rest of his life. He always believed in it. When he left the Admiralty he thought he was finished … . I thought he would never get over the Dardanelles; I thought he would die of grief.[7]

But despite all evidence to the contrary, he remained extraordinarily optimistic about the Dardanelles campaign, telling his brother, Jack, on 2 October 1915,

I am sure we shall carry the Dardanelles to ultimate victory. Do not despair whatever happens, or let others do so. I wish I were with you so much. Here with full knowledge & now lots of time on my hands it is damnable. But for the present this is my post.[8]

However, Winston's former colleagues in government did not share his views, and in the autumn of 1915 their appetite for the Dardanelles campaign waned progressively and, in early November, the 'Dardanelles Committee', the name by which the War Council was now officially known, was reduced in size and Winston was excluded from it, although he retained his seat in the Cabinet. Finally, the decision was made to withdraw the troops, whereupon, on 15 November, Winston felt that he had no choice but to resign from the government. Nevertheless, he remained as an MP. In his speech of resignation, made to the House of Commons that day, he described the Dardanelles campaign as 'a legitimate gamble'[9], words hardly likely to endear him to the families of the dead, the wounded or of those who were missing in action. Winston's use of the 'gamble' was no accident, for, as will be seen, he was a risk-taker by nature.

Not only did Winston become the principal scapegoat for the failure of the Dardanelles campaign but, because this overshadowed all else, his 'immense achievements' at the Admiralty, which were carefully enumerated by his biographer, Frederick Smith, 2nd Earl of Birkenhead, were conveniently forgotten. They included,

The conversion of the [British] Fleet to oil, the Anglo-Persian Oil Agreement which produced such a vast accumulation of wealth for Britain, the initiation and proving of the 15-inch gun and the creation of the incomparable Fast Division [a squadron of fast battle cruisers] made Winston's time at the Admiralty [October 1911-May 1915] memorable.[10]

And Professor A. M. Low, inventor and President of the Institute of Patentees, described how Winston 'fought to start the Royal Naval Air

Service [founded in 1912, whose task was to protect Britain's naval ports and oil storage facilities]', and also encouraged the development of the tank as a weapon of war.[11]

Why, it may be asked, was Winston so anxious to pursue to the bitter end a plan which, with hindsight, may be regarded as grandiose and unrealistic, and why did he fail to recognize this fact? Whatever the reason, and this will be discussed later, the outcome was that, by clinging to the belief that the Dardanelles operation would be a success, long after all hope of achieving a successful resolution had gone, together with the colossal loss of life which it had entailed, Winston became deeply unpopular. Also, this debacle, together with the failure of the Antwerp expedition of the previous autumn, for which Winston was also held to be responsible and which was still fresh in peoples' minds, led those around him to mistrust his judgement.

*   *   *

For Winston, personally, 1915 contained one tiny glimmer of light for, in June, when he was at his lowest ebb, there had occurred a remarkable incident which was to bring him lasting joy, instead of sorrow and frustration. Said Mary Soames,

> painting came to him as an amazing sort of rescue therapy after the Dardanelles in 1915, when, quite by accident, he saw his sister-in-law, Aunt 'Goonie' [Gwendeline, wife of Winston's brother, Jack] painting in watercolours in the garden.

The incident which Mary refers to occurred in June 1915 when brother, Jack, Gwendeline and family had paid a visit to the Churchills at Hoe Farm near Godalming in Surrey, which Winston and Clementine rented as a weekend retreat. Continued Mary,

> He was walking around like a bear with a sore head, miserable, because of the crisis, and she said to him, 'Winston, why don't you try this; it's such a lovely occupation?' And he tried two or three strokes with her paintbrush, and borrowed one of the children's paint-boxes and was hooked. And for forty years after that he painted whenever he could. Wonderful. I think it had a very, very profound affect on his whole psyche. He always said, you know, that it made him look at everything in a different way. I mean, he always liked a beautiful view, but after he started to paint he saw different

things in it, and more depth or colour, or whatever. And I think also it was a terrific occupation. A person with a mind like that can't do nothing.[12]

When Winston's secretary, Edward Marsh, stated that 'Winston had never seen anyone paint before' this was not strictly true, for, in fact, Winston had been introduced to painting at an early age, as will be seen, and the outcome was that

On the Monday morning he bought-up practically the entire contents of Roberson's colour-shop in Piccadilly – easels, palettes, brushes, tubes and canvases. The new enthusiasm, spurring him to rapid progress, was a distraction and a sedative that brought a measure of ease to his frustrated spirit.[13]

For Winston, who subsequently did Gwendeline the honour of painting her at Hoe Farm, this now became not only a lifelong hobby, but also a therapy.

Sir John Lavery, RA, was primarily a painter of portraits and of ceremonial occasions. He was also one of the Great War's official war artists. He and his wife, Hazel, the daughter of a wealthy industrialist from Chicago who was also a gifted painter, lived at 5 Cromwell Place, South Kensington, and were, therefore, near neighbours of the Churchills. Said he,

Mr Churchill has been called a pupil of mine, which is highly flattering, for I know few amateur wielders of the brush with a keener sense of light and colour, or a surer grasp of essentials. I am able to prove this from experience. We have often stood up to the same *motif*, and in spite of my trained eye and knowledge of possible difficulties, he, with his characteristic fearlessness and freedom from convention, has time and again shown me how I should do things. Had he chosen painting instead of statesmanship I believe he would have been a great master with a brush and as PRA [President of the Royal Academy] would have given a stimulus to the Art world.[14]

In the autumn of 1914 Lavery had painted a portrait of Winston in service uniform, prior to the latter's embarkation for the Western Front. Now, in 1915, Winston would paint Lavery as the latter, in turn, painted in his studio, and Lavery once again painted Winston, this time at his easel in the garden of Kingston Hill, Kingston-upon-Thames, Surrey, the home of General Sir Arthur Paget and his wife, Mary. Winston subsequently painted Lavery's wife, Hazel, and Lavery's studio itself. Winston's portrait of Sir John Lavery was shown 'in the exhibition held by the Royal Society of Portrait Painters in 1919'.[15]

Art historian and collector Professor Thomas Bodkin,[16] describes how, in early July 1915, when Winston was painting, Lady Lavery intervened and

> took over the command. Seizing the tyro's [novice's] biggest brush, she mixed a lavish quantity of pigment on his palette and proceeded to lay it on in bold swift strokes. Her practical demonstration demolished his unprecedented timidity. From that day forth he has held and practised the creed that 'audacity is a very great part of the art of painting'.[17]

Notes

1. Gilbert, Martin. *The Challenge of War: Winston S. Churchill 1914-1916*, H. H. Asquith to Venetia Stanley, 5 December 1914, p. 223.
2. NA Kew, ADM, 1437b.q.1251. In Birkenhead, Earl of. *Churchill 1874-1922*, p. 362.
3. Churchill, Winston S. *Thoughts and Adventures*, p. 7.
4. Bonham Carter, Violet. *Winston Churchill an Intimate Portrait*, p. 383.
5. Lloyd George, David. *War Memoirs of David Lloyd George*, p. 139.
6. Gilbert, Martin, op cit, p. 501.
7. Ibid, p. 473.
8. Ibid, Winston to Jack, 2 October 1915, pp. 542-3.
9. Ibid, p. 569.
10. Birkenhead, Earl of. *Churchill 1874-1922*, p. 285.
11. Eade, Charles (ed,), *Churchill by his Contemporaries*, p. 445.
12. *Churchill: The Greatest Briton of All Time*. A TW1/Carlton Production.
13. Marsh, Edward. *A Number of People*, p. 248.
14. Lavery, John. *The Life of a Painter*, p. 177.
15. Eade, Charles, op cit, p. 420.
16. Professor Thomas Bodkin, Director of the National Gallery of Ireland 1927-35, and Barber Professor of Fine Arts and Director of the Barber Institute of the University of Birmingham 1935-53.
17. Eade, Charles, op cit, p. 419.

CHAPTER 13

A Return to the Army

'An honourable door was [now] open' to Winston,[1] who, in 1915, held the rank of major in the Queen's Own Oxfordshire Hussars (otherwise known as the Oxfordshire Yeomanry in which his brother Jack also held a commission). He, therefore, crossed the Channel to France on 18 November 1915 to join his regiment and resume his life as a soldier. Two days later, Winston was informed of his transfer to the 2nd Battalion Grenadier Guards, which he joined at Laventie, in northern France's Pas de Calais. On 28 November 1915 Clementine wrote, 'I miss you terribly – I ache to see you.'[2] Early in December Winston wrote from France to British Conservative statesman George Curzon, First Earl of Kedleston, to say,

> What a release! Except for the distressing thoughts [which your] papers & letter revive I have been entirely happy & free from care. I do not know when I have passed a more joyous three weeks; & to let that tremendous melancholy situation of our affairs all over the world slide from one's mind after having fixed it so long in mental gaze, has felt exactly like laying down a physical load ... .[3]

A week later Winston told Clementine, 'My conviction that the greatest of my work is still to be done is strong within me ... . I feel a [great] assurance of my power: & now – naked – nothing can assail me.'[4] (In his imagery, Winston may have had in mind the gods of Greek mythology who are always depicted naked.)

Winston had hoped to be given command of a brigade, but this proposal was blocked by the Prime Minister, as Winston informed Clementine on 18 December 1915:

> Asquith wrote a note to French [Sir John French, Commander-in-Chief of the British Expeditionary Force], (wh[ich] French showed me v[er]y privately) saying that 'with regard to our conversation about our friend [i.e. Winston] – the appointment might cause some

criticism' & should not therefore be made – adding 'Perhaps you might give him a Battalion.'[5]

On 1 January 1916 Winston learned that he had, indeed, been given command of a battalion and, on 3 January, he commenced his duties as Lieutenant Colonel in command of the 6th Battalion Royal Scots Fusiliers, which shortly afterwards entered the front line. That day he declared to Clementine,

... I cannot help feeling the lack of scope for my thought & will power. I see so much that ought to be done, that [could] easily be done, that never will be done or only half done: and I can't help longing for the power to give those wide directions [which] occupied my Admiralty days.[6]

Five days later he wrote again to Clementine from France:

I am now deeply immersed in the v[er]y small things wh [ich] fall to my lot. I do all I can with zest: but I must confess to many spells of emptiness & despondency at the narrow sphere in wh[ich] I work & the severely restricted horizon.[7]

The evacuation of all Allied forces from the Gallipoli peninsula was completed two days later, on 8 January.

On the 10th it was clear that Winston's mind was still very much preoccupied with the recent past:

Whenever my mind is not occupied by war, I feel deeply the injustice with [which] my work at the Admiralty has been treated ... . Then the damnable mismanagement [which] has ruined the Dardanelles enterprise & squandered vainly so much life & opportunity cries aloud for retribution: & and if I survive, the day will come when I will claim it publicly.[8]

Winston was particularly aggrieved about Asquith who 'has cruelly & needlessly wronged me; & even in his power & prosperity has had the meanness to strike at me'.[9]

A week later Winston told Clementine that he had been busily organizing sporting activities, including mule races and concerts for the men, which they enjoyed 'immensely. Poor fellows – nothing like this has ever been done for them before. They do not get much to brighten their lives – short though these may be.'[10] On 24 January he told his wife,

It is splendid having you at home to think about me & love me & share my inmost fancies. What [should] I find to hold on to without you. All my great political estate seems to have vanished away – all my friends are mute – all my own moyens [means and capabilities] are in abeyance. [And he ends the letter] Most tender love & many many kisses – from your ever loving & devoted W.[11]

Meanwhile, Winston's batman, John McGuire, stated as follows,

I took Winston Churchill up over the top of the parapet into no-man's-land, and whenever we got to a certain hole in front of the German barbed wire we would crawl into it and we would lie there up to here [i.e. up to the neck] in water listening to the Germans talking, and we heard them stamping their feet on the duck-boards to warm their feet.[12]

On 6 February Winston learned that he was finally to have command of a brigade, consisting of five battalions of men who would be responsible for 4,000 yards of the front line.[13] Winston's advance headquarters was Laurence Farm at Ploegsteert, Belgium (which the British Tommies nicknamed 'Plug Street') and which he made a painting of during the time he was there.

Just as Winston painted in Belgium, whenever the opportunity presented itself, so, on the German side, did a young corporal called Adolf Hitler. And whereas Winston's paintings were characteristically light and colourful, reflecting the fact that he was happy when so engaged, Hitler's were more subdued, favourite subjects being castles, opera houses, churches, and cathedrals (although he also painted stilllifes, landscapes, and even the Madonna and child). Hitler's paintings of buildings display excellent draughtsmanship and perspective – reflecting the truth of the words of the Rector of Vienna's Academy of Fine Arts – who rejected him as a student, but told him that his sketches 'gave clear indication for my [i.e. Hitler's] aptitude for architectural designing'.[14]

On 22 February 1916 Winston informed Clementine that he was coming home for a week's leave and expressed the desire 'to have at least one day's painting in Lavery's studio'.[15] The following month Winston was anxious to return to England and to politics, but Clementine cautioned him to be patient until the time was right.[16] To this Winston replied, 'Tender love my dearest soul – I cannot tell you how much I treasure & count on y[ou]r aid & counsel.'[17] On 24 March, Clementine had clearly been unable to sleep as her letter to Winston indicated that it was written at 4.00am. Again, she wisely counselled him against returning to England,

It seems to me such an awful risk to take – to come back just *now* so lonely & unprotected with no following in the House [of Commons] & no backing in the Country … .[18]

Owing to heavy losses, the 6th Battalion Royal Scots Fusiliers transferred to 45 Brigade of 15th (Scottish) Division on 7 May 1916 and amalgamated with the 7th Battalion, whereupon Winston was obliged 'to give way to a senior colonel. His connection with the Royal Scots Fusiliers thus came to a natural conclusion … '. This gave him the opportunity to return to England and resume his parliamentary duties.[19]

Notes

1. Soames, Mary. *Winston Churchill: His Life as a Painter*, [*LP*] p. 24
2. Soames, Mary (ed.), *Speaking for Themselves: The Personal Letters of Winston and Clementine Churchill*, [*SP*] Clementine to Winston, 28 November 1915, p. 121.
3. Gilbert, Martin, *The Challenge of War: Winston S. Churchill 1914-1916*, Winston to Lord Curzon, 8 December 1915, p. 603.
4. Soames, Mary, *SP* op cit, p. 132.
5. Ibid, Winston to Clementine, 18 December 1915, p. 137.
6. Ibid, Winston to Clementine, 1 January 1916, p. 143.
7. Ibid, Winston to Clementine, 6 January 1916, p. 147.
8. Ibid, Winston to Clementine, 10 January 1916, p. 150.
9. Ibid, Winston to Clementine, 19 January 1916, p. 156.
10. Ibid, Winston to Clementine, 17 January 1916, p. 155.
11. Ibid, Winston to Clementine, 24 January 1916, p. 161.
12. *Churchill*. BBC Enterprises Ltd.
13. Ibid, Winston to Clementine, 6 February 1916, p. 169.
14. Hitler, Adolf, *Mein Kampf*, p. 30.
15. Soames, Mary, *SP* op cit, Winston to Clementine, 18 February 1916, p. 179.
16. Ibid, Winston to Clementine, 16 March 1916, p. 189.
17. Ibid, Winston to Clementine, 16 March 1916, p. 190.
18. Ibid, Clementine to Winston, 24 March 1916, p. 193.
19. Soames, Mary, *LP* op cit, p. 29.

CHAPTER 14

A Return to Politics: The USA enters the War; The Bolshevik Revolution: Victory

In June 1916 Asquith agreed to the appointment of a commission of enquiry to determine where the responsibility for the Dardanelles action lay. July found Winston still railing at his enforced exclusion from government, and on the 31st of that month he told Jack:

> It is [very] painful to me to be impotent & inactive at this time: but perhaps a little later on I may find a chance to be useful.[1]

In these sad and frustrating circumstances Winston resorted to what had now become his favourite leisure-time occupation, as Violet Asquith (who had married Liberal politician Maurice Bonham Carter, on 30 November 1915) describes. It was in August 1916 that Violet was a guest at Herstmonceux Castle, East Sussex – the home of Conservative politician, South African War veteran, and art collector, Colonel Claude W. H. Lowther, when Winston, who was also a guest of the Colonel, came into the garden to paint. Violet described the scene:

> His coming was heralded by a procession of gardeners bearing an easel, a large canvas, a chair, a box of paints and a bristling bundle of brushes – the whole armoury of his new art. He followed in their wake clad in a white coat and hat and, having observed the light, chosen his site, deployed his man power and his apparatus, set to work. As he painted his tensions relaxed, his frustration evaporated. He was as happy as a child with his new toys.[2]

Although Lloyd George became Prime Minister of a new, all-party coalition government on 7 December 1916, he failed to offer Winston a post in his Cabinet, whereupon, three days later, a frustrated and dejected Winston wrote to Sir Archibald Sinclair (his former second-in-command in the 6th Royal Scots Fusiliers) as follows:

I had an impulse & a gift [i.e. contribute] to give to the war energies of the country. But my treasure is rejected ... . You who know me so well will understand how unpleasant it is for me to be denied all scope in action at this time of all other times.[3]

In his speech to the House of Commons on 5 March 1917 during the Army Estimates debate, Winston declared it to be essential that warfare become mechanized, because 'machines save life ... [otherwise] I do not see how we are to avoid being thrown back on those dismal processes of waste and slaughter which are called attrition'.[4] In that same month the Dardanelles Commission of Enquiry published its first report, its conclusion being that Winston 'was not solely, or even principally responsible' for the failure of the campaign.[5]

On 6 April 1917 the USA finally entered the war on the side of the Allies. That spring the Churchills purchased Lullenden, a Tudor manor house and farm at East Grinstead in Sussex, which they used as a country retreat until November 1919. Here, Winston painted the house and garden to his heart's content.

At last, in July 1917, Winston finally got his wish and was recalled to office – as Minister of Munitions in Lloyd George's coalition government (but without a seat in the War Cabinet). 'It wasn't just as a friend but as a political force' that Lloyd George required Winston's services, said the Prime Minister's great grandson, Robert, subsequently:

Churchill was not someone you wanted on the other side. You wanted to have him with you. And Churchill was a very vigorous, energetic, valuable ally to have with you in the War Cabinet and I think that Lloyd George found that Winston was the most cheerful, the most supportive, the best person you could have on a daily basis to help you run a very difficult war.[6]

Winston travelled to France in mid-September in company with his private secretary Edward Marsh. Said Marsh, from the Front near Arras,

Winston was attracted by the sight of shells bursting in the distance – irresistible! Out [of the car] we got, put on our steel helmets, hung our gas-masks round our necks, and walked for half-an-hour towards the firing. There was a great deal of noise, shells whistling over our heads, and some fine bursts in the distance ... .[7]

This provides another illustration of Winston's willingness to take unnecessary risks and deliberately to place himself in harm's way, irrespective of the danger to himself, and to those in company with him. This was a characteristic which was deeply rooted in his psyche, and further examples of it will shortly be given.

*   *   *

In Russia the Bolsheviks seized power on 7 November 1917 and deposed, and subsequently murdered, the Tsar and his family. This was anathema to Winston, who for this and other reasons regarded the Bolsheviks as uncivilized savages. A 'White' army of anti-Bolsheviks was now created to oppose the 'Red' forces. The Whites fought on the following fronts – the Baltic Region, Poland, Ukraine, Caucasia, Turkestan and Western Siberia and, in their fight, they would be aided by every Allied government including Britain, France, Italy, the USA, Japan, Poland and Finland.

*   *   *

In February 1918, accompanied by his brother, Jack, Winston visited the Ypres Salient and Passchendaele, where, he said 'nearly 800,000 of our British men have shed their blood or lost their lives ... during 3½ years of unceasing conflict!' On the return journey, 'We passed the lunatic asylum blown to pieces by the sane folk outside!' he remarked dryly.[8]

On 1 June 1918 Lady Randolph, now aged sixty-four, was married, for the third time, to Montagu Phippen Porch of the Nigerian Civil Service; he was twenty-three years her junior.

In France again, in early August 1918, Winston remarked on the 'nearly 5,000 German prisoners [of war]' whom he passed on his way to visit the Front. 'They looked a fairly sturdy lot, though some of them were very young. I could not help feeling very sorry for them in their miserable plight and dejection, having marched all those miles from the battle-field without food or rest, and having been through all the horrors of the fight before that.'[9]

In contrast, on 15 September 1918, he declared, in respect of those Germans who were still engaged in combat, that 'the hamper of mustard gas is on its way. This hellish poison will I trust be discharged on the Huns [Germans] to the extent of nearly 100 tons by the end of the month.' (It should be remembered that it was the Germans who had first used mustard gas at

Ypres in July 1917. Mustard gas was first used by the British against the Germans on the night of 26/27 September 1918.)[10]

Finally, on 11 November 1918, the Armistice was signed between the Allies and Germany.

Notes

1. Gilbert, Martin. *The Challenge of War: Winston S. Churchill 1914-1916*, Winston to Jack, 31 July 1916, p. 791.
2. Bonham Carter, Violet. *Winston Churchill an Intimate Portrait*, pp. 381-2.
3. Gilbert, Martin. *World in Torment: Winston S. Churchill 1917-1922*, [*WT*] pp. 2-3.
4. Ibid, p. 8.
5. Matthew, H.C.G. and Harrison, Brian (eds), *Oxford Dictionary of National Biography*, Volume 11, p.663.
6. **Churchill: The Greatest Briton of All Time*. A TW1/Carlton Production.
7. Gilbert, Martin, *WT* op cit, p.48.
8. Soames, Mary (editor). *Speaking for Themselves: The Personal Letters of Winston and Clementine Churchill*, Winston to Clementine, 23 February 1918, pp.205-6.
9. Ibid, Winston to Clementine, 10 August 1918, p.209.
10. Ibid, Winston to Clementine, 15 September 1918, p.215.

CHAPTER 15

The Post-War Decade

The Churchills' fourth child, Marigold – nicknamed 'Duckadilly' – was born on 15 November 1918 but, alas, she died of septicaemia three years later.

In the 1918 general election, the results of which were announced on 28 December, the outcome was a landslide victory for the coalition of Conservatives, led by Andrew Bonar Law, and Liberals, led by David Lloyd George. The latter, who remained as Prime Minister, offered Winston the post of Secretary for War and Air but not the Admiralty, to which the latter had hoped to return. Nevertheless, for Lloyd George Winston had an undying admiration, both for his ability as a war leader and for his humanity, as the following remarks of his testify:

> When the English history of the first quarter of the twentieth century is written, it will be seen that the greater part of our fortunes in peace and in war were shaped by this one man. It was he who gave to orthodox Liberalism the highly new inflexion of an ardent social policy. All the great schemes of insurance which have entered for ever into the life of the British people, originated or flowed from him. He it was who cast our finances intently upon the line of progressive taxation of wealth as an equalizing factor in the social system. He it was who in the darkest year of the War seized the supreme power and wielded it undauntingly till overwhelming victory was won. He it was who for good or ill settled the Irish question … .[1]

Angry at the Cabinet's decision – made on 4 March 1919 – to withdraw Britain's 13,000 troops from northern Russia, Winston told Herbert A. L. Fisher, Minister of the Board of Education, 'After conquering all the huns – the tigers of the world – I will not submit to being beaten by the baboons.'[2] On 11 April, in a speech to the Aldwych Club, Winston declared, 'Of all tyrannies in history, the Bolshevik tyranny is the worst, the most destructive, the most degrading.'[3]

As Winston himself pointed out when, in January 1919, he was appointed Secretary for War and Air, 'The British Fleet was already in the Baltic & the Black Seas. The Caucasus had already been occupied. The Hampshire Regiment was already in Siberia', and munitions, including shells, artillery pieces, and tanks for the White general, Anton I. Denikin, and White admiral, Alexander V. Kolchak, 'had already been promised & definitely ordered …'. Since then, he declared, 'I have simply tried to discharge honourably and efficiently the obligations entered into by my predecessor & by the Cabinet within the limitations imposed.'[4]

The truth was, however, that had Winston had his way there would have been no 'limitations', and he would have proceeded 'to make war upon the Bolshevists [i.e. Bolsheviks] by every means in our power …'.[5] Nevertheless, from January 1919 up until the opening of negotiations between Britain and the Bolsheviks in London in May 1920, no one could have worked harder in mustering support for the White forces. Innumerable letters and memoranda were despatched – the long-suffering Lloyd George, whose patience was tried to the limit, being their principal recipient – and meetings convened, for, as with all his 'goal directed activities', Winston was utterly fixated upon his task. And his hopes might have been realized, for by October/December 1919 Denikin had advanced to within 200 miles of Moscow. However, the Bolsheviks finally gained the upper hand. Lloyd George insisted, however, that he and his Cabinet had 'never contemplated anything beyond supplying arms in anti-Bolshevik areas in Russia with necessary equipment to enable them to hold their own'.[6]

From Paris on 11 September 1919, Winston wrote to Clementine, who was always in his thoughts,

> My dear it is a rock and comfort to have y[ou]r love & companionship at my side. Every year we have formed more bonds of deep affection. I can never express my gratitude to you for all you have done for me & for all you have been to me.[7]

Eleven days later Lloyd George wrote to Winston, pointing out how British financial support for the White forces had reached such proportions that he was now obliged 'to cut down the enormous expenditure which is devouring the resources of the country at a prodigious rate'. He accused Winston of being 'obsessed by Russia':

> I invited you to Paris [to a meeting to discuss what future action was to be taken] to help me reduce our commitments in the East. You then produced a lengthy and carefully prepared memorandum on Russia.

I entreated on Friday to let Russia be for at least 48 hours; and to devote your weekend to preparing for the Finance Committee this afternoon. You promised faithfully to do so. Your reply is to send me a four-page letter on Russia, and a closely printed memorandum of several pages – all on Russia. I am frankly in despair.

The reconquest of Russia would cost hundreds of millions. It would cost hundreds of millions more to maintain the new government until it had established itself. You are prepared to spend all that money, and I know perfectly well that is what you really desire. But as you know that you won't find another responsible person in the whole land who will take your view, why waste your energy and your usefulness on this vain fretting which completely paralyses you for other work?[8]

Winston later described how the war and its aftermath had left for him an unhappy legacy:

When I was young, for two or three years the light faded out of the picture. I did my work. I sat in the House of Commons, but black depression settled on me. It helped me to talk to Clemmie about it.

Thoughts of suicide had come into his mind, where 'a second's action would end everything. And yet I don't want to go out of the world at all in such moments.' In other words, however strong the compulsion was to do so, he ultimately rejected the notion of taking his own life.[9]

Winston's depression, in turn, had a 'knock-on' effect on his wife Clementine, who, according to daughter Mary Soames, experienced 'periods of fatigue and tension', and 'bouts of mental and physical exhaustion'. Nor, said Mary, was Winston 'oblivious to the fact that he himself (however unwittingly) somehow contributed to her troubles'. For this reason, 'he ruefully recognized' that it was 'necessary from time to time for his wife to have breaks away from home – and away from him'.[10] Was Winston's 'Black Dog' and his suicidal 'ideation' (notion of committing suicide) simply a reaction to circumstances, or was it indicative of a deeper malaise?

On 24 March 1920 Winston set off on holiday with fellow painter, General Lord Rawlinson (Commander of the Fourth Army in the Great War) to Mimizan in southern France as guests of Hugh Richard Arthur Grosvenor, 2nd Duke of Westminster – nicknamed 'Bendor' – at his house, 'The Woolsack'.[11] Three days later, writing from Mimizan, les Landes, south-west France, Winston described how he and Rawlinson had been painting by the lake. 'How I wish [Sir John] Lavery were here to give me a few hints; it would bring me on like one o'clock ... .'[12]

According to Mary Soames, 'Winston, who always welcomed the unofficial viewpoint, had asked John Lavery [an Ulsterman and a Roman Catholic] to let him know his views on the Irish situation.' To which Lavery, 'probably at some time in the winter of 1920, when the partition of Ireland was imminent', had replied,

> I believe that Ireland will never be governed by Westminster, the Vatican, or Ulster without continuous bloodshed. I also believe that the removal of the 'Castle' [Dublin Castle, seat of British government in Dublin] and all its works, leaving Irishmen to settle their own affairs, is the only solution left.[13]

It was Lavery who had encouraged a friendly relationship to develop between Winston and Michael Collins, a member of the Irish delegation during the Anglo-Irish Treaty negotiations. Collins was the Director of Intelligence for the Irish Republican Army (IRA), a member of the Irish republican party, Sinn Féin, and Minister in the first Irish Parliament – Dáil Éireann – established in Dublin in 1919. (In August 1922 Collins, then Minister for Finance in the new Free State Government, was assassinated by his former IRA comrades.)

In January 1921 Winston sold several of his paintings at the Galerie Druet in Paris, having exhibited under the pseudonym Charles Morin.[14] The following month Lloyd George appointed him Colonial Secretary, in which capacity he would attend the Cairo Conference (12-22 March), which was convened to decide the future of the Middle East. Prior to setting out for Egypt, Winston announced that:

> I hope to paint a few pictures in the intervals between settling my business and naturally I'm taking all the right kind of colours. For the yellow deserts purple rocks and crimson sunsets.[15]

Sure enough, his hope was realized, and in one of several paintings of the pyramids, he included himself in the scene.

At the conference, where Winston's adviser on Arab affairs was T. E. Lawrence (Lawrence of Arabia, who became a lifelong friend), it was decided that Mesopotamia would become Iraq, and Palestine – east of the River Jordan – would become Transjordan. Also, a homeland for the Jews was promised in an area of Palestine west of the River Jordan in accordance with the Balfour Declaration of 1917.

Lady Randolph fell and broke the lower part of her left leg on 29 May 1921. A fortnight later gangrene set in and the leg had to be amputated above the knee. She died of post-operative complications on 29 June, aged sixty-seven. Now, said Lady Leonie Leslie, the late Lady Randolph's sister, 'It is Winston who weeps copiously but it is Jack, his brother, and poor Porchy [Lady Randolph's widowed husband, Montagu Porch] who are paying off her debts.'[16] Surely this is the final proof that, despite all her faults, real or imagined, Winston had come to love his late mother.

Writing from Dunrobin Castle, Scotland, home of the Duke and Duchess of Sutherland, on 19 September 1921, Winston told Clementine how he had 'painted a beautiful river in the afternoon light, with crimson and golden hills in the background'.[17]

The Anglo-Irish Treaty was signed on 6 December 1921. The treaty established the Irish Free State as an autonomous dominion within the British Empire, but gave Northern Ireland the opportunity of opting out and remaining a part of the United Kingdom, which it did. Both parliaments were 'home rule' parliaments – the King was still Head of State in Saorstát Éireann – and a Council of Ireland was to be established to promote co-operation between both. This cooperation was destroyed by Michael Collins who fomented an IRA campaign in Northern Ireland.

Writing from Cannes on 4 January 1922, Winston told Clementine:

> I must confess to you that I have lost some money here [presumably, either at cards or at the gambling table] – though nothing like so much as last year. [However] I have earned many times what I have lost by the work I have done here at my book [a reference to *The World Crisis*].[18]

Winston was surely aware that gambling, however pleasurable it may have been to him, was a risky business, particularly for a married man with a growing family and substantial outgoings. But, as already indicated, risk-taking was a feature of his modus vivendi.

Winston revealed that he was still feeling bitter about the way he had been treated over the Dardanelles campaign when, referring to Asquith, he declared in early February, 'I cannot forget the way he deserted me over the Dardanelles, calmly leaving me to pay the sole forfeit of the policy which at every stage he had actively approved.'[19]

In late July Winston revealed his meticulous attention to detail by forwarding to Clementine a 'DISSERTATION', the subject of which was 'DINING ROOM CHAIRS'. In it, he specified how many chairs were required for the dining room at Chartwell, a property in Kent which was to be the Churchills' new home, once renovations were complete, and what their precise shape and construction were to be.[20] Said he, 'I was ... taught to be very fond of Kent. It was, Mrs Everest said, "the garden of England".'[21]

At Deauville, France, in early August 1922, Winston declared, 'I got a little fitful sunshine in the afternoons & painted a small picture & daubed a few canvases.'[22] From Mimizan on 14 August, Winston wrote to his wife to say, 'The weather has not been specially good ... tho' I have painted every day.'[23] By that autumn, Chartwell had been renovated and was ready for occupation. Here, some existing outbuildings would serve as Winston's studio, premises which were subsequently enlarged in order to accommodate his substantial collection of paintings, which not only hung on the walls, but were also stacked on the floor.[24] On 15 September, the Churchills' fourth (surviving) and final child, Mary, was born.

At Chartwell, between the years 1925 and 1932, Winston built the greater part of a brick wall which separated the kitchen garden from the road to the farm.[25] And when he was subsequently invited to become an honorary member of the bricklayers' union 'he accepted this invitation with some pride'.[26]

In late 1922 the Conservatives withdrew from Lloyd George's coalition government and fought the November general election as an independent party. They won a comfortable victory and their leader, Andrew Bonar Law, became Prime Minister. Winston, however, lost Dundee to the Labour candidate, which, for the first time in twenty-two years, left him without a seat in Parliament. In his own words, 'In the twinkling of an eye I found myself without an office, without a seat, without a party, and without an appendix.' [He had recently had an appendicectomy.][27] On 18 November Winston received a letter of condolence for his defeat from T. E. Lawrence, who declared:

> In guts and power and speech you can roll over anyone bar Lloyd George ... . I know that your fighting sense is urging you to get back into the scrimmage at the first moment: but it would be better for your forces to rest & rearrange them & no bad tactics to disengage a little. I needn't say that I'm at your disposal when you need me – or rather if ever you do.[28]

A week previously, Lawrence, with whom Winston had once had a camel race in the desert, had said of Winston,

> The man's as brave as six, as good-humoured, shrewd, self-confident & considerate as a statesman can be: & several times I've seen him chuck the statesmanlike course & do the honest thing instead.[29]

As for Winston, he in turn was a great admirer of Lawrence not only for the latter's military exploits, but also as a man of letters. For example, he said of Lawrence's book, *Seven Pillars of Wisdom* (published in 1926),

> It ranks with the greatest books in the English language. When most of the great literature of the Great War has been sifted ... Lawrence's tale of the war in the desert will gleam with immortal fire.[30]

Winston's daughter Sarah described the impact Lawrence's visits had on the Churchill family at Chartwell, who

> were silenced by his quiet personality, and we would all listen in pindrop silence to what he had to say. I remember my father sitting back watching him with a half smile, and letting him run the conversation.[31]

(American journalist Walter Graebner stated that Lawrence was not the only one to whom Winston deferred: 'Churchill insisted on the limelight on most occasions, but he would sometimes give it up voluntarily to an exceptionally pretty and intelligent woman.')[32]

Winston now embarked on writing his monumental history of the First World War, entitled *The Great War*, in six volumes which were published between April 1923 and November 1931.

In the winter of 1922, at Cannes, where the Churchills rented a villa for a period of six months, Winston 'wrote and painted away to his heart's content'.[33]

Writing from 2 Sussex Square (the Churchills' home since April 1920) in mid-August Winston told Clementine, then in Norfolk, that 'The children come back tomorrow, and I have had a delightful letter from Diana. I am going to amuse them on Saturday and Sunday by making them an aerial house in the lime tree. [And then perhaps remembering the time when, as a child, he had leapt from a bridge with disastrous results – as already mentioned, continued] You may be sure I will take the greatest precautions to guard against them tumbling down.'[34] On 2 September he promised Clementine that in order to see her 'happy & prosperous & safe' he would 'indeed work my utmost and avoid imprudence of all kinds'.[35]

Writing from Mimizan on 17 February 1924, Winston told Clementine, 'I feel quite lonely & sometimes frightened without you to give me a kiss or a prog [his and her word for a prod].'[36] Clementine was staying at 'Lou Sueil', Eze-sur-Mer, on the French Riviera – the home of Consuelo Balsan, former wife of the 9th Duke of Marlborough and her husband, Jacques Balsan, a lieutenant colonel in the French air force, whom she had married in 1921.

In the general election of October 1924 the Conservatives won by a decisive overall majority and Winston was appointed Chancellor of the Exchequer in Stanley Baldwin's newly elected government. Sir Frederick Leith-Ross (Deputy Controller of Finance on the Finance Board of the War Reparations Committee – which was concerned with the reparations which Germany was required to make, following the First World War, under the terms of the 1919 Treaty of Versailles) made the following perceptive remark about Winston in this role:

> Winston ... was not the easiest Minister to work for but he was stimulating and full of ideas. About one in twenty of them were sound. You see Winston is really an artist.[37]

In early March 1925 Winston told Clementine how he had taken Diana and Sarah to London Zoo, where the new aquarium was 'wonderful'. He continued,

> Philip [Conservative politician and art collector Sir Philip Sassoon] came here [to the Treasury Chambers] last night and fell into raptures over the Sargent drawing. [A painting of Winston in the ceremonial robes of Chancellor of the Exchequer by US painter John Singer Sargent.] I was hard put to it to reconcile truth and politeness. I wanted to point out the awful concavity of my right cheek. However, one must not look a gift portrait in the mouth.[38]

Winston and Clementine frequently visited Sir Philip, a bachelor, at his country houses – Port Lympne, Hythe, on the Kent coast, and Trent Park, New Barnet, near London, where Winston combined socializing with painting.[39] On the 15th Winston asked Clementine, who was again staying on the French Riviera with the Balsans:

> When do you think you will return my dear one? Do not abridge y[ou]r holiday if it is doing you good – But of course I feel far safer from worry and depression when you are with me & when I can confide in y[ou]r sweet soul. The most precious thing I have in life is y[ou]r love for me. I reproach myself for many shortcomings. You are a rock & I depend on you & rest on you. Come back to me therefore as soon as you can. Your ever loving & devoted W.[40]

By mid-August Winston was heavily involved with the workmen, who, along with his personal bodyguard, Walter Thompson, were busy creating two new lakes at Chartwell and draining the old one.[41] In this project, Winston undoubtedly derived his inspiration from the late Charles, 9th Duke of

Marlborough, who at Blenheim had 'conceived a series of water-terraces from the house all the way down to the lake, marrying the two by the imaginative use of water'.[42]

In that year of 1925 an exhibition for amateur artists was held at Sunderland House, Curzon Street, London. The competition was judged by patron and benefactor of the arts Sir Joseph Duveen, historian Kenneth Clark and portrait painter Oswald Birley. Winston entered his painting of Chartwell under snow entitled 'Winter Sunshine', which duly won First Prize. There was no question of favouritism as the paintings were submitted anonymously.[43]

From 3 to 13 May 1926 there was a General Strike called by the General Council of the Trades Union Congress in an attempt to force the government to prevent the owners of coal mines from reducing their workers' wages. Sir Jack Layden, who came from a family of Yorkshire coal miners, described how uncompromising Winston's attitude was towards the strikers.

> Churchill's whole attitude to life, you know, was to beat you down and then, after you'd conceded tired, weak, nothing to offer, he'd want to talk to you.[44]

In early 1927 when Winston, accompanied by his brother, Jack, and fifteen-year-old son, Randolph, were cruising off the coast of Italy, Winston wrote to Clementine to say he had 'played a great deal of chess' with Randolph. 'I am shocked to see him wear nothing under his little linen shirt, & go about without a coat on every occasion. He is *hardy*, but surely a vest is a necessity to white people. I am going to buy him some … .'[45] Three days later Winston wrote to Clementine from Admiralty House, Malta to say, 'It is a new pleasure to me to show the world to Randolph. He is v[er]y well, v[er]y good mannered & seems to take things in. It ought to be a wonderful experience for him.'[46]

On 15 June Clementine was knocked down by an omnibus whilst crossing London's Brompton Road. She was badly bruised but otherwise not seriously injured. When British painter Walter Richard Sickert saw the report of the accident in the newspaper he called on her. Sickert had known Clementine's family since 1899, when, at the end of the season, her mother, Lady Blanche, who was by then estranged from her husband, Colonel Henry Hozier, had relocated with her children to Dieppe on the north coast of France. Clementine and her twin sister, Kitty, were then aged eleven.[47] Dieppe was also the home of Sickert who met the family; Clementine became a particular favourite of his.[48] Now, twenty-eight years later, Clementine introduced Sickert to her husband and the outcome was that the two men formed a friendship which was not only pleasant, but, for Winston, the budding artist, particularly fruitful.

Artist and art critic Adrian Daintrey states that

> Sickert, by some perversity, some saintliness perhaps, or some candour in his character, would have nothing to do with ... a world [which included] the top people of the time. Instead, his choice of subjects [was] mainly seedy streets, garish cafés and odd people, but by the lack of obvious attraction or prettiness in his colour schemes he had doubly bolted the door and made sure that the fashionable world would have nothing to do with him.

However, as far as 'top people' were concerned, said Daintrey, with Winston, Sickert made an exception.[49]

On the evening of 26 September 1927 Sickert and his third wife, Thérèse Lessore, whom he had married in the previous year, arrived at Chartwell as guests of the Churchills. Subsequently, said Winston, the two men

> worked very hard at various paintings and had many discussions. I am really thrilled by the field he is opening to me. I see my way to paint far better pictures than I ever thought possible before. He is really giving me a new lease of life as a painter.[50]

Violet Bonham Carter tells how Winston gave her

> a very amusing account of W. S. [Sickert] coming down to Chartwell to teach him to paint. W. [Winston] rushing in out of the garden where sunlight was blazing & begging W. S. to tell him how to transfer the marvellous greens & purples he saw onto the canvas – & W. S. refusing to put his nose out of doors.[51]

This was because Sickert 'spent most of his time inside, with the curtains drawn, reading French novels'.[52] Nevertheless, Sickert made copious notes for Winston, instructing him how to mix and apply his paints and, according to Mary Soames, it was he who taught Winston how

> by using a magic lantern [prototype of the modern-day slide projector] in conjunction with glass slides projected on to a canvas he could overcome his lack of expertise as a draughtsman ... .[53]

(This is known as the *panafieu* technique of painting in oils on top of the image of a black and white photograph which is projected onto a canvas screen.)

In that year, 1927, Sickert did Winston the honour of painting 'from life as well as from photographs' a portrait of 'the Rt Hon. Winston Churchill', currently serving as Chancellor of the Exchequer. The portrait was 'painted in two colours only, a deep green-blue and a hot pink'.[54]

Meanwhile, Irish portrait painter Sir William Orpen, RA

> advised Winston to invite James Sinton Sleator [Irish painter of portraits and stilllifes, and a pupil of Orpen] ... to come to Chartwell and paint in his company so that he might profit from observing dexterity resulting from long practice.[55]

In early October 1927 Winston, together with Professor Frederick Alexander Lindemann – nicknamed 'The Prof' – who was a physicist and also his special advisor on all matters scientific, set off for a two-week sojourn in Venice, where Clementine was convalescing after her road traffic accident.

The following April Winston told Clementine, 'I am becoming a Film fan, and last week I went to see "The Last Command", a very fine anti-Bolshevik film, and "Wings" which is all about aeroplanes fighting and perfectly marvellous.'[56] His personal bodyguard, Walter Thompson, confirms that this was a hobby that Winston and newspaper magnate and Liberal politician Lord Beaverbrook had in common.

> Beaverbrook is a great lover of films. Whenever Mr Churchill visited him at his house a film show was arranged. Before the War, Winston often used to go to Lord Beaverbrook's office and after business had been transacted the two men would adjourn to a private cinema on the premises.[57]

Three days later, Winston wrote to Clementine about Randolph, 'His mind is free & growing more powerful every day. It is quite startling to hear him argue. His present phase is rabid Agnosticism ... he is far more advanced than I was at his age.'[58] (Winston himself, as a young man, had, as already mentioned, gone even further, and, in his own words, 'passed through a violently anti-religious phase'.) On 7 August Winston told Clementine, 'I motored over to see Randolph in Camp [Randolph was currently attending at Eton College, and this was a reference to the Eton Officers' Training Corps summer camp] on Sunday ... .'[59] Shortly afterwards Winston declared that Randolph and Professor Lindemann were enjoying games of tennis and rounds of golf together. 'I have persuaded the Prof. to stay until Monday. He is a great companion both for me and for Randolph.'[60]

THE POST-WAR DECADE

Notes

1. Churchill, Winston S., *Thoughts and Adventures*, [*TA*] pp. 39-40.
2. Gilbert, Martin, *World in Torment: Winston S. Churchill 1917-1922*, [WT] pp. 275-6.
3. Gilbert, Martin, *WT* op cit, p. 278.
4. Ibid, Winston to Lloyd George, 6 September 1919, p. 326.
5. Ibid, Winston: memorandum to War Cabinet, 25 September 1919, p. 337.
6. Ibid, Lloyd George, Telegram to Winston, [arrived] 17 February 1919, p. 251.
7. Soames, Mary (ed.), *Speaking for Themselves: The Personal Letters of Winston and Clementine Churchill*, [SP] Winston to Clementine, 11 September 1919, p. 220.
8. Gilbert, Martin, *WT* op cit, Lloyd George to Winston, 22 September 1919, p. 331.
9. Moran, Lord, *Winston Churchill: The Struggle for Survival 1940-1965*, p. 167.
10. Soames, Mary, *Clementine Churchill*, p. 254.
11. Soames, Mary, *Winston Churchill: His Life as a Painter*, (*LP*) pp. 32 & 37.
12. Soames, Mary, *SP* op cit, Winston to Clementine, 27 March 1920, pp. 222-3.
13. Lavery, John, *The Life of a Painter*, pp. 211-12. Undated letter in Soames, Mary, *Winston Churchill: His Life as a Painter*, pp. 42-3.
14. Soames, Mary, *SP* op cit, p. 228.
15. Gilbert, Martin, *WT* op cit, Winston to Clementine, 20 February 1921, p. 533.
16. Sebba, Anne, *Jennie Churchill: Winston's American Mother*, undated notes prepared by Seymour Leslie for Anita Leslie, Tara King Papers, p. 319.
17. Soames, Mary, *SP* op cit, p. 241.
18. Ibid, Winston to Clementine, 4 January 1922, p. 247.
19. Ibid, Winston to Clementine, 4 February 1922, p. 250.
20. Ibid, Winston to Clementine, 20 July 1922, p. 259.
21. Churchill, Winston S, *My Early Life*, p. 13.
22. Soames, Mary, *SP* op cit, p. 260.
23. Ibid, p. 261.
24. Soames, Mary, *LP* op cit, p. 178.
25. Moran, Lord, op cit, p. 660.
26. Thompson, Walter H., *I was Churchill's Shadow*, p. 165.
27. Churchill, Winston S., *TA* op cit, p. 213.
28. Gilbert, Martin, *WT* op cit, T. E. Lawrence to Winston, 18 November 1922, pp. 889-90.
29. Ibid, TE Lawrence to R. D. Blumenfeld (US writer and journalist, and editor of the *Daily Express* from 1902-1932), 11 November 1922, p. 895.
30. Churchill, Winston S. *Great Contemporaries*, p. 120.
31. Gilbert, Martin, *Prophet of Truth: Winston S. Churchill 1922-1939*, p. 707.
32. Graebner, Walter, *My Dear Mister Churchill*, p. 30.
33. Soames, Mary, *LP* op cit, p. 87.
34. Soames, Mary, *SP* op cit, Winston to Clementine, 16 August 1923, p. 272.
35. Ibid, Winston to Clementine, 2 September 1923, p. 273.
36. Ibid. Winston to Clementine, 17 February 1924, p. 277.
37. Moran, Lord, op cit, p. 530.
38. Soames, Mary, *SP* op cit, Winston to Clementine, 8 March 1925, p. 290.
39. Soames, Mary, *LP* op cit, p. 48.

40. Soames, Mary, *SP* op cit, Winston to Clementine, 15 March 1925, pp. 291-2.
41. Ibid, Winston to Clementine, 19 August 1924, p. 284.
42. Rowse, A.L., *The Churchills: The Story of a Family*, p. 365.
43. Soames, Mary, *LP* op cit, p. 57.
44. *Churchill*. BBC Enterprises Ltd.
45. Soames, Mary, *SP* op cit, Winston to Clementine, 7 January 1927, p. 303.
46. Ibid, Winston to Clementine, 10 January 1927, p. 305.
47. Sturgis, Matthew, *Walter Sickert*, p. 278.
48. Ibid, p. 281.
49. Daintrey, Adrian, *I Must Say*, pp. 72-3.
50. Soames, Mary, *SP* op cit, Winston to Clementine, 26 September 1927, pp. 308-9.
51. Pottle, Mark (ed.), *Champion Redoubtable: the Diaries and Letters of Violet Bonham Carter 1914-1945*, p. 237.
52. Daintrey, Adrian, op cit, p. 73.
53. Soames, Mary, *LP* op cit, p. 72.
54. Baron, Wendy, *Sickert*, pp. 174 & 380.
55. Eade, Charles (ed.), *Churchill by his Contemporaries*, p. 420.
56. Soames, Mary, *SP* op cit, Winston to Clementine, 5 April 1928, p. 320.
57. Thompson, Walter H., op cit, p. 181.
58. Soames, Mary, *SP* op cit, Winston to Clementine, 8 April 1928, p. 320.
59. Ibid, Winston to Clementine, 7 August 1928, p. 326.
60. Ibid, Winston to Clementine, 10 August 1928, p. 327.

CHAPTER 16

The 'Wilderness Years':
The Influence of Clementine

On 30 May 1929 the Conservatives were defeated by Labour in the general election. Winston, however, retained his seat at Epping, Essex. The succeeding decade, from May 1929 until September 1939, when Winston was out of office (i.e. without a ministerial position in the government) has been described as his 'wilderness years', and so it was, as far as politics was concerned. But in other respects this was a far from apt description because, as Mary Soames relates,

> Within a few weeks [a fortnight, in fact] of his resignation Churchill began work on the mammoth undertaking he had been contemplating for some little while: the writing of the history of his great ancestor John, Duke of Marlborough [which appeared in four volumes between 1933 and 1938].

In addition, *My Early Life* was published in 1930 and *Thoughts and Adventures* and *The Unknown War* in 1931. 'Alongside these there was also an astonishingly long tally of articles for newspapers and magazines ... [and] political speeches, over which Churchill toiled with passionate care.'[1]

However, said Mary:

> politics always came first ... and all his other work and pleasures were subordinated to the times and seasons of Parliament and the uncertain but overriding commands of political events. Yet he found time – or made it – to enjoy himself; to be brilliant and convivial company; to reorganize the landscape at Chartwell; to build (with his own hands) walls and cottages; and to paint.

Friends of the Churchills were the Astor family of Hever Castle, Kent, which was about six miles distant from Chartwell. Colonel John Astor and the colonel's step-daughter, Lady Margaret Mercer-Nairne, both enjoyed painting and, said Mary Soames, as their guest during the 1920s and 1930s, 'Winston quite often painted at Hever, where there is a famous colonnaded Italian garden as well as beautiful lakeside scenes.'[2] Mary estimates that during the 1930s Winston produced no fewer than 250 paintings.[3]

In company with his son, Randolph, brother, Jack, and Jack's son, John (Johnny), Winston arrived at Quebec for an extended lecture tour of North America on 9 August 1929. But, nevertheless, there was still time for relaxation. For example, at Lake Emerald in British Columbia, Winston remarked on the 'extraordinary colour' of the water, 'more Turquoise or Jade than Emerald ... . I painted three pictures which give a very inadequate idea of the great beauty of this spot.'[4]

Between 13 and 17 September Winston and his party were entertained by US newspaper proprietor, film mogul, newspaper and radio magnate, and art collector, William Randolph Hearst, at his home, 'San Simeon', a self-designed castle on California's Pacific coast. Winston would have been grateful to Hearst for printing articles which he had written in his newspapers; the latter was the proprietor of no fewer than twenty-eight titles nationwide, in addition to books and magazines. However, the two men were opposed diametrically in that Hearst disapproved of Britain having an empire. Also, whilst Winston was alarmed and issuing warnings about the growing power and militarization of Germany, Hearst, on the other hand, was to become an avowed admirer of Adolf Hitler. At San Simeon, said Winston,

> we made g[rea]t friends with [another guest, film actor and director] Charlie Chaplin. You c[oul]d not help liking him. The boys [Randolph and Johnny] were fascinated by him. He is a marvellous comedian – bolshy in politics – delightful in conversation.[5]

Winston now travelled to Los Angeles and visited Chaplin at his studios at a time when the latter was making the film 'City Lights' – described as the last great silent movie. (When Winston returned to England it was his pleasure, at Chartwell, to watch Chaplin's films after dinner. Like millions of others throughout the world he was enthralled by the maestro's antics, whilst at the same time recognizing the intense pathos of Chaplin's portrayal of the tramp, a figure hitherto despised and discarded by society.)In October Winston was visiting and being fascinated by the battlefields of the American Civil War (1861-65), and the Civil War Museum at Richmond, Virginia, where the 'tattered rebel flag' still flew.[6]

Winston's visit to the USA was marred by the Wall Street stock market crash of October/November 1929, when he 'lost what to him was a small fortune'. However, on the positive side, whilst in the USA, he 'signed several highly lucrative contracts for articles in weekly magazines; his pen and his unfailing industry would keep the wolf from the door'.[7] He returned home on 30 November.

Over the years Winston's attitude to conflict changed, as is apparent by the following statement, made by him in 1930:

> War, which used to be cruel and magnificent, has now become cruel and squalid. Instead of a small number of well-trained professionals championing their country's cause with ancient weapons and a beautiful intricacy of archaic manoeuvre, sustained at every moment by the applause of their nation, we now have entire populations, including even women and children, pitted against one another in brutish mutual extermination, and only a set of bleary-eyed clerks left to add up the butcher's bill.[8]

Because of his opposition to the Conservative government's conciliatory attitude towards India and the pro-Indian independence movement, Winston resigned from Baldwin's Shadow Cabinet in January 1931. This meant that when the coalition government (of Labour, Liberals and Conservatives) was created in August 1931, headed by Labour Prime Minister Ramsay MacDonald, Winston was excluded. He was also excluded from the next coalition government, again led by Ramsay MacDonald, which was created following the general election held that October.

In early December Winston embarked on another lecture tour of America, this time in company with Clementine and Diana. Here, he would 'undertake a strenuous tour of forty lectures,[9] with the chief purpose of recouping some of the [financial] losses he had suffered two years before ... .'[10] However, on 13 December, he was involved in a serious road traffic accident while attempting to cross New York's Fifth Avenue. He was hospitalized for eight days, after which he spent three weeks convalescing in the Bahamas.

Winston returned to New York on 22 January 1932 to resume his lecture tour in which his theme was the 'the great opposing forces of the future', which would be 'the English-speaking Peoples and Communism', and how it was the duty of the USA and Britain to stand together to protect the peoples of Europe.[11] Winston also stressed how important it was, if peace was to be assured, that Britain and America retained mastery of the seas, and that France maintained a strong army.

In his younger days, Winston had been somewhat gung ho about warfare, as many young men are, but now, with the benefit of experience, he saw matters in a different light. In his book, *Thoughts and Adventures*, published in that year, 1932, when he was aged fifty-eight, he wrote:

> The story of the human race is War. Except for brief and precarious interludes, there has never been peace in the world; and before history began, murderous strife was universal and unending. [However,] It was not until the dawn of the twentieth century of the Christian era that War really began to enter into its kingdom as the potential destroyer of the human race.[12]
>
> Such, then, is the peril with which mankind menaces itself. Means of destruction incalculable in their effects, wholesale and frightful in their character, and unrelated to any form of human merit: the march of Science unfolding ever more appalling possibilities … .[13]

What of the League of Nations, an inter-governmental organization which had been created after the First World War to resolve international disputes by arbitration? In 1932 Winston declared that, to his great disappointment, the organization had been

> deserted by the United States, scorned by Soviet Russia, flouted by Italy, [and] distrusted equally by France and Germany. [However] To sustain and aid the League of Nations is the duty of all. To reinforce it and bring it into vital and practical relation with actual world politics by sincere agreements and understanding between the great Powers, between the leading races, should be the first aim of all who wish to spare their children torments and disasters compared with which those we have suffered will be but a pale preliminary.[14]

Accompanied by Professor Lindemann and military historian Lieutenant Colonel Ridley Pakenham-Walsh, Winston revisited the battlefield of Blenheim in August 1932. That winter found him working not on one book but on three: *Marlborough: His Life and Times*; *A History of the English-Speaking Peoples* and *Great Contemporaries*. However, according to Winston's granddaughter Celia Sandys, the year had not been a happy one and the 'Black Dog' had returned with a vengeance,

> 1932 was one of the lowest points in Winston's life. He was troubled by recurring periods of gloom and despondency, which he called his black dog. Three recent events affected him so badly that he thought he would never recover. A small fortune which he had accumulated as a successful author had been wiped out in the Wall Street Crash;

his Party had been voted out of office in Britain, and his years in the political wilderness had begun. He had also been severely injured when knocked down by a car in New York, taking many weeks to recover from his injuries.[15]

It goes without saying that Winston's recent experiences were enough to make anyone depressed. But again it should be asked, was there more to his depression than meets the eye?

How did Clementine cope, with a husband in this mood? Phyllis Forbes, who, as Phyllis Moir, was Winston's secretary from January to March 1932, during his American tour, declared of Winston and Clementine's marriage:

I was always astonished what a good marriage it was, in spite of the fact that he was a *terribly* demanding man. It seemed to me that Clemmie had worked out a way of managing him. He always rushed off to her with any new idea he had to ask her opinion, and she never hesitated to say if she liked it, or if she didn't, and very often they'd have a rather heated argument about it and he, afterwards, would say, 'You know, she's my pussycat. She spits at me.'[16]

Despite all, Winston, in his book, *Thoughts and Adventures*, which was published in that same year, 1932, declared that he was an optimist. If he visited Monte Carlo, he said, referring to the Casino, he 'staked my money on red, as I usually do, having a preference for the optimistic side of things'.[17] And in the same volume, in the chapter entitled 'Hobbies', he explained the coping mechanism which he employed in times of stress:

Many remedies are suggested for the avoidance of worry and mental overstrain by persons who, over prolonged periods, have to bear exceptional responsibilities ... Some advise exercise, and others, repose. Some counsel travel, and others, retreat. Some praise solitude, and others, gaiety. But the element which is constant and common in all of them is Change.[18]

Certainly, no one could say that Winston's life was not replete with change!

From 1933 to 1939 Winston made several visits to the Château de l'Horizon at Golfe-Juan near Cannes – home of Irish-American Miss Maxine Elliott, the former famous actress. Clementine did not always accompany him, as she was not enamoured of the Riviera. However, said Mary Soames, even though Winston was ostensibly on holiday 'he was nearly always working steadily to meet some imminent deadline with his publishers'.[19]

William Nicholson was a painter (of portraits, landscapes and still life), illustrator, and author of children's books, whose home and studio were at Apple Tree Yard, St James's, London. In the summer of 1934 he arrived at Chartwell in order to paint a charming 'conversation piece, which had been commissioned by a group of the Churchills' friends to mark their [Winston and Clementine's] Silver Wedding', which the couple had celebrated the previous year. Winston was doubtless aware that, in 1884, Nicholson, at the age of twelve, had painted 'Blenheim Bridge at Sunset' – the bridge in the grounds of Blenheim Palace; and that in 1917 he had painted the portrait of South African soldier and statesman Jan Christiaan Smuts – a person whom Winston would come greatly to admire. Entitled, 'The Churchills in the Dining Room at Chartwell', Nicholson's work depicted Winston and Clementine seated at a circular table having breakfast, together with 'numerous bantams strolling on the lookout for crumbs, and Tango, the adored cat, sitting on the newspapers on the table', and being offered morsels of food by Clementine.[20]

Nicholson subsequently became a regular visitor to Chartwell, where he gave Winston the benefit of his artistic knowledge and, on this account, earned the nickname *Cher Maître* (Dear Master). 'I think the person who taught me most about painting was William Nicholson,' Winston subsequently told Sir John Rothenstein, Director of the Tate Gallery.[21] Nicholson further endeared himself to the Churchills by painting Winston's beloved pair of black swans, and sketching daughter Mary's pug dog, her 'large family of ill-assorted dolls' and the marmalade cat.[22] As for Clementine, she so liked and admired his style that she urged her husband to paint '*au Nicholson*'!

In August 1934 Winston, accompanied by Randolph, again joined Maxine Elliott on the French Riviera. Meanwhile, Clementine visited Scotland with Sarah and Mary. In that month Winston told Clementine that he had painted the church of Notre Dame de Vie situated near the French village of Mougins 'a la Nicholson'.[23] He also informed his wife, perhaps hardly the wisest thing to have done, bearing in mind that she had cautioned him against it, that both he and Randolph had been gambling at the casino where they had both lost money.[24] Clementine embarked on a four-month cruise in December with British politician and businessman, Walter Guinness, Lord Moyne, on his yacht, the MY *Rosaura*. 'To see you vanishing away like that was a melancholy thing,' said Winston, having accompanied his wife to the railway station. 'I miss you v[er]y much & feel v[er]y unprotected.'[25] Such a separation, said Winston's daughter Mary, was viewed by her father 'with considerable dismay'.[26]

On 30 January 1935 Winston wrote to Clementine to say:

It makes me gasp to look at the map & see what enormous distances you have covered since I saw the last of your dear waving hand at Victoria Station: and it depresses me to feel the *weight* of all that space pressing down upon us both. How glad I shall be when you turn homewards.[27]

In the election of mid-November 1935, the Conservatives won, but without an absolute majority. Having been left out of the new government by Baldwin, who became Prime Minister once again, Winston declared, 'I do not pretend that, thirsting to get things on the move, I was not distressed.'[28] On 10 December Winston and Clementine departed for Spain and, when Clementine returned home on 20 December, Winston, in company with Professor Lindemann, journeyed on to Tangiers. From there, and in search of better weather, they proceeded to Marrakech, where they stayed at the Mamounia Hotel. There

Winston did not want for lively and agreeable company: Randolph had joined his father and 'the Prof' [Lindemann]; Lord Rothermere and his party were there; and so was Lloyd George, who was busy writing a book.[29] [Newspaper proprietor Lord Rothermere, had a house at Cap Martin, 'La Dragonnière', where the Churchills were always welcome].

January 1936 found Winston enjoying an eighteen-day sojourn at Marrakech, one of his favourite places for painting. King George V died on 20 January 1936 and was succeeded by Edward VIII. On 3 March Winston told Clementine that were he to be appointed Minister for Co-ordination of Defence, then he would 'work faithfully before God & man for *Peace*, & not allow pride or excitement to sway my spirit'.[30] But in the event, Winston was not appointed to the post.

Referring to the Spanish Nationalists, who, in July 1936, led by General Francisco Franco, had revolted against Spain's democratically elected left-wing Popular Front Movement, Winston declared, 'I am thankful the Spanish Nationalists are making progress ... . Better for the safety of all if the communists are crushed.'[31] In the event, Franco prevailed and, in October 1936, he was proclaimed Spain's head of state.

At the Defence Debate in the House of Commons on 12 November, Winston criticized the government for its failure to pay sufficient attention to Britain's national defence and, in particular, to strengthening the Royal

Air Force. Said he, 'So they go on in strange paradox, decided only to be undecided, resolved to be irresolute, adamant for drift, solid for fluidity, all powerful to be impotent.'[32]

On 10 December King Edward VIII abdicated the throne. Said Mary Soames:

> The period following the Abdication was probably the lowest point of Winston's political fortunes since the dark days immediately following the Dardanelles disaster. His warnings of the national peril ahead had been practically unheeded, and now discredit was cast on him by the feeling that his support of the King sprang from ulterior motives, and was largely prompted by antipathy to [Conservative Prime Minister Stanley] Baldwin. To those who knew him well this was malicious nonsense ... . Churchill had reacted to the King's plight spontaneously and naturally, as one would expect of someone possessing his instincts of loyalty and chivalry. Winston himself suffered at this time from feelings of almost fatalistic depression ... .[33]

July 1937 found Winston working on yet another book, entitled *Great Contemporaries*. At the same time he was working 'night & day' on his biography of his ancestor, John Churchill, 1st Duke of Marlborough.[34] His daughter Sarah described how, when her father was 'working at tremendous tension in his room' the slightest noise 'could make him very angry'.[35]

When Clementine was holidaying in the French Pyrenees in July 1938, Winston wrote to her from Chartwell to say, 'Now that y[ou]r garden is so beautiful & all sorts of things in wh you take an interest are alive & growing, it is vexing that you sh[oul]d not be here.' But, he added, 'I am sure a change [which] cuts you out of the household routine and leaves you free to recharge y[ou]r batteries is a wise step.'[36] When, in late November 1938, Clementine sailed to Jamaica in order to embark on another voyage with Lord Moyne on his yacht, Winston declined to go, as such cruises 'took him too far away and too far out of touch'.[37] In December Winston revealed once again that he was missing the presence of his principal 'affirmer' when he asked Clementine for reassurance, writing,

> Do you love me? I feel so deeply interwoven with you that I follow y[ou]r movements in my mind at every hour & in all circumstances. Darling do always cable every two or three days. Otherwise I get depressed – & anxious about you and y[ou]r health.[38]

He told her that he had been 'toiling double-shifts' in his writing of *A History of the English-Speaking Peoples*, and had averaged in excess of a thousand words a day since 1 August.

Writing from Maxine Elliot's home, Château de l'Horizon, on 18 January 1939 Winston declared, 'We [i.e. 'I'] have averaged fifteen-hundred words a day, although nominally on holiday.'[39]

Said Stefan Lorant, Editor of *Picture Post* and a promoter of Winston's views, when he interviewed the latter at Chartwell early in 1939:

> And so we had lunch, and I remember it was steak and kidney pie and I didn't like steak and kidney pie, but I took a little bit but Mr Churchill had steak and kidney pie in a bowl, and instead of taking the spoon, as I did, he took the bowl to his mouth and he took the spoon and *shovelled* the steak and kidney pie in. And I was just looking at him, and at what he was doing. [Then, said Lorant, he took his cigar,] puffed a couple of times, put it back, shovelled again, then he had … quite a big glass, of brandy. So he drank a little brandy and then I looked at him – I didn't believe it – there was a piece of chocolate and while he shovelled the steak and kidney pie, he stopped for a second and put a chocolate in his mouth. And I said [to myself] I don't believe it. There is no such a thing![40]

This was an occasion in which Winston was uninhibited in his behaviour, and it would not be the last, for, as will be seen, this was another feature of his make-up.

Sir John Colville (Cabinet Secretariat, 1939-45) paid tribute to Winston's unstinting generosity:

> He was lavish with his hospitality and there was no streak of meanness apparent. If something good came his way he wished to share it with all at hand.[41]

Notes

1. Soames, Mary. *Winston Churchill: His Life as a Painter*, [*LP*] p. 73.
2. Ibid, p. 162.
3. Ibid, p. 74.
4. Soames, Mary (ed.), *Speaking for Themselves: The Personal Letters of Winston and Clementine Churchill*, [*SP*] Winston to Clementine, 1 September 1929, p. 343.
5. Soames, Mary, *SP* op cit, Winston to Clementine, 29 September 1929, p. 347.

6.   Gilbert, Martin. *Prophet of Truth: Winston S. Churchill 1922-1939*, [*PT*] p. 349.
7.   Soames, Mary, *LP* op cit, pp. 75-6.
8.   Churchill, Winston S., *My Early Life*, p. 73.
9.   Soames, Mary, *SP* op cit, p. 356.
10. Soames, Mary, *LP* op cit, p. 76.
11. Gilbert, Martin, *PT* op cit, p. 424.
12. Churchill, Winston S.. *Thoughts and Adventures*, [*TA*] pp. 184-5.
13. Ibid, p. 190.
14. Ibid, pp. 190-1.
15. **Chasing Churchill: In Search of my Grandfather with Celia Sandys: To The Other Country*. 2008. Discovery Knowledge.
16. **Churchill*, BBC Enterprises Ltd.
17. Churchill, Winston S, *TA* op cit, p.1.
18. Ibid, p. 226.
19. Soames, Mary, *LP* op cit, p. 97.
20. Ibid, p. 86.
21. Rothenstein, Sir John. *Time's Thievish Progress*, III, p. 129.
22. Soames, Mary, *LP* op cit, p. 85.
23. Soames, Mary, *SP* op cit, Winston to Clementine, 25 August 1954, p. 360.
24. Ibid, Winston to Clementine, undated, probably 27 August 1934, p. 362.
25. Ibid, Winston to Clementine, 31 December 1934, p. 368.
26. Ibid, p. 363.
27. Ibid, Winston to Clementine, 30 January 1935, p. 379.
28. Gilbert, Martin, *PT* op cit, p. 686.
29. Soames, Mary, *LP* op cit, pp. 101-2.
30. Soames, Mary, *SP* op cit, Winston to Clementine, 3 March 1936, p. 414.
31. Ibid, Winston to Clementine, 5 September 1936, pp. 415-16.
32. Gilbert, Martin, *PT* op cit, p. 797.
33. Soames, Mary. *Clementine Churchill*, p. 274.
34. Soames, Mary, *SP* op cit, Winston to Clementine, 3 August 1937, p. 428.
35. Churchill, Sarah., *A Thread in the Tapestry*, p. 47.
36. Soames, Mary, *SP* op cit, Winston to Clementine, 8 July 1938, p. 435.
37. Soames, Mary, *LP* op cit, p. 123.
38. Soames, Mary, *SP* op cit, Winston to Clementine, 19 December 1938, p. 442.
39. Ibid, Winston to Clementine, 18 January 1939, p. 448.
40. **Churchill*, BBC Enterprises Ltd.
41. Wheeler-Bennett, Sir John (ed,), *Action this Day: Working with Churchill*, pp. 56-7.

CHAPTER 17

Painting as a Pastime:
What Winston's Paintings Reveal

In his book *Painting as a Pastime*, Winston describes the benefits which hobbies can bestow:

> Change is the master key. A man can wear out a particular part of his mind by continually using it and tiring it … . [However] it is not enough merely to switch off the lights which play upon the main and ordinary field of interest; a new field of interest must be illuminated. It is no use saying to the tired 'mental muscles' – if one may coin such an expression – 'I will give you a good rest', 'I will go for a long walk', or 'I will lie down and think of nothing'. The mind keeps busy just the same. If it has been weighing and measuring, it goes on weighing and measuring. If it has been worrying, it goes on worrying. It is useless to argue with the mind in this condition. The stronger the will, the more futile the task. One can only gently insinuate something else into its convulsive grasp. And if this something else is rightly chosen, if it is really attended by the illumination of another field of interest, gradually, and often quite swiftly, the old undue grip relaxes and the process of recuperation and repair begins. The cultivation of a hobby and new forms of interest is therefore a policy of first importance to a public man.[1]

Winston then proceeded to quote reading, joinery, chemistry, book-binding and bricklaying as suitable diversions. However, 'best of all and easiest to procure are sketching and painting in all their forms'. Finally, said he, 'Painting came to my rescue in a most trying time.'[2]

Parodying the Gospel of St Matthew, Chapter 5, Verses 3-11, Winston declared:

> Happy are the painters, for they shall not be lonely. Light and colour,

peace and hope, will keep them company to the end, or almost to the end, of the day.[3]

However, Winston was humble enough to realize that, not having served the kind of 'long, hard, persevering apprenticeship' that the 'real artist' undergoes, those such as he must therefore 'not be too ambitious. We cannot aspire to masterpieces. We may content ourselves with a joy-ride in a paint-box.'[4] He then described how, when he departed from the Admiralty at the end of May 1915, and was left with 'long hours of utterly unwonted leisure', there suddenly appeared Hazel, 'the gifted wife of Sir John Lavery', who came to the rescue. Said she, 'Painting! But what are you hesitating about? Let me have a brush – the big one.'[5] Trying to paint a picture, said Winston, was

> like trying to fight a battle. It is the same kind of problem as unfolding a long, sustained, interlocked argument. It is a proposition which, whether of few or numberless parts, is commanded by a single unity of conception.[6]

One autumn, when he was visiting France's Côte d'Azur, Winston said that he

> fell in with one or two painters who revelled in the methods of the modern French school. These were disciples of Cézanne. They view Nature as a mass of shimmering light in which forms and surfaces are comparatively unimportant ... but which gleams and glows with beautiful harmonies and contrasts of colour.[7]

Winston read artist and art critic John Ruskin's teaching manual, *The Elements of Drawing*, and was taken by a 'French friend', Walter Sickert, to see the art galleries of Paris. Said he, 'Never having taken any interest in pictures till I tried to paint, I had no preconceived opinions. I just felt, for reasons I could not fathom, that I liked some much more than others.'[8] As for painting as a pastime:

> I know of nothing which, without exhausting the body, more entirely absorbs the mind. Whatever the worries of the hour or the threats of the future, once the picture has begun to flow along, there is no room for them in the mental screen. They pass out into shadow and darkness.

Winston also declared painting to be a 'spur to travel. Every country where the sun shines and every district in it, has a theme of its own ... each

Blenheim Palace: tapestry depicting the 1st Duke receiving the surrender of Marshal Tallard after the Battle of Blenheim. (*Photo: by courtesy of His Grace, the Duke of Marlborough*)

Blenheim Palace: the bedroom, just off the Great Hall, in which Winston was born on 30 November 1874. (*Photo: by courtesy of His Grace, the Duke of Marlborough*)

Lord Randolph Churchill and Jennie Jerome, on the occasion of their engagement.

(Photo: Churchill Archives Centre, Other Deposited Collections relating to Sir Winston Churchill, WCHL 4/41 pt 2)

Winston as a schoolboy at Harrow School. *(Photo: by permission of the Harrow School Archive)*

Winston's nanny, 'Mrs' Elizabeth Ann Everest. *(Photo (unknown origins): Churchill Archives Centre)*

Winston with Consuelo, 9th Duchess of Marlborough on the steps of the South Portico, Blenheim Palace, c.1902/3. (*Photo: Churchill Archives Centre, The Papers of Clementine Ogilvy Spencer-Churchill, Baroness Spencer-Churchill of Chartwell, CSCT 5/4/25*)

Winston Spencer Churchill of the 4th Hussars, 1895. (*Photo: Churchill Archives Centre, Other Deposited Collections relating to Sir Winston Churchill, WCHL 4/41 pt 2*)

Violet Bonham Carter by Cecil Beaton, c.1915.

Jack Churchill. (*Photo courtesy of Tarka King*)

Winston's sketches of 'A tranquil pug' and of 'The galloping pug'. (*Churchill, Randolph S.,* Winston S. Churchill, Vol II, Young Statesman 1900-1914)

Winston leaving the Admiralty with the Rt Hon. Robert Borden in 1912. (*Library and Archives Canada/C-002082*)

Winston and Clementine boating on the river Thames, c. 1940s. (*Photo: Churchill Archives Centre, The Papers of Clementine Ogilvy Spencer-Churchill, Baroness Spencer-Churchill of Chartwell, CSCT 5/4/5*)

Winston and President Roosevelt on board HMS *Prince of Wales* in August 1941. (*Photo: Churchill Archives Centre, The Papers of Clementine Ogilvy Spencer-Churchill, Baroness Spencer-Churchill of Chartwell, CSCT 5/4/33*)

Distinguished visitors to the Canadian Corps Headquarters at Headley Court in Surrey in 1941. (L-R) General Wladyslaw Sikorski, Lt Gen A. G. L. McNaughton, Winston and General Charles de Gaulle. (*Library and Archives Canada/C-064027*)

Welcoming the Canadian Prime Minister, the Rt Hon. W. L. Mackenzie King, to London in August 1941. (*Library and Archives Canada/C-047565*)

Addressing the House of Commons, Ottawa, 30 December 1941. (*Library and Archives Canada/C-022140*)

Winston and Mackenzie King leaving the House of Commons, Ottawa, 30 December 1941. (*Library and Archives Canada/C-015132*)

Studying a map at Canadian Corps Headquarters, Headley Court, Surrey, with Lt Gen A. G. L. McNaughton. (*Library and Archives Canada/PA-l19399*)

President Roosevelt, the Rt Hon. Mackenzie King, Prime Minister of Canada, and Winston at the Quebec Conference in August 1943. (*Library and Archives, Canada/C-014170*)

At the Quadrant Conference in Quebec, 18 August 1943, with (seated) Mackenzie King and Roosevelt. Standing are (L-R) General Henry Arnold (US Army Air Forces), Air Chief Marshal Sir Charles Portal (Chief of the Air Staff), General Sir Alan Brooke (Chief of the Imperial General Staff), Admiral Ernest King (US Chief of Naval Operations), Field Marshal Sir John Dill (Head of UK Military Mission in Washington), General George Marshall (Chairman US Joint Chiefs of Staff), Admiral Sir Dudley Pound (First Sea Lord), Admiral William Leahy (US Navy and Chief of Staff to the President).

With Mackenzie King and Canadian Cabinet ministers at the Chateau Frontenac during the Octagon Conference at Quebec, 14 September 1944. (*Library and Archives Canada/C-071095*)

McGill University
conferring honorary
degrees to Winston and
President Roosevelt
during the Octagon
Conference at Quebec
on 16 September 1944.
(*Library and Archives
Canada/C-026931*)

Arriving for the Octagon Conference at Quebec in September 1944. (*Library and Archives Canada/C-026942*)

At the Commonwealth Prime Ministers' Conference in London, 1 May 1944. (L-R) Rt Hon. W. L. Mackenzie King (Canada), General Jan Smuts (South Africa), Winston, Rt Hon. Peter Fraser (New Zealand) and Rt Hon. John Curtin (Australia). (*Library and Archives Canada/C-068672*)

Visiting First Canadian Army's front in March 1945 with General H. D. G. Crerar, the Army Commander, and Field Marshal Sir Alan Brooke. (*Library and Archives Canada/PA-145738*)

On the Rhine, March 1945. (L-R) Crerar, Lt Gen G. G. Simonds, Field Marshal Sir Alan Brooke and Field Marshal Sir Bernard Montgomery. (*Library and Archives Canada/PA-143952*)

At the Potsdam Conference, Winston is greeted by Admiral William Leahy. (*US National Archives and Records Administration*)

With Truman and Stalin at the Cecilienhof Palace, outside Churchill's official residence for the Potsdam conference. (*US National Archives and Records Administration*)

Leaving Potsdam. President Truman shakes hands with Mary Churchill, Winston's daughter, as Winston descends the steps of the 'little White House'. Admiral Leahy is just behind Truman and General Dwight D. Eisenhower is behind Mary Churchill. (*US National Archives and Records Administration*)

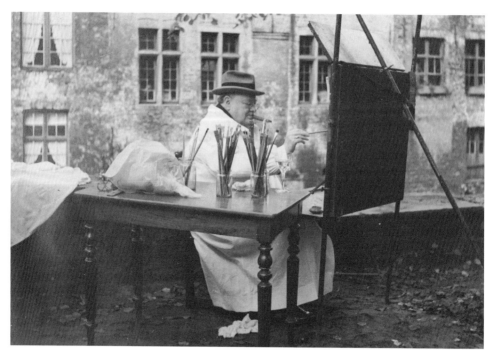

Winston painting in Belgium, 1948. (*Photo: The Papers of Clementine Ogilvy Spencer-Churchill, Baroness Spencer-Churchill of Chartwell, CSCT 5/6/160*)

At Rockliffe Airport, Ottawa, on 29 June 1954, Winston and Anthony Eden are greeted by Canada's Prime Minister, St Laurent (left) and Mr L. B. Pearson. (*Library and Archives Canada/C-004047; National Film Board of Canada*)

Field Marshal The Earl Alexander of Tunis and Errigal. 'Alex' was Winston's beau idéal as a soldier. (*Photo: Lord Alexander*)

Lord Moran, Winston's doctor throughout the war years. (*Photo: St Mary's Hospital*)

Winston Churchill. Ottawa, 30 December 1941. (*Yousuf Karsh/Library and Archives Canada/PA-165806*)

has its native charm.' It was for this reason that Sir William Orpen advised him to visit Avignon in France, and also Egypt and Palestine.[9] Orpen, as one of the First World War's official war artists, had painted Winston's portrait in 1916.

As far as subject matter was concerned, for Winston it was what he loved best. For instance, he painted Blenheim Palace and Park from almost every aspect, including the 'Marlborough Tapestries' – depicting the military exploits of his ancestor, John Churchill, the 1st Duke – Long Library, State Room, Drawing Room, Great Hall, West Front, Lake, and Boathouse. At Chartwell, his own miniature Blenheim Palace, Winston painted the house in the snow, the lakes, the goldfish pool and the swimming pool.

He loved painting water and the life that goes on around it. For example, England's River Thames, France's River Meuse, Germany's River Rhine; harbour scenes with yachts; canal scenes including Venice's Grand Canal; the Italian and Swiss Lakes, and Loch More and Loch Choire in Scotland were all included in his portfolio. Morocco's snow-capped Atlas Mountains were another favourite subject. He also enjoyed painting religious buildings, such as the Church of Notre Dame de Vie near Mougins, north of Cannes; the mosque at Marrakech; Greek temples and village churches. He painted castles, such as the fortress at Carcassone, and the Pont du Gard – the impressive Roman aquaduct at Nîmes in Provence. Gardens, such as that of the Mamounia Hotel, Marrakech, were another delight for him to paint.

Although human beings were not his forte, Winston's nearest and dearest *did* have the honour of appearing in his portfolio. For example, he painted (from a photograph) Randolph, Mary and himself, as his daughter laid the foundation stone for the brick summerhouse at Chartwell; Randolph, reading in the pergola and Diana in the dining room. In 'Tea at Chartwell' (c.1928, and also based on a photograph), he depicts himself seated at Chartwell's dining table, together with Clementine, Randolph, Diana, Walter and Thérèse Sickert, Diana Mitford (daughter of Baron Redesdale), Edward Marsh (Winston's private secretary) and Professor Lindemann. His 'Painting Lesson from Mr Sickert' (1927-8), which is based on a picture from a newspaper cutting, depicts pupil (himself) and master (Sickert) in animated conversation, and reveals Winston's humility in that he was not afraid to admit that he had taken lessons from the French maestro. In 'Children Laughing', painted in the 1920s and also based on a newspaper cutting, Winston depicts children enjoying a 'Punch and Judy' show, their delighted faces reflecting his own pleasure at seeing young people being happy and enjoying themselves.

With Winston, a pretty face, such as that of his secretary Cecily Gemmell, was also likely to inspire a painting. Doris, Viscountess Castlerosse, appears in no less than three of his paintings: in one, she is sitting on the terrace at Maxine Elliot's Château de l'Horizon, and in another, painted from a photograph, she and he are sitting together on the rocks below the Château.

Professor Thomas Bodkin made the following observations about Winston's paintings:

> A striking characteristic of his pictures is their quite extraordinary decisiveness. Each is a clear and forcible pronouncement. He does not niggle nor retouch. His paint is laid once and for all with no apparent hesitation or afterthought. It is never fumbled or woolly in texture.
>
> Spaces are filled with obvious speed. His colours are bright, clean and well harmonized. His drawing makes factual statements, though these may not always be quite accurate in detail.
>
> His ability to devise a good composition might well be envied by many a successful modern professional. He does not try to say two or more things at the same time. Each of his pictures is the presentation of a distinct theme: a tower, a village, a church, a lake, a harbour, a range of mountains, a pool, a group of palm trees, an English grove, a Grecian temple. The dominant motive is never obscured by irrelevancies.
>
> He is primarily interested in landscape, but shows no desire to subject natural appearances to romantic or dramatic conventions. He does not attempt to deal with storms, night-scenes or, even, lurid sunsets. Light and peace, those qualities which all wise men most value in life, are indubitably those which chiefly distinguish the scenes that he prefers to paint.[10]

In his book *Painting as a Pastime*, Winston, for reasons best known to himself, made no mention of one very important fact. Whereas he gives the impression that it was Hazel Lavery, in May 1915, who first stimulated his interest in painting, Jack's son, Peregrine, affirmed that both Winston and Jack were taught to draw and paint by their mother.[11] As for Lady Randolph, she, in turn, had received professional tuition from painter Henrietta Ward,[12] who declared that

> Lady Randolph Churchill showed a decided talent for painting ... and on more than one occasion was accompanied by her son Winston, a delightful little boy in short trousers.[13]

This, of course, is further corroboration of Lady Randolph's affection for, and attentiveness towards, her children.

Notes

1. Churchill, Winston S. *Painting as a Pastime*, [*PP*] pp. 7-8.
2. Ibid, pp. 10 & 13.
3. Ibid, p. 13.
4. Ibid, pp. 15-16.
5. Ibid, pp. 16-17.
6. Ibid, p. 19.
7. Ibid, p. 25.
8. Ibid, pp. 25-7.
9. Ibid, pp. 30-32.
10. Eade, Charles (ed.), *Churchill by his Contemporaries*, pp. 416-17.
11. Lee, Celia and John, *The Churchills: A Family Portrait*. Information derived from the 1882 diary of Lady Randolph Churchill by Celia and John Lee, and quoted in *The Churchills*, p. 24.
12. Henrietta M.A. Ward, 1832-1924, wife of painter, Edward M. Ward.
13. Ward, Mrs E.M., *Reminiscences*, quoted in Lee, Celia and John, *The Churchills: A Family Portrait*, p. 24.

CHAPTER 18

The Menace of Nazism: Winston's Warnings: The Phoney War

Throughout the 1930s, as the records testify all too well, Winston issued a stream of warnings about the dangers of a resurgent Germany, for the harsh terms which the post-Great War Treaty of Versailles had imposed on that country had left a bitter legacy, a fact which Winston was not slow to appreciate. Following a visit to that country in 1932, Winston described its young people in the following terms,

> These bands of sturdy Teutonic youths, marching through the streets and roads of Germany, with the light of desire in their eyes to suffer for their Fatherland, are not looking for status. They are looking for weapons, and when they have the weapons, believe me they will then ask for the return of [their] lost territories and lost colonies.[1]

In a speech delivered at the Conservative Party Conference in Birmingham in October 1933, Winston drew a comparison between Germany and Britain, stating that,

> during the last four or five years the world had grown gravely darker. We have steadily disarmed, partly with a sincere desire to give a lead to other countries, and partly through the severe financial pressure of the time. But a change must now be made. We must not continue longer on a course on which we alone are growing weaker while every other nation is growing stronger.[2]

In a BBC radio broadcast on 15 November 1934, Winston declared:

> It is startling and fearful to realize that we are no longer safe in our island home. Only a few hours away by air there dwells a nation of nearly 70 million of the most educated, industrious, scientific,

disciplined people in the world, who are being taught, from childhood to think of war and conquest as a glorious exercise, and death in battle as the noblest deed for man.[3]

Winston was in no doubt of Germany's future intentions, nor was he in any doubt that Britain was ill-prepared, should there ever be another war with that country. And in coming to this conclusion he did not rely simply on his own government's statistics and propaganda. Two of his unofficial 'informants' were Squadron Leader Charles Torr Anderson of the Royal Air Force, and British Government Foreign Office official Ralph Wigram. They made him aware of the discrepancy 'between the facts then known to the [Foreign Office] Departments and the use made of them by the Government',[4] and through them, and others, he learnt of the woeful state of the RAF, both in terms of equipment, manpower and training. For example, on 28 November 1934, Baldwin had told the House of Commons that 'His Majesty's Government are determined in no condition [i.e. in no circumstances] to accept any position of inferiority with regard to what air force may be raised in Germany in the future'.[5] However, the fact was that, in April 1935, it was predicted, by extrapolating from the Air Ministry's own figures, that by October 1936, German front-line strength in aeroplanes would be 1,296, compared with a British front-line strength in aeroplanes of only 710.[6]

In a speech made to the House of Commons on 12 November 1936 during the defence debate, Winston declared:

Two things, I confess, have staggered me, after a long parliamentary experience in these debates. The first has been the dangers that have so swiftly come upon us in a few years, and have been transforming our position and the whole outlook of the world. Secondly, I have been staggered by the failure of the House of Commons to react effectively against those dangers.[7]

In late February 1937 Winston met Hungarian Jew Imre Révész, known as Emery Reves, who not only became his friend but also assisted him in the following way. In Berlin in 1930 Reves had founded the staunchly anti-Nazi 'Co-operative Press Service for International Understanding', an agency for the press syndication of political articles. Having been forced to flee Nazi tyranny in 1933 he had relocated to Paris, where he opened a new office. Reves was now instrumental in placing articles written by Winston, warning of the dangers of German military resurgence, in the newspapers of Europe.

To the House of Commons on 22 February 1938, Winston said:

I predict that the day will come when, at some point or other, on some issue or other, you will have to make a stand and I pray to God that, when that day comes, we may not find through an unwise policy, that we have to make that stand alone.[8]

Seven months later, on 30 September, the Munich Pact, an agreement signed by Britain, France, and Italy, but not by Czechoslovakia, permitted the annexation of the Czech Sudetenland, a province of that country which contained about 3 million ethnic Germans, by Nazi Germany. And that same day, British Conservative Prime Minister Neville Chamberlain famously declared, 'I believe it is peace for our time.' Winston, however, was horrified by this policy of appeasement and, on 16 October in a radio broadcast to the USA, he warned of the consequences of 'the abandonment and ruin of the Czechoslovak republic'. And in case anyone should misconstrue the stance which he had adopted and consider it to be warmongering, he asked his audience the question:

Does anyone pretend that preparations for resistance against aggression amounts to the unleashing of war? I declare it to be the sole guarantee of peace.[9]

At the end of the decade, what Winston had long prophesied came true, on a massive scale, and with alarming rapidity. On 15 March 1939 Hitler breached the terms of the Munich Pact by forcing Emil Hácha, President of the Czech Republic, to cede the remainder of his country (i.e., those regions which had not already been annexed by Hungary and Poland) to Germany. The *New York Times* published an article with the caption NOW THEY LISTEN TO CHURCHILL on 13 August. And the article continued, 'Kept out of Conservative Cabinets for years, Winston Churchill comes back as a political power because his warnings proved true.'

In that month Winston invited Walter H. Thompson, formerly a Detective Inspector in Scotland Yard's Special Branch, who had previously served as Winston's personal bodyguard for over a decade, between 1920 and 1932, to be his personal detective. Winston had the highest regard for Thompson, so much so that when the latter retired for the first time from Winston's service, he was presented with one of Winston's paintings.[10] And not only that, Winston had signed the painting for him, a rare honour. Thompson would provide some unique insights into Winston's mind and modus operandi, as will soon be seen.

On 1 September 1939 Germany invaded Poland and, two days later, Britain and France declared war on Germany. On that day Chamberlain appointed Winston First Lord of the Admiralty, a post which he had first held almost three decades previously, from 1911 to 1915.

Much as Winston loathed the policy of appeasement, he did not seek to criticize Neville Chamberlain for attempting to make peace with Germany. Neither did he seek to make political capital out of the debacle; quite the reverse in fact, for it was his belief that Chamberlain

> acted with perfect sincerity according to his lights and strove to the utmost of his capacity and authority ... to save the world from the awful, devastating struggle in which we are now engaged.[11]

* * *

On 11 September British newspaper publisher Lord Camrose noted that Winston had 'prophesied that while we would get the submarine [U-boat] menace in hand fairly quickly, there would be a very large recrudescence of submarine warfare in about a year's time. He said this was what happened in the last war.'[12] Sure enough, in late-1940, during the early phase of the Battle of the Atlantic (1939-45), the destruction wrought by German U-boats and surface warships on Allied convoys almost brought Britain to her knees. The British Expeditionary Force (BEF) began deploying to France and, by 11 October, 158,000 men had crossed the Channel; their number would double by March 1940.

This was the time of the Phoney War, the period between September 1939 and May 1940 when there was little military activity on the ground on the continent of Europe. For Britain, said General Sir Ian Jacob, Military Assistant Secretary to the War Cabinet 1939-1945, this lull was a blessing:

> In the early months of the war ... there was a certain feeling of relief that in the air and on the land we were granted a breathing-space, as this would enable our fighter [aircraft] strength to be built up, and our Army to expand somewhat and receive the modern equipment of which pre-war parsimony had kept it so deficient. It was not very long, however, before we realized that the drive which should have been exerted to ensure that we profited from our respite was sadly lacking. Naturally Churchill, who was the embodiment of the offensive spirit, and was never content unless action was afoot, chafed in this situation, and did what he could to prod and question in all directions. A good deal of friction resulted. Memoranda

125

addressed to the Prime Minister, and sometimes to his colleagues, flowed from his office on every conceivable subject.[13]

He [Winston] was under-employed because he had such an active mind and worked so hard and long, that he really hadn't got enough to do with simply the Admiralty business and he kept on interfering in the affairs of the other service ministers – the Minister of Supply, or anybody – and rather annoyed some of them, I think.[14]

Winston's enormous energy and capacity for work and innovation is confirmed by Walter Thompson, who described, for example, how the former, as First Lord of the Admiralty, created the War Room at Admiralty House, an idea subsequently emulated by US President Roosevelt. In the War Room, 'the movements of ships and troops of every nation' were plotted on 'huge coloured maps and charts', and in its conference room, the war at sea was planned.[15] (In 1943, the War Room was transferred to the Annexe at Downing Street.) 'In the first two months of the War he [Winston] did manage to take an odd week-end's relaxation at Chartwell. But soon the week-ends became as strenuous as the weeks.'[16]

On 8 April 1940 German forces overran Denmark and invaded Norway. Meanwhile, from 1940 to 1946, Clementine was President of the Young Women's Christian Association's (YWCA) War Time Appeal, and also Chairman of Fulmer Chase Maternity Hospital for Wives of Junior Officers at Fulmer in Buckinghamshire. Clementine had officially launched the aircraft carrier HMS *Indomitable* on 25 March and Winston subsequently painted a portrait of her, based on a photograph taken on that occasion.

Notes

1. Gilbert, Martin, *Prophet of Truth: Winston S. Churchill 1922-1939*, [*PT*] Winston, Speech to the House of Commons, 23 November 1932, p. 451.
2. Winston's speech was quoted in *The Times* newspaper, and recalled by him on 12 November 1936, in a subsequent speech to the House of Commons.
3. BBC Radio Broadcast entitled 'Winston', 15 November 1934.
4. Gilbert, Martin, *PT* op cit, p. 630.
5. Ibid, p. 577.
6. Ibid, p. 631.
7. Ibid, p. 797.
8. Ibid, Winston, Speech to House of Commons, 22 February 1938, p. 906.
9. Churchill, Randolph S. (compiler), *Into Battle: Speeches by the Right Hon. Winston S. Churchill, C.H., M.P.*, pp. 83-91.

10. Thompson, Walter H, *I was Churchill's Shadow*, p. 168.
11. Moran, Lord, *Winston Churchill: The Struggle for Survival 1940-1965*, p. 435.
12. Gilbert, Martin, *Finest Hour: Winston S. Churchill 1939-1941*, Notes of interviews,
11 September 1939: Camrose Papers, p. 24.
13. Wheeler-Bennett, Sir John (ed.), *Action this Day: Working with Churchill*, p. 159.
14. *Churchill*. BBC Enterprises Ltd.
15. Thompson, Walter H., op cit, p. 29.
16. Ibid, p. 21.

CHAPTER 19

Winston as Prime Minister: A Whirlwind Strikes No. 10

Whehn Neville Chamberlain resigned on 10 May 1940 a wartime coalition government was formed with Winston as Prime Minister (and also Minister of Defence, for he was convinced that in wartime 'the two offices were inseparable').[1] That in accepting the post he had embraced fully the greatest challenge of his life – to save the free world from nothing less than total oblivion – whilst at the same time recognizing the enormity of what that challenge entailed, is revealed in the following speech, made by him to the House of Commons on 13 May:

> We have before us an ordeal of the most grievous kind. We have before us many, many long months of struggle and of suffering. You ask, what is our policy? I will say: it is to wage war, by sea, land and air, with all our might and with all the strength that God can give us: to wage war against a monstrous tyranny, never surpassed in the dark, lamentable catalogue of human crime. That is our policy.
>
> You ask, what is our aim? I can answer in one word: It is victory, victory at all costs, victory in spite of all terror, victory, however long and hard the road may be; for without victory, there is no survival. Let that be realised; no survival for the British Empire; no survival for all that the British Empire has stood for …

But he ended on a note of optimism:

> I feel sure that our cause will not be suffered to fail among men. At this time I feel entitled to claim the aid of all, and I say, 'Come, then, let us go forward together with our united strength.'[2]

And such optimism was an essential ingredient in the make-up of Britain's new wartime leader, for, on the very day of his appointment as Prime Minister, Germany invaded Holland, Belgium and France.

There were those who were apprehensive of Winston in his new role. According to Sir John Colville,[3]

The mere thought of Churchill as Prime Minister sent a cold chill down the spines of the staff at 10 Downing Street ... . His verbosity and restlessness made unnecessary work, prevented real planning and caused friction.[4]

However, within a fortnight, said Colville, 'all was changed. I doubt if there has ever been such a rapid transformation of opinion in Whitehall.'[5] And, he continued,

No delays were condoned; telephone switchboards quadrupled their efficiency; the Chiefs of Staff and the Joint Planning Staff were in almost constant session; regular office hours ceased to exist and week-ends disappeared with them.

Winston's energy was ceaseless and dramatic, and his ideas flowed out to the Chiefs of Staff or the Ministries in the form of questions and minutes, to which more often than not in those early weeks he attached his bright red label, 'ACTION THIS DAY'. Most of the matters were of major importance relating to the battle that was raging or to aircraft production, but he always found time for the trivialities too. [For example] what was to be done with the animals in the [London] Zoo in the event of bombardment?[6]

He [Winston] is always having ideas which he puts down on paper in the form of questions and despatches to Ismay and the Chief of the Imperial General Staff. Sometimes they relate to matters of major importance and sometimes to quite trivial questions.[7]

However, said Sir Norman Brook, Personal Private Secretary to Sir John Anderson, Lord President of the Council in Winston's War Cabinet, Winston 'never frittered away his time attending social functions, public dinners and the like'.[8]

Colville described Winston as having

an imagination of a remarkable kind, and a constant flow of ideas, some of which were brilliant; some of which were not so good. On the other hand, he used to try his ideas out on everybody and sometimes people thought that he'd gone mad in proposing to do something totally idiotic. What he was actually doing was to fly a kite and see how people reacted.[9]

Should Colville's view of Winston, as expressed above, be taken at face value, or was there more to Winston's behaviour than Winston's Assistant Private Secretary realized? For example, was the 'constant flow of ideas' which Colville refers to a reflection of the fact that Winston was experiencing what psychiatrists call 'flights of ideas', where thoughts and speech race from one topic to another? And was Colville's description of Winston's 'totally idiotic' proposals further evidence of Winston's proneness to put forward grandiose and unrealistic plans, and to the fact that his attention was drawn easily to unimportant or irrelevant matters? Although this may, at first, appear fanciful, evidence will be produced shortly to support the notion that this was indeed the case.

In the meantime, said Marian Holmes, Winston's secretary from 1940 to 1945,

The whole place exploded. It was as if a current of high-voltage electricity was let loose, not only in No. 10 itself, but throughout the fusty corridors of Whitehall. And elderly civil servants were seen running along the corridors.[10]

Recalled Thompson,

From 1940 to the end of the war, Winston Churchill worked a regular 120-hour week. Of course, I never used to go to bed until he did.[11]

Lord Willis (Edward H. Willis, formerly of the Royal Fusiliers and subsequently of the Ministry of Information) noted that,

In 6 months of Churchill there were 5 years of change. He put Beaverbrook into aircraft production [i.e. appointed him Minister of Aircraft Production and subsequently Minister of Supply, 1941-42], for example, and within a very short time Beaverbrook had *doubled* the number of aircraft we produced, simply by cutting through the red tape, and Churchill was a real red-tape cutter.[12]

Said Brook,

So far as we were concerned he [Winston] drew no sharp distinction between his private life and his official duties. This was partly due to the fact that he never stopped work, wherever he was, and wanted some of us to be continuously on hand; but it also flowed from the generosity shown towards his staff by himself and by Lady Churchill. Those of us who were in personal attendance on him were taken freely into the family circle, both at No. 10 and at Chequers [in

Buckinghamshire, the traditional country residence of Britain's prime ministers].[13]

I remember an occasion when he wanted information from some senior member of the Air Staff and was told that this particular officer was away on a few days' leave. He just could not understand how a man who was doing such an important and interesting job could possibly leave it, even for a few days rest and relaxation, in time of war ... . The members of his personal staff were expected to conform to the same standards. Everything that he wanted had to be done at once: all demands, however exacting and unreasonable, had to be met; anything that was not of immediate importance and concern to him was of no value; when he wanted something done, everything else had to be dropped. The work was heavy and the pace was hot.[14]

[However] though he seemed to take our work for granted, and might allow some time to pass without showing any special interest on [in] it or in us, he would at intervals find time to say or write a few words of appreciation which showed a quite exceptional generosity and kindness.[15]

Sir Norman Brook describes how, when Winston requested information, the request was couched, typically, as follows:

Pray let me have, by this evening, on one sheet of paper, an account, for example, of the development of our tank-production programme or of some other project of similar magnitude.[16]

Sir John Martin, Private Secretary to Winston, 1940-41, and Principal Private Secretary, 1941-45, states how Winston chivvied and cajoled his staff, bombarded them with minutes, and insisted on correct English in their correspondence. In Winston's

office work he did not spare himself, dictating not only his own speeches but also (with few exceptions) his letters, other than the most formal official ones, and his personal Minutes.[17]

He shot off ceaselessly the famous stream of Minutes to Ministers and Service chiefs – enquiring, proposing, criticizing, prodding and on occasion praising.[18]

He would sometimes quote the authority of Fowler's *Modern English Usage*, to which for example, he referred the Director of Military Intelligence in correcting the misuse of 'intensive' for 'intense'. He was intolerant of sloppiness and jargon in official letters – which he did not like to be signed only with Christian names. (His interest in Basic English was, I think, inspired by political rather than linguistic reasons: it was a means of promoting 'the English-speaking club.') He waged continual war against verbosity in official documents, especially Foreign Office telegrams. 'It is sheer laziness,' he said, 'not compressing thought into a reasonable space.'[19]

Sir Ian Jacob described the cauldron of activity, both at No. 10 Downing Street and at Chequers, and the lengths to which Winston went to ferret out the information which he required,

He insisted on being informed constantly about details, and had a continuous flow of statistics and graphs prepared for him either by us or by his private statistical office under Professor Lindemann. He was extremely suspicious of concealment or sloth, and, if it was ever suggested that the flow might be curtailed or condensed by the staff, he immediately imagined that someone was trying to hide something from him and became more insistent than ever on receiving the full information as before.[20]

There were no social activities. Except during the hours of sleep every moment could be used for work. Meal-times and journeys by train or car were never wasted, because useful conversations could be held or Minutes dictated.[21]

Said Jacob, Winston spent 'nearly every weekend' at Chequers,

going down on Friday night as a rule, and there was a stream of guests for one night or two, or for lunch or dinner. The routine at Chequers was like that at No. 10 but more so. That is to say the work and the flow of papers, telegrams, minutes, etc., was just as intense, but in addition there were the meal-times, at which discussion could take place, and there was the night.

Elizabeth Nel, Winston's personal secretary, told how, when dictating his speeches, Winston behaved like a driven man, and expected those around him to behave in a similar way:

I can remember now, I sat there writing all this down and we went on and on and on, and after a bit he swung round on me and said, 'Are you tired?' I said, 'No, no, I'm not tired,' because I was getting stewed up too [i.e. by the drama of the occasion], you see, and he said, 'We must go on and on, like the gun horses, till we drop.'[22]

Lord Bridges, Secretary to the Cabinet 1938-46, described the lengths to which Winston went to ensure that his orders were fully understood:

> He was not only a master of the written word, he was a great believer in it as a discipline. So at the outset of the war he gave an instruction that no order from him was to be regarded as valid unless it was in writing. He thus imposed a discipline on himself and gave certainty to others.[23]

One instruction which Winston gave but which was not intended to be taken seriously, said Bridges, was to Sir Leslie Rowan, Private Secretary 1941-45, when he advised the latter to have four children. 'One to reproduce your wife, one to reproduce yourself, one for the increase in population, and one in case of accident.'[24]

Said Sir Ian Jacob, in late May 1940, during the operation to evacuate the British Expeditionary Force from the beaches of Dunkirk, code-named Operation DYNAMO, when

> it looked almost certain that the greater part of the British Expeditionary Force would be lost ... the Prime Minister, who felt the full tragedy of the situation and had on top of it all the responsibility to bear, gave no outward sign of depression, and, as usual, was simply concerned to make sure that every conceivable action was being taken. He showed himself at his very best in moments such as that.[25]
>
> His mental courage was remarkable ... . He was quite impervious to depression, despair, or indeed to the sinking of the morale which assails people when the news is constantly bad and disaster looms ahead.[26]

These words of Jacob's indicate that Winston had managed to banish, for the time being at any rate, his 'Black Dog' of despair.

On 4 June 1940 Winston made a speech to the House of Commons which included the following immortal and stirring words:

> We shall go on to the end. We shall fight in France, we shall fight on the seas and oceans, we shall fight with growing confidence and growing strength in the air, we shall defend our island, whatever the cost may be. We shall fight on the beaches, we shall fight on the landing grounds, we shall fight in the fields and in the streets, we shall fight in the hills; we shall never surrender ...

After the speech, Lord Willis declared:

I can tell you that every man there, they rose in spirits. You could almost measure it. We would have gone down to the beaches then and beaten the Nazis off with broom handles. Such was the magic effect of Churchill.[27]

Labour MP George Strauss commented:

He was a good fighting man and this is a time when you want as your leaders, fighting people, not politicians, whatever their views, and they [the people of Britain] were solidly behind him.[28]

On 10 June Italy declared war on Britain and France and, four days later, German troops marched in triumph through the streets of Paris.

Winston's oratory and in particular his use of imagery, was always calculated to inspire, and to those who heard his speeches, this, and his mastery of prose, was unforgettable. For example, in a speech to the House of Commons, made on 18 June 1940, Winston declared:

What General Weygand [Commander-in-Chief, Allied forces in France] called the 'Battle of France' is over. I expect that the battle of Britain is about to begin. Upon this battle depends the survival of Christian civilization. The whole fury and might of the enemy must very soon be turned on us. Hitler knows that he will have to break us in this island or lose the war. If we can stand up to him, all Europe may be free, and the life of the world may move forward into broad, sunlit uplands. Let us therefore brace ourselves to our duty and so bear ourselves that if the British Empire and its Commonwealth lasts for a thousand years men will still say, 'This was their finest hour.'[29]

Meanwhile, in that same month of June 1940, Emery Reves, who had become a British subject, was forced to escape from the Germans once again, this time by fleeing from Paris to London. However, he spent most of the wartime years in the USA where he promoted the publication of Winston's newspaper articles and also published anti-Nazi literature himself, including two of his own books, *A Democratic Manifesto* (1942) and *The Anatomy of Peace* (1945).

Thompson stated that during the Blitz, the German bombing campaign against the towns and cities of Britain, from 7 September 1940 to 10 May 1941, Winston led by example, and that

during the whole period of the bombing the Prime Minister, the other members of his Government and the Chiefs of Staff remained doing their normal work in London. Mr Churchill took the view, and the others agreed with him, that it was essential that they took, at least, the same chances as the remainder of the population of London.[30]

Colville declared that,

To Churchill courage was the greatest virtue. He revered it in others, and he himself was brave both physically and morally. If he thought a course of action right, he would proceed with it fearless of the consequences and sometimes, too, regardless of political expediency. He might worry about a speech, but not about his own safety. One morning in October 1940 we told him that an unexploded landmine was in St James's Park and that, unless it could be defused, No. 10 was in grave danger. We might have to evacuate. He merely looked up from his papers at the Cabinet Room table and expressed concern for the ducks and the pelicans [species which were introduced to the park in 1664 as a gift from the Russian Ambassador].[31]

According to Thompson, however, Winston went even further, by

taking deliberate risks during the blitz. He insisted upon seeing for himself what was going on. His worst habit, from my point of view as his bodyguard, was of going on to the roof of the [Downing Street] Annexe to watch the raids.[32]

Marian Holmes records that,

On one occasion it was very lively around St James's Park [with] heavy bombing. And he said, 'Are you frightened Miss Holmes? Are you sure you're not frightened?' 'I said, "No, I'm not." It was impossible to be frightened in his presence.'[33]

This illustrates, once again, how Winston could think nothing of exposing himself to unnecessary risks, and at the same time be unmindful of the risks posed by his reckless behaviour to those in his company.

In a BBC broadcast, made on 9 February 1941, Winston directed the following message to President Roosevelt,

We shall not fail or falter; we shall not weaken or tire. Neither the sudden shock of battle, nor the longdrawn trials of vigilance and exertion will wear us down. Give us the tools, and we will finish the job.[34]

In a further broadcast on 27 April, by which time the Germans had invaded the Balkans and overrun both Greece and Yugoslavia, and when so many merchant ships were being lost in the Battle of the Atlantic that Britain's supplies not only of war materials but of food were being seriously jeopardized, Winston quoted some lines by English poet Arthur Hugh Clough and, in so doing, revealed his enduring love of poetry:

> For while the tired waves, vainly breaking,
> Seem here no painful inch to gain,
> Far back, through creeks and inlets making,
> Came silent, flooding in, the main.
>
> And not by eastern windows only,
> When daylight comes, comes in the light;
> In front the sun climbs slow, how slowly,
> But westward, look, the land is bright.[35]

At a luncheon given by the London County Council on 14 July, Winston declared, in reference to the enemy's bombing of Britain's cities, 'We will mete out to the Germans the measure, and more than the measure, they have meted out to us.'[36] On a personal note, as a schoolboy at Harrow School Winston had, to his shame, ducked the challenge thrown down by the bullies. For him, *Nemo me impune lacessit* (No one provokes me with impunity – a motto with which he was doubtless familiar) would now best describe his attitude to those who struck blows against Britain and her Allies.

On 4 August Winston and his Chiefs of Staff set out to cross the Atlantic in the battleship HMS *Prince of Wales*, bound for Ship Harbor, Placentia Bay, Newfoundland, there to rendezvous with President Roosevelt, who arrived in the heavy cruiser USS *Augusta* for four days of talks. At Divine Service, held for the crews of both vessels aboard the *Prince of Wales*, Patrick Kinna, his shorthand writer 1941-45, described how Winston, this 'very kind-hearted, emotional man [was] clearly visibly affected by the service and by the hymn singing' (the British Prime Minister having chosen the hymns).[37] On 14 August a joint declaration was issued, the so-called Atlantic Charter, which defined the aims of the Allied Powers, not only in the current war, but also for the post-war years.

An exasperated Winston wrote to his son Randolph on 30 October to complain that 'The Admirals, Generals and Air Marshals chant their stately hymn of "Safety First". In the midst of this I have to restrain my natural pugnacity by sitting on my own head. How bloody!'[38] In late December he paid another visit to the USA for further discussions with President Roosevelt.

The fall of the Libyan seaport of Tobruk on 21 June 1942, said Lord Moran, Winston's doctor since he had become Prime Minister in May 1940, left 'not only Cairo and Alexandria, but the Suez Canal and all the oilfields of the Near East ... at the mercy of [Field Marshal Erwin] Rommel'. Winston, however, 'had refused to take the count ... and [remained] full of fight'.[39]

Said Lord Bridges,

> From May 1940 to, say, the middle of 1942, were the greatest years of Churchill's life. Everything depended upon him and upon him alone. Only he had the power to make the nation believe that it could win.[40]

Like all good leaders, Winston's finger was always on the proverbial pulse for it was his habit, where possible, to visit the various theatres of operation in order to discover the facts of the matter for himself. Brigadier Sir Edgar Williams (Chief Intelligence Officer to General Montgomery, British Eighth Army, North Africa) wrote that:

> He loved being the man on the spot and he loved the smell of powder. He liked taking part in these things; he would visit the forward troops, and if there were any guns about that he could possibly get his hands on, so to speak, he would like to have fired them. I think he just felt he'd been a soldier in his day and he now was an old warhorse sniffing powder ...[41]

> In Egypt, on 6 August 1942 for example, he sensed that 'There is something wrong somewhere. I am convinced there has been no leadership out here. What has happened is a disgrace. Ninety-thousand men all over the place ... .'[42]

The outcome was, rightly or wrongly, that on 8 August Auchinleck was relieved by General Sir Harold Alexander and, on 13 August, Lieutenant General Bernard Montgomery was made Commander of Eighth Army, command of which Auchinleck had assumed on 25 June 1942. Churchill's first choice for the latter post, Lieutenant General William Gott, had been killed on 7 August 1942 when the aircraft in which he was flying was shot down by the enemy. Very soon, for Britain and her Allies in North Africa, the tide of war would turn.

Notes

1. Wheeler-Bennett, Sir John (ed.), *Action this Day: Working with Churchill*, pp. 50-1.
2. Gilbert, Martin, *Finest Hour: Winston S. Churchill 1939-1941*, Winston, speech to the House of Commons, 13 May 1940, p. 333.
3. John Colville, Assistant Private Secretary to Neville Chamberlain in May 1940; Winston's Assistant Private Secretary, 1943-45; Joint Principal Private Secretary 1951-55.
4. Wheeler-Bennett, Sir John, op cit, p. 48.
5. Ibid, p. 49.
6. Ibid, p. 50.
7. Gilbert, Martin, op cit, Colville, *Diary*, 29 May 1940: Colville Papers, p. 427.
8. Moran, Lord. *Winston Churchill: The Struggle for Survival 1940-1965*, p. 677.
9. *Churchill*. BBC Enterprises Ltd.
10. *Churchill*. BBC Enterprises Ltd.
11. Thompson, Walter H., *I was Churchill's Shadow*, p. 21.
12. *Churchill*. BBC Enterprises Ltd.
13. Wheeler-Bennett, Sir John, op cit, p. 26.
14. Ibid, pp. 24-5.
15. Ibid, pp. 24-5.
16. Ibid, p. 23.
17. Ibid, p. 144.
18. Ibid, p. 144.
19. Ibid, pp. 146-7.
20. Ibid, p. 177.
21. Ibid, p. 175.
22. *Churchill: The Greatest Briton of All Time*. A TW1/Carlton Production.
23. Wheeler-Bennett, Sir John, op cit, p. 257.
24. Ibid. In fact, Rowan did take Winston's advice, and subsequently declared, 'I was able to report to him in 1958 that I had carried out his instructions to the letter.' p. 264.
25. Ibid, p. 171.
26. Ibid, p. 184.
27. *Churchill*, BBC Enterprises Ltd, 1993.
28. *Churchill*, BBC Enterprises Ltd, 1993.
29. Gilbert, Martin, op cit, Winston: speech to the House of Commons, made on 18 June 1940, pp. 570-1.
30. Thompson, Walter H, op cit, p. 61.
31. Wheeler-Bennett, Sir John, op cit, pp. 117-18.

32. Thompson, Walter H., op cit, pp. 58 & 62.
33. *Churchill*, BBC Enterprises Ltd, 1993.
34. Gilbert, Martin, op cit, Winston: BBC broadcast, 9 February 1941, p. 1010.
35. Ibid, Winston: BBC broadcast, made on 27 April 1941, p. 1070.
36. Eade, Charles (compiler), *The Unrelenting Struggle*, p. 187.
37. *Churchill*. BBC Enterprises Ltd.
38. Gilbert, Martin, op cit, Winston to Randolph, 30 October 1941: Churchill Papers, I/362, p. 1227.
39. Moran, Lord, op cit, p. 38.
40. Wheeler-Bennett, Sir John, op cit, p. 236.
41. *Churchill*. BBC Enterprises Ltd.
42. Moran, Lord, op cit, p. 51.

CHAPTER 20

Winston and the Levers of Power

For Britain's wartime leader many qualities were required, including the ability to maintain morale, both of the public and of the armed services. However, the first prerequisite of such a leader, needless to say, was mastery of the House of Commons. Leslie Hore-Belisha, Liberal Member of Parliament and Member of the War Cabinet (1939-40), described how Winston achieved this through his 'remarkable ability to impress, persuade and dominate in his speeches, in conversation, in committee [and] in the Cabinet itself'.[1] The apparent spontaneity of Winston's delivery belies the fact that, as Phyllis Forbes confirms, he went to immense pains to rehearse his speeches, each of which, said she

> was a wonderful bit of creativity. It was exactly like a director of a great orchestra. I always enjoyed it. He would march up and down, using his cigar as a baton, trying out different words, or their rhythm; discarding some, whispering to himself. And when he finally got the rhythm, then he would go on with the speech, and that was the moment that I really enjoyed. As I say, it was like seeing a great piece of music. People, you know, suppose that he was naturally an orator, but he really wasn't. It came as the hardest work I have ever seen.[2]

A study of Winston's body language during his speeches indicates that this too was as much studied as it was spontaneous. So how may this body language be interpreted? When he placed his hands over his heart, with palms facing downwards, this indicated loyalty, honesty, frankness and devotion. When he gripped his lapels, this signified dominance, superiority and aggression, these latter three sentiments of his being undoubtedly directed towards the Nazis. When he spread his arms, with palms facing outwards, this was a signal of positivity; and when he made abundant eye contact with his audience this was intended to promote mutual confidence. All these gestures, whether consciously or subconsciously made, were designed to establish a total rapport between himself and his audience and, almost always, the attempt was successful, as the ensuing warm cheers of support and adulation testified.[3] But the wielding of power did not end with the domination of the House of Commons, for Winston was astute enough to realize that, if he was to succeed, it was essential that he carried the people with him and that they trusted him to be honest and open with them. Commented Colville:

> His charm, his energy, the simplicity of his purpose, his unfailing sense of fun and his complete absence of personal vanity – so rare in successful men – were the Secret Weapons which outmatched any that Hitler could produce. There was another facet of his character which gradually dawned on those who worked with him and ensured their lasting affection: he pretended to a ruthlessness which was entirely foreign to his nature and while the thunder and lightning could be terrifying, they could not disguise the humanity and the sympathy for those in distress which were the solid basis for his character. I never knew him to be spiteful.[4]

And he continued: 'Churchill was by no means an arrogant man, even if he was overbrimming with self-confidence.' He then made the following insightful remark:

> Perhaps because his own youth had been unhappy, he went out of his way to be kind to young people. On journeys by battleship he never failed to visit the gun-room and to spend hours answering the midshipmen's questions ... .[5]

There were many others who testified to Winston's personal concern for the people of Britain. For example, Sir John Martin, who described how Winston's 'Minutes' afforded many examples of

> his practical efforts to provide better bus services, to improve the air-raid shelters and their comfort, and amenities to reduce the petty restrictions of what he called the policy of 'misery first'.[6]

Sir Ian Fraser, who, as a soldier, was blinded in the First World War and became National President of the British Legion, Chairman of the Executive Council of St Dunstan's (the organization for men and women blinded on war service) and also a Member of Parliament said that

> Churchill kept a sure touch with what the men in the Forces were thinking and feeling. That was partly because in his wartime visits to the troops at home and abroad he used to seize every opportunity of

mixing with men of all ranks, but in the main it was because he has always, at heart, been a soldier and has never lost the instincts of the ordinary fighting man.[7]

Thompson stated that Winston

was never too busy to be bothered with the troubles of humble folk. He regarded investigation and redress of legitimate grievances as being the essential part of a democratic representative.[8]

For example, he came to the aid of an ex-serviceman who had been denied his Army gratuity simply because he had 'failed [i.e. omitted] to sign a paper [official form] that gave him the right to lodge a claim'.[9] On another occasion, having examined a bombed restaurant in the Kent seaside resort of Ramsgate and seen that its proprietor 'was in great distress', Winston told Sir Kingsley Wood, then Chancellor of the Exchequer, 'We must arrange for compensation for shopkeepers in cases like this. Please get a scheme worked out with no delay. We must help them. This man has lost his business and his livelihood.'[10]

During the Blitz, Thompson continued, Winston saw to it 'that the people of London had the maximum ack-ack [the contemporary phonetic alphabet for anti-aircraft guns or fire] cover ...'. For Winston realized just how important it was for the morale of Londoners and others, to feel that Britain was hitting back at the enemy.[11] However, the damage done by the Luftwaffe was considerable, and, over the course of a few months, Winston paid visits to over sixty different towns and aerodromes, all of which had been subjected to heavy enemy bombing.[12] Thompson also attests to Winston's thoroughness and attention to detail,

Wherever we went: dockyards, factories, aerodromes, ships, barracks – nothing seemed to escape him and much neglect on other people's part was remedied because Churchill saw what was happening more clearly than they did.[13]

Sir John Peck, Private Secretary 1940-45, describes how,

In the outer suburbs somewhere, a rather poor region of London – little shops and things – there was a large queue of people outside a shop. So he [Winston] instantly told the driver to stop and told his detective to go and see what the queue was about. This was important because queues of anything, in conditions like that, are a danger signal. Serious shortages may herald discontent ... . So the detective went off to find out what it was and he came back, and Churchill said, 'What are they queuing for?' 'Birdseed, sir.' And Winston – well he did weep, I mean the thought of these wretched people queuing in the dusk, the raids just beginning, for their canaries.[14]

Thompson described Winston as a person of 'absolute honesty and integrity of purpose', which, of course, is why he was able to gain the absolute trust and confidence of the British people:

> There is about him an old-fashioned strictness and a complete straightforwardness that would mark him out in a generation less lax in personal matters than the present one. Winston regards a promise as sacred. I have never known him to depart from his covenant unless he was forced to do so by circumstances quite outside his control. He is always prepared to do what he can for those in need of personal assistance.[15]

However, there were certain people with whom Winston, despite his best efforts, was unable to establish a good rapport, as the following comment, made by him in a letter to Clementine, sent from Algiers on 29 May 1943, indicates.

> De Gaulle is due to arrive to-morrow and everyone here is expecting that he will do his utmost to make a row and assert his personal ambition.[16]

This was a reference to Charles de Gaulle, French general and leader of Free France, whom Mary Soames once aptly described as 'haughty'.

For Winston, manipulating the levers of power also involved, of course, the wooing of potential allies, for it was abundantly clear that Britain could not win, or even survive, on her own. However, the British Empire could be counted on to provide a vast reservoir of manpower, for which Britain was eternally grateful. In respect of the Union of South Africa, it was largely through the efforts of General Jan Christiaan Smuts, its Prime Minister from 1939 to 1948 (and Field Marshal from 1941), that this country declared war on Germany on 6 September 1939. Said Thompson, 'The outstanding comradeship and friendship existing between the two leaders was ever apparent' and when Field Marshal Smuts visited the UK in October 1942, 'Mr Churchill took great delight in showing him those parts of England [which] they had time to visit.'[17] As for India, which had declared war on Nazi Germany in September 1939, Winston, in March 1942, authorized a mission to that country, led by Labour politician Sir Stafford Cripps. Its object was to offer India her independence, once the war had ended, in return for her continuing loyalty to the Allied cause. But what of the other great world players?

The USA

On 18 May 1940 Winston, 'with great intensity', told his son Randolph, 'I think I see my way through ... . I shall drag the United States in [i.e. into the war].'[18] This, for Winston, was the 'Holy Grail'; if he could achieve this, then ultimate victory was assured. In the event, the USA *did* enter the war, but belatedly, and only then through circumstances beyond Winston's control.

In Winston's attempt to enlist the help of the USA in the Second World War, it must be borne in mind that there was a strong isolationist element to be overcome in that country, and also an anti-imperialist element, in that Britain was still a colonial power which had once held colonies in the USA itself. Nevertheless, Winston did his utmost and crossed the Atlantic on several occasions, despite his hectic schedule at home, in order to meet with President Roosevelt. And when he did so, he summoned up all the charm and powers of persuasion that he could muster.

March 1941 marked the commencement of the Lend-Lease programme, whereby the USA undertook to supply Britain and other Allied nations with war materials on a massive scale. However, for Winston, this was not enough, for, as Colville recorded in his diary on 30 August 1941, he was adamant that

> We must have an American declaration of war, or else, though we cannot now be defeated, the war might drag on for another 4 or 5 years, and civilization and culture would be wiped out. If America came in, she could stop this. She alone could bring the war to an end – her belligerency might mean victory in 1943.[19]

In the event, Winston's argument was advanced, not by himself, but by the Japanese who, on 7 December 1941, attacked the US Naval base at Pearl Harbor, Hawaii, with devastating consequences. The reaction was virtually instantaneous, for the following day the USA and Britain declared war on Japan. On 11 December 1941 Germany and Italy declared war on the USA.

At Roosevelt's invitation, Winston addressed a Joint Session of Congress on 26 December and began by reminding his audience that his mother was an American national. Displaying that sense of humour for which he was famous, he declared, 'I cannot help reflecting, that if my father had been American and my mother British, instead of the other way round, I might have got here on my own.' Referring to General Auchinleck's recent and successful campaign against the Italo-German *Panzergruppe Afrika* (of which Afrika Korps comprised most of the German element) in Cyrenaica (Eastern Libya), he continued:

I am glad to be able to place before you, members of the Senate and of the House of Representatives, at this moment when you are entering the war, proof that with proper weapons and proper organization we are able to beat the life out of the savage Nazi.

In a masterstroke, Winston then lumped Britain and the USA together, when he posed the question:

What kind of a people do they [the Japanese] think we are? Is it possible they do not realize that we shall never cease to persevere against them until they have been taught a lesson which they and the world will never forget?[20]

Then came a potion which the American parliamentarians found harder to swallow:

If we had kept together after the last war, if we had taken common measures for our safety, this renewal of the curse need never have fallen upon us. Five or six years ago it would have been easy, without shedding a drop of blood, for the United States and Great Britain to have insisted on the fulfilment of the disarmament clauses of the treaties which Germany signed after the Great War. That chance has passed. It is gone. Prodigious hammer-strokes have been needed to bring us together again.[21]

May 1943 found Winston once again in the USA, attempting unsuccessfully to convince President Roosevelt that 'the only fitting sequel to the victory in North Africa was to drive Italy out of the war and to bring Turkey in as our ally'.[22] This was indeed 'goal-directed activity' on a grand scale. In September 1943, having journeyed once more 'across the pond', Winston made a speech at Harvard University, Cambridge, Massachusetts, in which he emphasized the common bond between the British and American peoples, and how it was essential for them to act in unison with each other. 'If we are together, nothing is impossible. If we are divided we will fail.'[23]

At Cairo with President Roosevelt in late November 1943 Winston's thoughts were very much with the front-line troops. As he commented to his daughter Sarah, who was accompanying him:

War is a game played with a smiling face, but do you think there is laughter in my heart? I never forget the man at the front, the bitter struggles, and the fact that men are dying in the air, on the land, and at sea.[24]

Reinforcing this, Sir John Martin said of Winston, 'His deep sensitivity enhanced his appreciation of the agony of war (as well as its glory).'[25]

At the conference of the so-called Big Three – Winston, Roosevelt and Stalin – held in Teheran (Iran's capital city) from 28 November to 1 December 1943, there was a difference of opinion between Winston, whose focus was on Italy, and the Americans, who were anxious to proceed with the invasion of France. Roosevelt responded by having meetings with Stalin to which Winston was not invited. When Winston pointed out 'the strategic importance of Turkey and [the Greek island of] Rhodes', the President intervened sharply, saying, 'We are all agreed, that OVERLORD [codename for the invasion of northern France] is the dominating operation, and that any operation which might delay OVERLORD cannot be considered by us.'[26] From then on, said Moran, Winston 'sees [that] he cannot rely on the President's support'.[27] Furthermore, according to Hugh Lunghi, interpreter at the Teheran conference, 'Stalin saw that there was a split between them [i.e. Winston and Roosevelt], so he was very ready to exploit that split.'[28] Winston confided to Violet Bonham Carter that

> when I was at Teheran [November-December 1943] I realized for the 1st time what a very *small* country this is [i.e. Britain]. On one hand the big Russian bear with its paws outstretched – on the other the great American Elephant – & between them the poor little British donkey – who is the only one that knows the right way home.[29]

This prompted Lord Moran to say of Winston on 10 December, 'He knows without my help that he is at the end of his tether. Teheran seems to have got him down.'[30]

The USSR

Winston detested Communism, and all that it stood for, saying,

> The Communist theme aims at universal standardization. The individual becomes a function: the community is alone of interest: mass thoughts dictated and propagated by the rulers are the only thoughts deemed respectable.[31]

The Communist plan, said Winston, was 'fatal to personal freedom and a gospel founded upon Hate'.[32] But, on the other hand, he realized that it was absolutely imperative to keep the USSR in the war and, to this end, to support that country militarily, as far as was possible.

Nevertheless, Winston did acknowledge that western democracy was a far from perfect system, which

> as a guide or motive to progress has long been known to be incompetent. Democratic governments drift along the line of least resistance, taking short views, paying their way with sops and doles and smoothing their path with pleasant-sounding platitudes. Only the Communists have a plan and a gospel.

Winston arrived in Moscow on 12 August 1942 to meet Stalin and apprize the Soviet leader that the Allies would be unable, that year, to mount an invasion of northern France. Stalin expressed his bitter disappointment and, according to Moran, said 'we had broken our word about a Second Front'. Whereupon, Winston was at pains to point out to Moran that in the last convoy of ships sent laden with supplies to the Soviet Union 'only three out of fourteen got through' – a fact which he had undoubtedly brought to the attention of the Soviet leader.[33] (From 1941, ships laden with food and munitions were sent from the UK to the northern Russian ports of Murmansk and Archangel.) At about this time, Thompson heard Winston say, in respect of the possible opening of a second front, 'I do not intend to throw thousands of lives away unnecessarily. When the time is ripe our preparations should ensure that our losses will not be too heavy.'[34]

While Winston was in Moscow, however, the good news came that the siege of Malta had been lifted (13-15 August). Further good news came with the victory of Allied forces, led by General Bernard Montgomery, over Rommel in the desert in the Battle of El Alamein between 23 October and 4 November. And on 8 November, in Operation TORCH, the first contingent of British and American troops landed on the North African coast at Algiers and Oran, in Algeria, and at Casablanca in Morocco.

In a speech delivered on 10 November 1942 at the Lord Mayor of London's Luncheon, held at the Mansion House, Winston declared, 'The bright gleam has caught the helmets of our soldiers and warmed and cheered all our hearts', and then he added a note of cautious optimism, 'Now this is not the end. It is not even the beginning of the end. But it is, perhaps, the end of the beginning.'[35]

Incidentally, it is calculated that, during the Second World War, Winston travelled in excess of 100,000 miles by land, air, and sea, to meet and liaise with other national leaders. Had he been paid by the hour, with extra rates for overtime, the cost to the Exchequer would have been substantial.

WINSTON CHURCHILL

Notes

1. Eade, Charles (ed), *Churchill by his Contemporaries*, p. 395.
2. *Churchill*. BBC Enterprises Ltd.
3. Pease, Allan, *Body Language*.
4. Wheeler-Bennett, Sir John (editor). *Action this Day: Working with Churchill*, pp. 53-4.
5. Ibid, pp. 65 & 79.
6. Ibid, p. 142.
7. Eade, Charles, op cit, p. 259.
8. Thompson, Walter H. *I was Churchill's Shadow*, pp. 164-5.
9. Ibid, pp. 162-4.
10. Ibid, p. 64.
11. Ibid, p. 59.
12. Ibid, pp. 62-3.
13. Ibid, p. 21.
14. *Churchill*. BBC Enterprises Ltd.
15. Thompson, Walter H., op cit, pp. 162-3.
16. Soames, Mary (ed.), *Speaking for Themselves: The Personal Letters of Winston and Clementine Churchill*, Winston to Clementine, 29 May 1943, p. 484.
17. Thompson, Walter H., op cit, p. 105.
18. Gilbert, Martin, *Finest Hour: Winston S. Churchill 1939-1941*, Randolph Churchill, *Recollections*, dictated at Stour, East Bergholt, on 13 February 1963, p. 358.
19. Ibid, Colville, *Diary*, 30 August 1941: Colville Papers, p. 1180.
20. Cannadine, David (ed.), *The Speeches of Winston Churchill*, Winston, speech to Joint Session of Congress, 26 December 1941, pp. 225-33.
21. Gilbert, Martin, *Road To Victory: Winston S. Churchill 1941-1945*, [*RV*] p. 29.
22. Moran, Lord, *Winston Churchill: The Struggle for Survival 1940-1965*, p. 93.
23. Gilbert, Martin, *RV* op cit, p. 493.
24. Churchill, Sarah, *A Thread in the Tapestry*, p. 63.
25. Wheeler-Bennett, Sir John, op cit, p. 146.
26. Moran, Lord, op cit, p. 137.
27. Ibid, pp. 140-41.
28. *Churchill: The Greatest Briton of All Time*. A TW1/Carlton Production.
29. Pottle, Mark (ed), *Champion Redoubtable: the Diaries and Letters of Violet Bonham Carter 1914-1945*, pp. 312-13.
30. Moran, Lord, op cit, p. 147.
31. Churchill, Winston S., *Thoughts and Adventures*, p. 195.
32. Ibid, p. 212.
33. Moran, Lord, op cit, p. 57.
34. Thompson, Walter H., op cit, p. 135.
35. Gilbert, Martin, *RV* op cit, p. 254.

CHAPTER 21

Further Insights into Winston's Character: His 'Safety Valves'

A Second World War poster depicts Winston, attired like 'John Bull', standing defiantly and holding a rifle with bayonet fixed. 'John Bull' was a cartoon character who came to personify Britain in general, and England in particular. Paradoxically, he was invented by a Scotsman, Dr John Arbuthnot, who in 1705 became Physician Extraordinary to the monarch, Queen Anne.

John Bull first appeared in *Law is a Bottomless Pit*, published in 1712 as the first of five pamphlets that were aimed at bringing the War of the Spanish Succession (1701-14) to an end. In this war, John Churchill, 1st Duke of Marlborough, was Supreme Commander of British and Dutch forces. (His wife Sarah, the Duchess, was a one-time friend of the Queen.) John Bull is portrayed as a stout man with tailcoat, breeches and top-hat. He is described by Arbuthnot, his creator, as 'an honest, plain-dealing fellow, choleric [irascible], bold, and of a very inconstant temper'. By the twentieth century he had come to wear a waistcoat in the colours of the Union flag and to be accompanied by a bulldog.

Just as, in his day, John Bull epitomized common sense and a fighting spirit, so Winston, in his day, did the same. Furthermore, just as Bull was instantly recognizable, so Winston was not slow to realize that the public expected to see him in characteristic pose – cigar in mouth, and making his famous victory sign. He was also in the habit of doffing his hat to them, holding it aloft on his walking stick, or using it to orchestrate their applause. He was always careful to select that headgear which was most appropriate to the occasion, whether it was a naval cap, a top hat, bowler hat, pith helmet, and, once, even a sombrero. Yet, when the occasion demanded solemnity or seriousness, he could be seen marching purposefully and at pace, with lips pursed and eyes blazing with defiance, his furrowed brow, protruding jaw, and craggy features being the epitome of resilience and defiance – just like John Bull's bulldog!

Whereas John Bull got his message across by means of cartoons and the written word, Winston relied upon his brilliant speechmaking ability. In the words of Caspar Weinberger (US Army soldier and intelligence officer during the Second World War), 'I was, of course, deeply impressed, not only with the deep, rolling cadences and the prose, but with the substance … .' And finally, in the manner of John Bull's bulldog, Winston's voice often descended into a growl. But whereas Winston shares many characteristics with John Bull, there is far more to the former than this caricature suggests.

Unselfconscious and uninhibited
The fact that Winston was capable of behaving in a completely uninhibited manner has been commented on previously. Phyllis Forbes describes, for example, how, for Britain's leader, dictating speeches or minutes was an all-consuming project, during which process he entered into what can only be described as a trancelike state:

> Well, he was really the most unselfconscious person I have ever met. He never seemed to care what anyone else thought of him. I can remember one instance of that: he was undressing for dinner, meanwhile of course, dictating to me. I watched with some apprehension as he shed first his coat, his tie, his collar and then he began to loosen his braces which held his trousers up. Well, I realized that he was absolutely wrapped up in what he was dictating and he really didn't even know I was there. But when it came to really letting his trousers down, I rose to my feet and I said very firmly, 'Mr Churchill!' I saw a startled look come over his face and he pulled his trousers up and he said, 'Oh dear, I do apologize, but you know don't you that when I've got an idea in my mind I'm simply not aware of anything that's going on around me.'
>
> I very soon realized that as a secretary I was no more to him than a fountain pen that required no time to eat or time to rest. I was on the go perpetually. Often, I wouldn't have time to eat and I'd suddenly, late in the afternoon, realize that I needed some food so I'd snatch a cup of coffee and a sandwich and then go on – sometimes till 2 or 3 in the morning. He was a terribly inconsiderate man. In fact, I've never known anyone who was so inconsiderate and it wasn't that he was cruel, but he was so involved in his own wishes, his own desires to get the work done that he never thought about the person who had to do it.[1]

Denis Kelly, Winston's literary researcher, painted the following hilarious portrait of Winston:

> I went to see him when he was working in his bed during the morning and there was Rufus (I don't whether it was Rufus I or Rufus II) lying across his ankles [the Rufuses were poodles] with the ginger cat (we had no other name for it) on his lap and there was Toby the budgerigar sitting on his head, and here he was dictating away on some immensely important political document with his secretary behind him, and these three animals were hopping round him. Very moving.[2]

A decreased need for sleep

With Winston, the working day did not end at 5.00pm, or even in the evening. For example, according to Sir Ian Jacob, when he was at Chequers:

> Recreation took the form of a film each night after dinner, and this was followed by a serious discussion with those invited down to stay. Dinner rarely ended before 10 pm, and the film lasted till midnight, so that bedtime was often not before 2.30am.[3]

According to Walter Thompson, however, bedtime could be even later.

> Many an official has had a disappointment when expecting to go to bed after one of the film shows. Mr Churchill thought nothing at Chequers of staying up until four in the morning discussing affairs, dealing with correspondence and dictating replies.[4]

Meanwhile, said Sir John Martin, 'all the London newspapers, in their various editions, starting with the first brought by despatch rider from Fleet Street at midnight, were carefully scrutinized' by the Prime Minister.[5]

Winston's nocturnal habits appalled his personal physician, Lord Moran, whose reaction, when on 25 June 1942 he learned that Winston had been dictating to his 'exhausted secretary' until 4 o'clock that morning, was 'I can hardly credit it.'[6] On another occasion, said Moran,

> When it was nearly midnight he demanded cards and began to play bezique with [Averell] Harriman [U.S. Ambassador to the Soviet Union]. 'Damn the fellow will he never give himself a chance?'[7] [The occasion referred to was in late January 1945 when Winston was in Malta, en route to the Yalta Conference.]

Neither Moran, nor anyone else at the time, could understand why Winston required so little sleep.

Even Winston, however, was not superhuman, and Jacob describes how, when the opportunity arose, he caught up on his sleep by 'cat napping':

> Another characteristic that was of great importance to him was his capacity to sleep at once and at any time. If he was travelling by car he still had his sleep, either by stopping somewhere or by tying a bandage round his eyes and sleeping in the car.[8]

Irritable and aggressive towards those who failed to endorse his ideas and plans

Jacob said of Winston that

> When his mind was occupied with any particular problem it was relentlessly focused upon it and would not be turned aside. His usual method was to decide at the start what he wanted to do, and then to beat down opposition and drive through his course of action … .
>
> It often happened that it was the Chiefs of Staff who had to examine his proposals and who had to fight against them. Sometimes he prevailed, and sometimes he gave way; but only having driven them to the limit in the process. If the Prime Minister and the Chiefs of Staff were in agreement, then he followed matters up without pause, until everything had been put in train. I never heard him say that he hadn't time to do something, or that it was too late at night, or that something could be put off.[9]

Conservative MP Victor Cazalet wrote in his diary for 5 July 1940, 'We are disturbed somewhat about Winston. He is getting very arrogant and hates criticism of any kind.'[10] A year later, when the Chiefs of Staff had ruled out both British military action in Norway and a raid on the coast of France, and faced with newly-appointed Commander-in-Chief, Middle East Command, General Sir Claude Auchinleck's reluctance to commit to an early offensive in North Africa, Elizabeth Layton, Winston's secretary, declared of the latter:

> He was in a bad temper all this week and every time I went to see him he used a new and worse swear word. However, he usually rounded it off by beaming good night at me, so one can't bear any malice or even let it worry one.[11]

Walter Graebner commented:

> He always wanted to have his own way, and on the rare occasions when he failed to get it he was cross and unhappy. It was not easy to take up a

problem with him of any kind, and it was almost impossible to get him to change his mind about a thing. Nothing was so difficult as to talk to Churchill on the telephone about any serious subject. He had a devastating way of failing to hear any objections to his own scheme or any points the person might be making at the other end of the line – unless he wanted to.[12]

Even on minor questions he was always happier when his friends agreed with him. On large matters of politics or economics, he became thoroughly annoyed if anyone slowed down his train of thought by raising objections.[13]

And Jacob concurred, saying of Winston, 'He cared little whether others were disgruntled, as long as he got his way.'[14]

'Flights of ideas' and racing thoughts

Some of the drawbacks which resulted from a mind which was overactive, which rapidly jumped from one topic to another, which could easily be distracted by trivial matters, and which had grandiose notions of its own abilities – all characteristics of Winston's persona – were illustrated as follows by his colleagues. The opinion which Jacob, for example, formed of Winston

> was of a tireless and brilliant mind, yet unpredictable and meddlesome, and quite unsuited to handle [handling] his colleagues in a team. Organization did not loom large in Churchill's mind ... .[15]

Sir Alan Brooke said of Winston, in May 1943:

> [he] thinks one thing at one moment and another the next moment. At times the war may be won by bombing, and all must be sacrificed to it. At others it becomes necessary for us to bleed ourselves dry on the Continent because Russia is doing the same. At others our main effort must be in the Mediterranean directed against Italy or the Balkans alternately, with sporadic desires to invade Norway and 'roll up the map in the opposite direction [that] Hitler did.' But more often than all he wants to carry out all operations simultaneously, irrespective of shortage of shipping.[16]

This view was endorsed by Sir John Colville:

> Throughout the war years plans were changed with no thought for others, and meetings were arranged, cancelled and rearranged to suit nobody's convenience but his own. Cabinet meetings would drag on interminably, and often unnecessarily.[17]

Sir John Peck drew a distinction between Winston's methods and those of Labour Party leader Clement Attlee. Said Peck, whenever Winston was abroad or otherwise unavailable,

> Attlee, as Deputy Prime Minister, took the Chair at the Cabinet and was a very good stand-in because he was as business-like as Churchill was diffuse ... . The number of man-hours he [Churchill] must have wasted one way and another was quite incredible, but that was his working method. Attlee, very crisp and precise, got through the business very well. [However, despite this] There was really a very, very good understanding between those two wildly different men.[18]

Having inflated ideas about himself and his abilities

Alan Brooke stated that, 'Winston never had the slightest doubt that he had inherited all the military genius of his great ancestor, Marlborough.' But Brooke believed that this was true only in part, for it was his opinion that, Winston's 'military plans and ideas varied from the most brilliant conceptions at the one end to the wildest and most dangerous ideas at the other. To wean him away from these wilder plans required superhuman efforts ... .'[19]

Sir David Hunt, Chief Intelligence Officer to Field Marshal Alexander, declared:

> Churchill thought of himself as a very great strategist. He was having lots and lots of ideas. He was always proposing a different strategy to what his Chiefs of Staff favoured. One of the reasons for this was because he simply hated having to accept what we would now call the 'establishment view' and thought he was cleverer still. And he would argue and argue until he had driven [Alan] Brooke, for example, practically out of his head.[20]

*   *   *

Brilliant though Winston was in so many ways – and full tribute to his brilliance will be paid shortly – given the unpredictable nature of his character and the apparent random nature of his thought processes, it was essential that those around him should urge restraint when it came to his wilder notions and plans. This, of course, required considerable courage, given Winston's formidable intellect and stature.

One person who was not in the least intimidated by Winston was his wife, Clementine, as Sir John Colville indicated:

Lady Churchill ... was, perhaps, the only human being who, on matters which were not political, could influence his decisions in a sense contrary to his own judgment and volition. She was indeed the only person who was never, in any circumstances, even the slightest bit overawed or afraid [of her husband].[21]

In fact, Clementine was quite capable of giving her husband a strict dressing down, if she felt he deserved it. For example, on 27 June 1940 she wrote to him to say:

One of the men in your entourage (a devoted friend) has been to me & told me there is a danger of your being generally disliked by your colleagues & subordinates because of your rough, sarcastic, & overbearing manner. I must confess that I have noticed a deterioration in your manner; & you're not so kind as you used to be.

Finally, she told Winston, 'You won't get the best results by irascibility & rudeness. Please forgive your loving devoted & watchful Clemmie.'[22]

Another person capable of standing up to Winston was the Chief of the Imperial General Staff, General, later Field Marshal, Sir Alan Brooke. Said Moran, 'Time and again his [Winston's] pet schemes were dismissed by the CIGS with a bleak negative; they were, he would say, expensive diversions which we could not afford.' In other words, Winston's attention was easily drawn to unimportant and irrelevant matters – another of his character traits. But when Moran asked Winston if he had ever considered dismissing Alan Brooke, the answer was an unequivocal 'Never'.[23]

The same might be said of General Montgomery (Monty), in whom, as far as stubbornness was concerned, Winston met his match. Said General Sir Ian Jacob, Military Assistant Secretary to the War Cabinet from 1939 to 1946:

Monty, like all generals, annoyed Winston at various times because they didn't always do what he wanted them to do, at the time he wanted them to do it. Monty wouldn't be hurried; he wouldn't be pushed about.[24]

As for the Joint Planning Staff, which was responsible to the Chiefs of Staff, this, to Winston, was like a red rag to a bull. Jacob observed that this was 'a body that Churchill never understood or appreciated':

He found so often that they produced papers which proved

conclusively that what he wanted to do was out of the question. He referred to them on one occasion as 'the whole of machinery of negation'.[25]

Soon, all Winston's idiosyncratic character traits, such as those mentioned above, will be brought together, and an attempt made to make sense of them.

* * *

Sir Ian Jacob stated that Winston 'had a remarkable independence of mind. No one ever had the Prime Minister "in his pocket".'[26] And Leslie Hore-Belisha spoke of Winston's

> dogged determination. If he cannot win his way in an argument he will probably propose the adjournment of the meeting to another day, when he will appear again, reinforced with new and even weightier evidence, facts and information and renew the attack. He never gives up and he never accepts a negative for an answer.[27]

This view, that Winston was *totally unreceptive* to other people's ideas, was not shared by others. However, said Lord Bridges, if Winston was to be persuaded to alter his views, then he required delicate handling:

> One thing that I soon learned was that a perpetual fault-finder achieved nothing. You had to make Churchill feel that you were on his side, that you sympathized with his general views, and that any criticism you made was genuinely intended to be helpful. Once convinced of this, he would listen to what you had to say, and you became, so to speak, the licensed critic. [Nevertheless] Churchill enjoyed a good battle ... and, of course, he enjoyed having his own way ... .[28]

Sir Norman Brook also endorsed the fact that, although Winston 'certainly was a man of strong will' he was not 'impervious to argument', and 'opportunity was always given to full discussion', even though such an 'argument' might be 'tense and long'. And it was also the case that Winston was capable of learning from (often bitter) experience:

> He was careful throughout the war to avoid over-ruling his military advisers, in the sense of requiring them to undertake operations to which they were opposed. This was a conscious and deliberate restraint which he imposed on himself – largely, I believe, because of his experience over the Dardanelles in the First World War, which

had taught him that a brilliant concept can end in disaster if its execution is entrusted to military staffs who have no confidence in it. He had learned this lesson in a hard school, and he never forgot it.[29]

And Walter Thompson described how Winston was man enough to admit when he was wrong, or when he had acted unfairly:

If he [Winston] has criticized and subsequently found the criticism to be unfounded he has always been big enough to make his apologies. There is about the man no seeking after cheap popularity, no talking down to the crowd in order to win favour. His outstanding characteristics are his fearlessness, his honesty and his sense of destiny and responsibility.[30]

As a result, said Lord Bridges,

Relations between the politicians and the soldiers were infinitely better in the Second than in the First World War; and ... I cannot recollect a single Minister or civil servant who was removed from office because he stood up to Churchill and told Churchill that he thought his policy or proposals were wrong.[31]

A classic example of Winston in 'receptive mood' is given by Julian Amery*, who stated that, when he was on leave in London from North Africa, he had asked to see Winston to inform him that the British Army in North Africa had lost confidence in its commanders. Amery was invited round to No. 10 Downing Street immediately, where, on 2 July 1942, he declared,

There was Churchill, at the Cabinet table with Sir Alan Brooke, Chief of General Staff, sitting beside him ... . He asked me about the situation, and I explained that I thought the army was demoralized. Sir Alan Brooke looked pretty cross, that a junior officer who was only a captain should press that sort of opinion, and he tried to intervene, but Churchill shut him up and said, 'Go on.' So I explained and Churchill then said, 'Is there anything we can do?' So I said well you can't get the tanks there any quicker, but if you were to go out yourself, show yourself to the army and visit the regiment, make a speech or two, it might make all the difference.[32]

And, as has already been mentioned, this is exactly what Winston did.

---

* Amery served in Special Forces from 1940 to 1946 and was in the Desert campaign.

WINSTON CHURCHILL

Notes

1.   *Churchill*. BBC Enterprises Ltd.
2.   *Churchill*. BBC Enterprises Ltd.
3.   Wheeler-Bennett, Sir John (ed.), *Action this Day: Working with Churchill*, pp. 179-80.
4.   Thompson, Walter H., *I was Churchill's Shadow*, p. 50.
5.   Wheeler-Bennett, Sir John, op cit, p. 143.
6.   Moran, Lord., *Winston Churchill: The Struggle for Survival 1940-1965*, p. 40.
7.   Ibid, p. 217.
8.   Wheeler-Bennett, Sir John, op cit, pp. 179-81.
9.   Ibid, p. 176.
10. Gilbert, Martin., *Finest Hour: Winston S. Churchill 1939-1941*, Victor Cazalet, Diary, entry for 5 July 1940, quoted in Robert Rhodes James (editor), *Victor Cazalet: A Portrait*, p. 231.
11. Ibid, Layton diary, 18 July 1941; Nel Papers, p. 1138.
12. Graebner, Walter., *My Dear Mister Churchill*, p. 46.
13. Ibid, p. 28.
14. Wheeler-Bennett, Sir John, op cit, pp. 162-3.
15. Ibid.
16. Bryant, Arthur, *The Turn of the Tide 1939-1943*, p. 626.
17. Wheeler-Bennett, Sir John, op cit, pp. 56-7.
18. *Churchill*. BBC Enterprises Ltd.
19. Bryant, Arthur, op cit, p. 415.
20. *Churchill*. BBC Enterprises Ltd.
21. Wheeler-Bennett, Sir John, op cit, p. 65.
22. Soames, Mary (ed.), *Speaking for Themselves: The Personal Letters of Winston and Clementine Churchill*, Clementine to Winston, 27 June 1940, p. 454.
23. Moran, Lord, op cit, p. 713.
24. *Churchill*. BBC Enterprises Ltd.
25. Wheeler-Bennett, Sir John, op cit, pp. 195-6.
26. Ibid, p. 177.
27. Eade, Charles (ed.), *Churchill by his Contemporaries*, p. 398.
28. Wheeler-Bennett, Sir John, op cit, pp. 226-7.
29. Ibid, p. 27.
30. Thompson, Walter H., op cit, p. 169.
31. Wheeler-Bennett, Sir John, op cit, p. 235.
32. *Churchill*. BBC Enterprises Ltd.

CHAPTER 22

D-Day and Onward to Victory: Stalin – A Challenge Too Far

As D-Day approached and as the workings of Winston's mind reached fever pitch, he came up, said the military historian General Sir David Fraser, with an alternative plan for the Allied invasion of Normandy:

Churchill, quite suddenly, late one evening, said to whoever was with him at the time, 'Why are we doing this? Why are we going to throw away the lives of hundreds and thousands of our young men once again in invading the coast of France? Why don't we approach occupied France through the territory of our oldest ally – Portugal – which was of course, neutral?' So there was rather a stunned silence, as to whether this enquiry was seriously intended. But it was, and Churchill said that he wished to hear the Chiefs of Staff upon this subject. And Alan Brooke couldn't believe it at first. He was absolutely furious that he was to be invited to speak [i.e. devote his attention] to this, as he saw it, total irrelevance. And he said to his briefer, 'Do you know the Pyrenees? I do. I spent my boyhood there.' Which he had. 'I know every track, every road. It is absolutely absurd and impossible, leaving on one side the political issues of invading a neutral country and opening up a new centre of operation.' [To which the reply was] 'Well, that's what the Prime Minister wants.' So Alan Brooke said, 'Very well. Then you shall get it.' And all through that night the planning staff were set to working out a perfectly rational statement of the pros and the cons, and the difficulties and the logistic problems which would arise from such an operation, such an expedition. And next morning Churchill adverted to this point. And Alan Brooke said, 'Right, Prime Minister.' And he then gave a completely cool, objective, factual account of the pros and cons – there weren't any pros … . And when he had finished, he, as it were,

159

closed the file and looked at Churchill and he said, 'Now Prime Minister, I'm going to tell you what I think about your wasting of the time of my staff on an absurd and irresponsible irrelevance of that kind, at a time when we are trying to conduct the war according to principles which we have *all*, you not least, established and agreed for some time,' and really went for him.

Nevertheless, one of the great things about Churchill was that he did, in the last resort, never overrule his Chiefs of Staff on a matter where professionally, they were as it were, doing their own duty.[1]

According to Thompson, at Southampton Docks Winston asked troops, preparing for the Normandy invasion, 'Do you men get enough to eat?' To which the reply was, 'Yes, sir – quite enough.' Nevertheless, 'he continued his enquiries with the cooking staff. He wanted to see exactly what was being given.'[2] But the next day, as the troops embarked, Winston 'did not want to speak, he was too full of emotion, so he called out: "Good luck boys".'[3]

On 5 June 1944 (the original D-Day, which was postponed to 6 June because of adverse weather conditions), the possibility of forthcoming bloodshed was very much on Winston's mind. Said he to Clementine, 'Do you realize that by the time that you wake up in the morning twenty-thousand men may have been killed?'[4]

Said Professor R. V. Jones (Scientific Intelligence 1939-46) of Winston,

He decided that he was going on D-Day – the landings in Normandy – and he said, 'I could not see why I should not witness the preliminary bombardment and, if possible, be landed on the beaches in the afternoon,' and he got himself a berth in [the cruiser] HMS *Belfast* … . Well, one could imagine the sort of consternation this caused because obviously this was going to be pretty risky, and finally it went up to Eisenhower as Supreme Allied Commander, and Ike [nickname for Eisenhower] was given very short shrift when he told Winston that he should not go. He [Winston] said, 'You may be Supreme Allied Commander but you have no right to try and regulate the complement in one of His Majesty's ships and I'm going.' And we wondered how this would ever be solved, and I remember I told some Americans that this was one of the real advantages of the monarchy because it was solved in a way that none of us foresaw. The King heard about it, and he came down to breakfast the following morning and said at the breakfast table, 'Do you know what? Winston wants to go on D-Day. Tell him, I was a naval officer.

I was at Jutland. If Winston can go, I can damn well go.' And effectively he said to Winston, 'Look, I can't stop you. If you go, I go.' And Winston said 'Well, it's much too dangerous for you, Sir.' To which the King said, 'Look, it's too dangerous for me, and it's too dangerous for you and you're much more important in this war than I am.'[5]

Nonetheless, six days later, Winston persuaded the King to allow him to cross the Channel.

On 12 June 1944, by which time the Allies had established 'a comprehensive bridge-head' in France, Winston, accompanied by Smuts and Alan Brooke, crossed the Channel in the destroyer HMS *Kelvin* and visited General Montgomery's headquarters. (On 1 September Montgomery was promoted to Field Marshal.) Winston's detective, Walter Thompson, mindful of the fact that, at that stage, the minefields had not yet been cleared, and that not all German stragglers had been rounded up, declared in exasperation, 'How can you protect someone who insists on getting in amongst the fighting?'[6]

On the return journey the destroyer sailed along the French coast and Thompson heard the order ring out for several salvos to be fired at German coastal artillery defences. And he subsequently heard Smuts say to Winston, 'I think the captain of the ship was rather cross with you for ordering him to fire on the German batteries.' 'Why?' asked Mr Churchill. 'Because the destroyer was well within the range of the German guns and they might have fired at us.' 'That's what I did it for. I wanted them to fire!' said Winston.[7]

Mary T. G. Shearburn had, since 1939, been a member of Winston's personal secretarial staff. She married Walter Thompson – whom she called Tommy – after the latter's retirement. The reason that Tommy had not proposed to her earlier, she said, was because of 'the feeling he had that he would never survive the war because of Churchill's habit of continually [and deliberately] walking into danger'.[8] A possible explanation of why Winston felt it necessary to risk his life unnecessarily in this way will be given shortly.

When the first flying bombs (V-1s) began landing on London and south-east England on 13 June 1944, Winston sent a 'Personal Minute' to Chief of Staff Lord Ismay, suggesting a possible line of retaliation:

I want you to think very seriously over this question of poison gas. I would not use it unless it could be shown either that (a) it was life or death for us, or (b) that it would shorten the war by a year. It is absurd to consider morality on this topic when everybody else used it in the last war without a word of complaint from the moralists or the Church. I want a cold-blooded calculation made as to how it would pay us to use poison gas, by which I mean principally, mustard. Although one sees how unpleasant it is to receive poison gas attacks … [nevertheless] nearly everyone recovers … . We could drench the cities of the Ruhr and many other cities in Germany in such a way that most of the population would be requiring constant medical attention. We could stop all work at the flying bomb starting [i.e. launching] points.[9]

Having participated in the First World War it is inconceivable that Winston was ignorant of the effects of mustard gas, which can cause agonizing blistering and excoriation of the skin, and a slow, lingering death from asphyxiation. Winston, therefore, in describing the effects of mustard gas poisoning as 'unpleasant', was being economical – to say the least – with the truth. In the event, his Chiefs of Staff argued, successfully, against his proposed use of poison gas.

According to R. V. Jones, when Winston was warned by his scientists that an even more sinister weapon – the V-2 ballistic missile – would soon be used against Britain, he reacted in much the same way, by saying, 'Shouldn't we try to stop this by threatening to retaliate with poison gas if they did bomb us with the V-2?' Jones confirmed that the gas in question

was not anthrax, which some of the accounts have said, it was poison gas, particularly mustard gas and this [i.e. the idea] was that we wouldn't do it, but we would threaten to do this if they opened the V-2 bombardment. But no one really supported him and the Chiefs of Staff particularly, and of course, he backed down.[10]

On 4 August Winston expressed his concern to Moran about the threat from the east. Said he, 'Good God, can't you see that the Russians are spreading across Europe like a tide; they have invaded Poland, and there is nothing to prevent them marching into Turkey and Greece!' As for the American landings in the south of France, Operation DRAGOON, which commenced on 15 August 1944, Winston saw, in his own words, 'no earthly purpose' in them. Instead, to Winston's way of thinking, 'those 10 [American] divisions should have been landed in the Balkans'.[11]

From 11 to 23 August Winston was in Italy where, at Naples, he had a meeting with Marshal Josip Tito, Communist leader of Yugoslavia's resistance movement. From there, on the 17th, he wrote to Clementine to tell her that he had enjoyed bathing and visiting the islands of Ischia and Capri, about which he enthused.[12] That very day he had visited the battlefield of Monte Cassino. The following day, he told Clementine, 'I am just off to see a bit of the [front] line near Florence where fighting is still going on.'[13]

Moran noted on 21 August that Winston was 'sorely perturbed about Greece. His mind is full of forebodings about what will happen when the Germans leave Athens. The Communists will seize power, and he is resolved to thwart their purpose'.[14] On 8 September the first V-2 fell on London.

Five days after the arrival of that first V-2, at a dinner at the Citadel, the operational centre for the Admiralty in London's Horse Guards Parade, the subject arose as to how another war could be prevented. Whereupon, Henry Morganthau, US Secretary of the Treasury, advocated the closing down of Germany's Ruhr – the largest industrial region in Europe – in order 'to help British exports, especially steel'. Winston, however, opposed the idea, saying,

> I'm all for disarming Germany, but we ought not to prevent her living decently. There are bonds between the working classes of all countries, and the English people will not stand for the policy you are advocating.[15]

In other words, there was to be no repetition of the infamous Treaty of Versailles, whereby, after the First World War, Germany had been subject to punitive reparations which caused bitter and lasting discontent in that country, and gave Hitler an excuse for re-arming and going to war.

By late September, said Moran, the advance of the Red Army had 'taken possession of his [Winston's] mind',[16] and Winston had already come to the conclusion that 'the only way to save a country from the Russians was to occupy it'[17], for 'once they [the Soviets] got into a country it would not be easy to get them out'. However, when Roosevelt declined his suggestion of having a meeting with Stalin, Winston decided to 'go it alone'.[18]

Between 9 and 18 October Winston met with the Soviet leader in Moscow. On the very first day, the 9th, Winston wrote down, on a 'half-sheet of paper', his notion of what percentage of influence Britain and the Soviet Union were to have in each of the following countries of Europe: Rumania, Greece, Yugoslavia, Hungary and Bulgaria. For Greece, Winston proposed that the figures should be: Britain 90 per cent, the Soviet Union 10 per cent, it being his view that if British power in the Mediterranean was not to be threatened then it was imperative to keep communism out of Greece. When he showed this so-called 'naughty document' to Stalin, the Soviet leader did not demur. However, on his return, said Moran, Winston's mood was one of pessimism.

'The PM seemed to realize that he had got nothing out of Stalin and that Poland had been left in the grip of Russia.'[19]

From Malta, on 1 February 1945, Winston wrote to Clementine to say:

My heart is saddened by the tales of the masses of German women and children flying [i.e. fleeing] along the roads everywhere in 40-mile-long columns to the West before the advancing armies. I am clearly convinced that they deserve it; but that does not remove it from one's gaze. The misery of the whole world appalls me and I fear increasingly that new struggles may arise out of those we are successfully ending.

And he ended the letter, 'Tender Love my darling I miss you much I am lonely amid this throng. Your ever loving Husband W.'[20]

Another conference of the 'Big Three' was held from 3 to 11 February, this time at Yalta in the Crimea on the northern coast of the Black Sea. The challenge for Winston was to enlist the support of Roosevelt in countering Stalin's colonization of Eastern Europe, the countries of which the latter regarded as the spoils of war. Sadly, this was a challenge too far, as Moran confirms:

Only a solid understanding between the democracies could have kept Stalin's appetite under control. The PM has seen that for some time, but the President's eyes are closed. What is more remarkable – for Roosevelt is a sick man – the Americans [a]round him do not seem to realize how the President has split the democracies and handcuffed the PM in his fight to stem Communism. They cannot see that he [Roosevelt] is playing Stalin's game. The PM has for some time been thinking of the outcome of the war; and he can see that the map of Europe will be redrawn in red ink. Far more than at Teheran he is conscious of his own impotence.[21]

Roosevelt had not been a well man since contracting poliomyelitis in 1921, which left him with weakness in the legs. By 1945 he was suffering from hypertension and cardiac failure.

Winston was later criticized by the Poles, including Josef Kowal, who served in the Polish Army from 1939 to 1945, for not fighting hard enough to wrest Poland from Stalin's grasp. But Sir Frank Roberts, British minister to Moscow, 1945, did not agree, saying:

More of a fight! We'd had more discussions at Yalta on Poland than on any other single subject. Of course he fought. I asked the Pole what he would have wanted us to do effectively; would he have wanted us to go to war, and if so how? Were we to drop the atom bomb? And some Poles think that Roosevelt should have threatened to drop an atom bomb on the Russians – he only had two, or three I think, at that time, which were being reserved for Japan. But then, how could that have been done with the public opinion in America and Britain which was full of gratitude and admiration for the Russian war effort?[22]

The irony of the situation was, of course, that in September 1939 Britain had gone to war with Germany following that nation's invasion of Poland, and now, at Yalta, Britain was a signatory to the surrendering of Poland to the Soviets. Said Marian Holmes:

The impression of Mr Churchill's mood at Yalta was that he was melancholic; rather depressed. Perhaps he felt his teeth were drawn and he was not going to have much influence over affairs in the future and it was the two giants, protagonists – Soviet Union and United States [who would henceforth determine matters].[23]

Winston's grandson and namesake, Winston (born 10 October 1940, the son of Randolph Churchill and Pamela, née Digby), described how,

There were many conversations to which Churchill was not privy and, above all, what pulled the rug from under our feet, as an alliance, was the fact that Roosevelt announced to Stalin, that as soon as the war was won the United States would not hang about in Europe; that there would be a massive demobilization of American troops and they would be withdrawn from Europe, and that was music to Stalin's ears because he had no intent to demobilize his forces at all.[24]

Even the American military were aware of Roosevelt's shortcomings, as this statement by Colonel H. Merrill Pasco, who, from 1941 to 1945, was on the personal staff of American General George C. Marshall, US Army Chief of Staff and Chief Military Advisor to Roosevelt, reveals:

It was not long before Marshall realized that Mr Churchill was correct, and he [Marshall] thought that Mr Roosevelt was very slow in appreciating the Russian threat and I think that explains to some degree, the results of the Yalta conference. He [Marshall] felt that if they had bargained harder they need not have given him [Stalin] anything like the control that they did.[25]

Roberts believed that Winston, also, was to some extent duped by Stalin:

Churchill had moved away, as Roosevelt had, from their initial suspicion of hostility into a sort of feeling of we're all comrades together, and they had this, to me, rather fantastic idea that if you treated – by that time he was being called 'Uncle Joe', which was almost an affectionate term – if you treated Uncle Joe like a member of the club, one day he'd behave like one, which I always felt was a rather false assumption because he had a club of his own and didn't want to be a country member of ours. But still, that had been the approach, and was still Roosevelt's approach at the time of Yalta.[26]

Winston's personal secretary Elizabeth Nel revealed that,

There was one side of Mr Churchill which was almost naïve: he couldn't project himself into the mind of somebody like Stalin, and I always felt that that was very, very sad, that he felt he'd made a friend of Stalin, and all the time Stalin was laughing at him behind his back.[27]

Another interpretation of the situation is that Winston was all too aware of Stalin's strategy, but was powerless, without the benefit of Roosevelt's support, to do anything to counteract it, and he realized that the only weapon available to him was charm.

The Conservative MP Sir Alec Douglas Home wrote that:

Winston made a claim which I couldn't stomach. He said that the agreement at Yalta was an act of justice. And so I felt bound to get up and say that I couldn't accept it as an act of justice; it might be an act of expediency, but certainly not justice. And he didn't much care for this.[28]

General Sir David Fraser states that

Alan Brooke, I think, recorded Churchill … gazing into the middle-distance with a very despondent expression and saying, 'We shall end this whole business with the barbarians in the heart of Europe.'[29]

From Downing Street, on 12 February 1945, Winston told Clementine:

People here are getting upset at the conditions in France. Quite apart from the humanitarian aspect, don't you think it's dangerous to have the whole Nation cold, hungry & unemployed. Do you think you could influence General [George] Marshall or the President

[Roosevelt] to release enough lorries to distribute the food and coal already in France.[30]

BBC War Correspondent Robert Barr described Winston's antics on 25 March 1945:

In warm, brilliant sunshine this afternoon the Prime Minister, Mr Churchill, basked on his balcony overlooking the Rhine and discussed, casually, with General Eisenhower and Field Marshal Montgomery just how the Ninth Army bridgehead had been established. Downstream he could see the town of Wesel, which the British commandos had just completely cleared. Through his binoculars the Prime Minister was inspecting the bridgehead just across the slow-flowing Rhine, when quite suddenly he decided to cross. Our planes were still pounding the German positions across the river when Mr Churchill walked down to the river's edge and got into a landing craft. With him went Sir Alan Brooke, Chief of the Imperial General Staff; Field Marshal Montgomery; General Omar Bradley [Commander of the US 12th Army Group], and General [William H.] Simpson, Commander of the [US] Ninth Army [under British command]which had forced the river at this point. We cruised across the Rhine in the tracks of the infantry and the Prime Minister scrambled up the gravel bank along the same narrow wired path that the infantry had used, and scaled a high earth dike to get a good view. He studied the bridgehead and discussed the morning's battle with the American generals and then he decided to have a short cruise on the Rhine. After the short cruise the landing craft turned back to shore.[31]

Now, once again, having manoeuvred himself as close as possible to the scene of the action, Winston behaved with characteristic and deliberate recklessness. According to Thompson:

He was not content until he, himself, stood on the east bank of the Rhine. He insisted on going up very near to the front line. A shell fell near him but he was rather more pleased than worried about this.[32]

Said Sir John Colville, in respect of this visit made by Winston to Montgomery's headquarters,

When, in March 1945, I accompanied him on to German soil to watch the 21st Army Group [composed primarily of British and US forces] cross the Rhine I remember how upset he was by the strained look on the faces of the civilian inhabitants, particularly the children. By this time, indeed, he was again advocating clemency: let a list of a hundred or so of the principal war criminals be drawn up, and let them, on capture, be tried by drum-head court-marshal, sentenced to death and shot on the ratification of any officer with the rank of Major General or above. After that no more bloodshed.[33]

On 28 March 1945 Clementine wrote to Field Marshal Montgomery:

Winston loved his visit to you. He said he felt quite a reformed character & that if in earlier days he had been about with you I should have had a much easier life! referring I suppose to his chronic unpunctuality & to his habit of changing his mind (in little things) every minute![34]

Roosevelt died of a stroke on 12 April 1945. He was succeeded by Harry S. Truman. Said Winston of the former, 'No one realizes what he has meant to this country. He was a great friend to us. He gave us immeasurable help at a time when we most needed it.'[35] And Colville related how Winston's faith in the late American President had continued right up until the end:

Nothing the Americans did: the futile landing in the South of France; Warsaw [The refusal by Roosevelt to permit US bases in Italy to be used by the RAF to fly supplies to General Bór Komorowski, Commander of Poland's Home Army, which had risen up against the Nazi occupiers]; Yalta [Conference, 4-11 February 1945], nor Churchill's deep distress at [Dwight D.] Eisenhower's [Supreme Commander of Allied Forces in Europe] failure to take Berlin and Prague when they lay within his grasp, for one moment dampened his faith in the essential virtue of the United States. His confidence in victory, even in the darkest days, was at least partly based on his certainty that Roosevelt would not desert us.[36]

In late-April 1945 the Soviet Government invited Clementine to tour Russia 'on behalf of her Red Cross Aid to Russia Fund', of which she had been chairman since its launch, in mid-October 1941. (She would remain so until 1946.)[37] Subsequently, on the evening of 9 May – Victory Day in Russia – Clementine broadcast on Moscow Radio.[38] Meanwhile, on 2 May 1945, Winston wrote to her from the Foreign Office to say, 'We have just heard that Hitler is dead.'[39] Hitler had committed suicide in his Berlin bunker on 30 April. Two days earlier, Italy's fascist dictator, Benito Mussolini, had been executed by Italian partisans.

D-DAY AND ONWARD TO VICTORY

On Monday 7 May Germany surrendered in Western Europe, and on Tuesday 8 May – which was declared VE (Victory in Europe) Day – Germany surrendered on the Eastern Front. VE Day, said Thompson, was a day that Winston

> enjoyed like a schoolboy on an outing. He had waited long and lived laborious days to witness this culmination. To my knowledge he had worked unceasingly since September 1939, and [now] for forty-eight hours he felt justified in abandoning himself to the joy of achievement.[40]

The Japanese, however, fought on.

Notes

1. *Churchill*. BBC Enterprises Ltd.
2. Thompson, Walter H., *I was Churchill's Shadow*, p. 137.
3. Ibid, p. 138.
4. Pawle, Gerald, *The War and Colonel Warden*, p.302, in Soames, Mary (ed). *Speaking for Themselves: The Personal Letters of Winston and Clementine Churchill*, p. 497.
5. *Churchill*. BBC Enterprises Ltd.
6. *Churchill's Bodyguard*, Nugus/Martin Productions Ltd.
7. Thompson, Walter H., op cit, p. 141.
8. *Churchill's Bodyguard*, Nugus/Martin Productions Ltd.
9. Gilbert, Martin, *Road To Victory: Winston S. Churchill 1941-1945*, Winston to Lord Ismay, 6 July 1944, Serial No. D.217/4, pp. 840-1.
10. *Churchill*. BBC Enterprises Ltd.
11. Moran, Lord, *Winston Churchill: The Struggle for Survival 1940-1965*, p. 161.
12. Soames, Mary (ed.), *Speaking for Themselves: The Personal Letters of Winston and Clementine Churchill*, [SP] Winston to Clementine, 17 August 1944, p. 500.
13. Ibid, Winston to Clementine, 18 August 1944, pp. 502-3.
14. Moran, Lord, op cit, p. 172.
15. Ibid, p. 177.
16. Ibid, p. 191.
17. Ibid, p. 206.
18. Ibid, p. 191.
19. Ibid, p. 206.
20. Soames, Mary op cit, Winston to Clementine, [SP] 1 February 1945, pp. 512-13.
21. Moran, Lord, op cit, pp. 232-3.
22. *Churchill*. BBC Enterprises Ltd.
23. *Churchill*. BBC Enterprises Ltd.
24. *Churchill*. BBC Enterprises Ltd.

25. *Churchill*. BBC Enterprises Ltd.
26. *Churchill*. BBC Enterprises Ltd.
27. *Churchill: The Greatest Briton of All Time*. A TW1/Carlton Production.
28. *Churchill*. BBC Enterprises Ltd.
29. *Churchill*. BBC Enterprises Ltd.
30. Soames, Mary, *SP* op cit, Winston to Clementine, 12 February 1945, p. 516.
31. Hawkins, Desmond (compiler and ed.), *War Report D-Day to VE-Day*, p. 269.
32. Thompson, Walter H., op cit, p. 151.
33. Wheeler-Bennett, Sir John (ed,), *Action this Day: Working with Churchill*, p. 88.
34. Soames, Mary, *Clementine Churchill*, [*CC*] Clementine to Montgomery, 28 March 1945. p. 367.
35. Thompson, Walter H., op cit, p. 153.
36. Wheeler-Bennett, Sir John (ed.), *Action this Day: Working with Churchill*, p. 95.
37. Soames, Mary, *SP* op cit, p.519, and Soames, Mary, *CC* op cit, p. 323.
38. Ibid, p. 531.
39. Ibid, Winston to Clementine, 2 May 1945, p. 530.
40. Thompson, Walter H., op cit, p. 159.

CHAPTER 23

Japan Fights On:
Electoral Defeat for Winston

On 13 May 1945, five days after VE Day, Winston addressed the nation in a BBC broadcast made from No. 10 Downing Street. Alluding to the Soviets, who had now replaced the Nazis as occupiers of the countries of Eastern Europe, he expressed his fear, lest

> totalitarian or police governments were to take the place of the German invaders. We seek nothing for ourselves. But we must make sure that those causes which we fought for find recognition at the peace table in facts as well as words, and above all we must labour to ensure that the World Organization which the United Nations are creating at San Francisco does not become an idle name, does not become a shield for the strong and a mockery for the weak.[1]

This was a reference to the United Nations Organization, which came into existence on 24 October 1945 and succeeded the League of Nations. Its aims were the promotion of international law, security, economic development, social progress, human rights and world peace.

On 23 May 1945 the coalition government resigned due to the Labour Party's unwillingness to maintain it further, and Winston became Prime Minister of a caretaker government, pending the result of a general election to be held on 5 July. Winston would have preferred it if the general election had been postponed until the end of hostilities with Japan. That nation continued to fight. Meanwhile, 21 June saw the completion of the capture of the Japanese island of Okinawa by US forces in a bloody campaign that made it apparent that any invasion of the Japanese mainland would involve the Allies in immense loss of life.

As there was a delay before the election results were announced, Winston and Clementine travelled, on 7 July, to the French coastal resort of Hendaye for a week's holiday.[2] There they were joined by Bryce Nairn, British Consul in Bordeaux, and his wife, Margaret, formerly a professional artist, who was able to advise Winston on his painting technique.[3]

On 15 July, Winston, in company with Lord Moran, flew on to Berlin for the Potsdam Conference (17 July – 2 August), this time of the 'Big Four' – Truman, Stalin, and both Winston and Clement Attlee, neither of whom knew, pending the election results, which would be Britain's next prime minister. Prior to the commencement of the conference, Winston visited the Reichs Chancellery where the German Führer, Adolf Hitler, had met his end.[4]

Moran subsequently described how the atmosphere at the Potsdam Conference was 'quite different' from that of the previous conferences at Teheran and Yalta. This was because

> When Stalin gets tough Truman at once makes it plain that he, too, can hand out the rough stuff. If only this had happened at Yalta. It is too late now. He [Truman] knows that the time to settle frontiers has gone. The Red Army is spreading over Europe. It will remain.[5]

Moran also described how, during the visit, and out of concern, Winston 'had looked very carefully at the children [of Germany] for signs of malnutrition'.[6]

Winston confided to Moran on 23 July that 'we [by which he meant the Americans] have split the atom. A bomb was let off in some wild spot in New Mexico. It was only a thirteen-pound bomb, but it made a crater half a mile across.'[7] (In fact, the atom had first been 'split' – i.e., a nuclear reaction had been produced – many years previously, in 1932. What Winston was referring to was the setting-off of the first atomic bomb on 16 July 1945.)

When, on 26 July 1945, the results of the general election were finally declared, it was much to Winston's dismay and consternation. The Labour Party had won a landslide victory with a majority of 145 seats, and Attlee duly became Prime Minister. Nevertheless, Winston retained his seat at Woodford, with a 17,000 majority. As for Randolph, he lost his parliamentary seat (and never regained it). Moran, however, was not wholly surprised. Said he, 'For some time I have had a growing disquiet that he [Winston] has lost touch with the way people are thinking; but I was not prepared for this debacle.'[8] Walter Graebner was of the opinion that:

> It was probably hurt vanity and pride which partly accounted for his utter dejection after his defeat in the 1945 election, which perhaps pained him as much as anything [that occurred] in his lifetime. The thought of defeat so soon after the end of the war had never crossed his mind, and for months he was hardly able to comprehend the

actual fact of it. 'No sooner was our peril over than they turned me out,' he muttered sadly to me many weeks later.[9]

Patrick Kinna also witnessed Winston's reaction at first hand:

He started reminiscing, and then he began to look very, very sad, and there was a pause, and he said, and now the British people don't want me any more. Tears were rolling down his cheeks, and mine too. I've never seen anyone so broken-hearted. It didn't occur to him that it could happen.[10]

When, on 2 August 1945, Moran went to visit him at Claridges Hotel, Winston, who had just finished breakfast and was still in his bedroom, pointed to the balcony and said, 'I don't like sleeping near a precipice like that. I've no desire to quit the world, but thoughts, desperate thoughts come into the head.' Said Moran, 'Winston was grinning at the time, but his remarks clearly reflected the very low state of his spirits.'[11] This provides further evidence that Winston had a preoccupation with death and suicidal ideation (i.e. of having the idea of committing suicide).

A few days later, Winston said to Moran,

It's no use, Charles, pretending I'm not hard hit. I can't school myself to do nothing for the rest of my life. It would have been better to have been killed in an aeroplane or to have died like Roosevelt. After I left Potsdam, Joe [Stalin] did what he liked. The Russians' western frontier was allowed to advance, displacing another eight million poor devils. I'd not have agreed and the Americans would have backed me. I get fits of depression. You know how my days were filled [i.e. when he was Prime Minister]. I go to bed about twelve o'clock [which was uncharacteristically early for Winston].

Ah, Charles, blessings become curses. You kept me alive and now ... .

'He turned his back,' said Moran, 'and when he looked at me his eyes were full of tears.'[12]

Goal-directed activity, conducted at a furious pace, was an essential ingredient of Winston's modus vivendi, so it is hardly surprising that the prospect of inactivity was making him depressed. However, as might be predicted, Winston did not remain inactive for long. He now, said daughter Mary Soames, 'started to work again on the [A] History of the English-Speaking Peoples which had been interrupted by the outbreak of the war'.[13] In fact, Mary was reasonably upbeat in her assessment of Winston's mental state during this troubled time:

Even in these bleak hours my father's sense of irony and humour did not desert him. During the day my mother had said, 'It [i.e. his party's electoral defeat] may be a blessing in disguise,' to which my father replied: 'Well, at the moment it's certainly very well disguised.'

But despite all, said Mary,

My father still maintained his courageous spirit … . Winston did not lurk long licking his wounds; when Parliament reassembled on 1st August, less than a week after the election results, he took his new place on the Opposition Front Bench.[14]

However, life at home was far from happy, as this letter from Clementine to Mary, dated 26 August 1945, reveals:

I cannot explain how it is but in our misery we seem, instead of clinging to each other to be always having scenes, I'm sure it's all my fault, but I'm finding life more than I can bear. He is so unhappy & that makes him very difficult.[15]

As for his political career, said Mary,

It would never have occurred to my father to stop. I mean, he would rather win an election than lose an election. He would rather be prime minister than not prime minister. But it would never occur to him not to go battling on in politics. *Never*![16]

On 6 August 1945 the US Army Air Forces[17] dropped an atomic bomb on the Japanese city of Hiroshima and, on 9 August, another on the city of Nagasaki. On 15 August the Japanese surrendered. Paradoxically, however, because of time zone differences, it was 14 August 1945 that was designated as VJ (Victory over Japan) Day.

Nonetheless, said Colville,

Never at any stage did I hear Churchill express vindictiveness to the Axis powers, or propose anything but chivalrous treatment of them in defeat.[18]

Notes

1. Gilbert, Martin, *Never Despair: Winston S. Churchill 1945-1965*, pp. 12–13
2. Moran, Lord, *Winston Churchill: The Struggle for Survival 1940-1965*, p. 258.
3. Ibid, p. 266.
4. Ibid, p. 270.

5.   Ibid, pp. 284-5.
6.   Ibid, p. 271.
7.   Ibid, p. 280.
8.   Ibid, p. 287.
9.   Graebner, Walter, *My Dear Mister Churchill*, p. 46.
10. **Churchill: The Greatest Briton of All Time*, A TW1/Carlton Production, 2002.
11. Moran, Lord, op cit, p. 280.
12. Ibid, Moran, Lord, *Winston Churchill: The Struggle for Survival 1940-1965*, pp. 289-90.
13. Soames, Mary, *Winston Churchill: His Life as a Painter*, p. 148.
14. Soames, Mary, *Clementine Churchill*, pp. 386-7 and 390-1.
15. Ibid, pp. 390-1.
16. **Churchill: The Greatest Briton of All Time*. A TW1/Carlton Production.
17. It was not until 1947 that the US Air Force was created as a separate service.
18. Wheeler-Bennett, Sir John (ed.), *Action this Day: Working with Churchill*, pp. 85-6.

CHAPTER 24

Leader of the Opposition

The question now was how would Winston react to being in opposition, rather than in government? Would he become bitter, resentful and disillusioned, or would other avenues open up towards which he could divert his prodigious energies?

As Leader of His Majesty's Opposition, Winston's mind remained as active as ever, but with the responsibility of government now having been lifted from his shoulders, he had more time to enjoy his other interests – travelling, socializing and, most importantly, painting. On 2 September 1945, the day Japan formally signed the documents of surrender, Winston, his daughter Sarah Clementine, and Lord Moran set off for Italy, there to stay for a month as guests of Field Marshal Sir Harold Alexander (Alex, Supreme Commander of Allied Forces in the Mediterranean theatre) at a villa, 'La Rosa', on the shores of Lake Como. Here, said Moran, Winston became totally absorbed in his painting.

When he was satisfied that he had found something he could put on canvas, he sat solidly for 5 hours, brush in hand, only pausing from time to time to lift his sombrero and mop his brow.[1]

The following day, Winston wrote to Clementine to say,

This is really one of the most pleasant and delectable places I have ever struck. Every conceivable arrangement has been made for our pleasure and convenience. Yesterday we motored over the mountains to Lake Lugano, where I found quite a good subject for a picture. I made a good beginning and hope to go back there tomorrow, missing one day.[2]

And two days later, Winston declared,

We have had three lovely sunshine days, and I have two large canvasses under way, one of a scene on the Lake of Lugano and the other here at Como. It has done me no end of good to come out here and resume my painting. I am much better in myself, and am not worrying about anything.[3]

However, on that same day, Moran recorded in his diary that his patient was far from being a well person:

In a sense Winston is tough, yet he is hardly ever out of my hands. His eyes, his ears, his throat, his heart and lungs, his digestion and his diverticulitis have given him trouble at different times.[4]

Nonetheless, continued Moran, the holiday in Italy appeared to be doing Winston good, for he had

made up his mind to cut his losses. He will not spend the rest of his days brooding on the past. Whatever happens, nothing can hold up for long the stream of ideas that rush bubbling through his head.[5]

Winston related how Alexander had visited him at the villa and 'produced a very good picture, considering it is the first time that he has handled a [paint] brush for six years'. As for Winston, he produced four paintings which he considered to be better than any he had ever painted before. Painting, he said, is, 'a great pleasure to me, and I have really forgotten all my vexations. It is a wonderful cure, because you really cannot think of anything else.' He then described, in a letter to Clementine, how he had converted his large bathroom into a studio with makeshift easels.[6]

During Alexander's stay, said Moran, he and Winston had visited a place 'where a great willow cast its shadow over the placid lake, and in the background a small yellow building caught the sunlight'. This, they decided, was the ideal subject for a painting.[7] The following day, Winston confessed to Moran that he had 'not been so happy for a long time. With my painting I have recovered my balance.'[8]

Winston's daughter Sarah told how, on the subject of painting, the two men were not always of the same mind. Alex always liked 'a touch of pure black on the palette'; Winston preferred 'Neutral Tint perhaps' and declared, 'I don't like the sepulchral finality of black.' When he arrived in heaven, said Winston, he expected to paint with 'a whole range of wonderful new colours which will delight the celestial eye'.[9] Of Winston's paintings, Alexander gave this candid, if rather blunt assessment, 'He loved colours, and used far too many. That's why his paintings are so crude. He couldn't resist using all the colours on his palette.'[10]

Winston told Clementine that he had been completely absorbed by his painting and had 'thrown myself into it until I was quite tired'. He felt confident that, after a few more months of regular practice, he would be able to paint better than ever before. Again, with Winston, even when he was supposedly at leisure, an excessive indulgence in goal-directed activity was, more often than not, par for the course.

Winston would now receive a visit from an old friend whom he had first met in 1915, during the First World War. This, said Moran, was 'M. Charles Montag, who represents Switzerland in Paris as Fine Arts Commissioner', and whose arrival 'helped to dispel the gloom' that Winston continued to experience following his election defeat. 'Winston has asked him to stay for a few days, and hopes that Montag will give him a few tips about painting.'[11] And Winston himself declared that Montag, a Swiss, who was known chiefly as a landscape painter, had 'a vast knowledge [of the subject], and one cannot paint in his presence without learning'.[12]

Moran also offered words of comfort to Winston, telling him that although the country was now hostile to the Tories (Conservatives), a recent Gallup poll showed that the people regarded him as the best person to have conducted the war.[13] 'But was there not something more behind this despair?' Moran wondered. 'Could it be that the shock of his defeat had stirred up the inborn melancholia of the Churchill blood?'[14] What Winston's doctor was alluding to here, the possibility that Winston's 'Black Dog' was a disorder which he had inherited from his forebears, will be discussed shortly. Meanwhile, Moran had his own personal view – which he did not disclose to Winston – of why the Conservatives had lost the last election:

> While the struggle [against Nazi Germany] lasted the country [Britain] was ready to put up with a dictator, but when peace came people wanted to have more say in things. The feeling grew that Attlee and the party he led [i.e. Labour] were in closer touch with their problems and in fuller sympathy with their aspirations than Churchill, with all his dazzling achievements, could be.[15]

Winston returned to England in the first week of October 1945 when 28 Hyde Park Gate became the Churchills' London home. It would remain so for the remainder of Winston's life.

At 11.00am on Armistice Day, commemorating the twenty-seventh anniversary of the armistice signed by the Allies and Germany on 11 November 1918 at the end of the First World War, Winston, his former deputy Anthony Eden, and General de Gaulle 'walked in line abreast from the Arc de Triomphe down the Champs Elysées through crowds that the French police had the utmost difficulty in controlling'.[16] During this visit to Paris,

Winston stayed at the British Embassy with Duff Cooper, the British Ambassador, and his wife, Lady Diana, who described 'Duckling', her nickname for Winston, as 'a picture of cherubic curves and glowing health – with boiler suit discarded in favour of civvies'.[17]

In early January 1946 Winston and Clementine embarked on the liner *Queen Elizabeth* for the USA where, on 5 March, he delivered his famous 'Iron Curtain' speech at Westminster College, Fulton, Missouri. In it, he referred, metaphorically speaking, to the 'Iron Curtain' which had descended over Europe, just as he had predicted it would.

Walter Graebner, London representative for *Time-Life* magazine, first met Winston in April 1946 at Chartwell, where the Sound Scriber Company of America was testing a machine to record Winston talking.[18] (And he subsequently spent time with Winston, when the latter was on holiday at Marrakech, Aix-en-Provence, or Monte Carlo.) Graebner remarked that:

Churchill was always doing something; there was never any time when, like most people, he simply did nothing at all. That is not to say that he always worked, for much of his time in the years before and after the war was spent playing. But he lived every minute so fully, with so much gusto, that anyone who was with him for three or four hours felt as if he had spent a day in his company. His tempo of living exhausted everyone but himself.[19]

According to his grandson and namesake, Winston himself admitted that he was a driven man, when he said:

Before my head touches the pillow I invigilate myself as to what I have achieved that day. Have I made a speech? Have I written an article? Have I done a chapter of a book?

And Winston (junior) continued:

It was often said during his time as Prime Minister that he was a slave-driver, but the slave that he drove was himself. He really drove himself, and that is the explanation for the colossal output that he achieved. He said, 'Not to achieve something positive in the day is like going to bed without cleaning one's teeth.'[20]

Continued Graebner:

Churchill's day began at 8 [a.m.] no matter when he went to bed. At that hour all the London daily newspapers were brought in … . He remained in bed all morning as a rule. Within easy reach of his bed, whether at Chartwell, Hyde Park Gate or 10 Downing Street, stood a narrow table with two telephones – a direct line to his secretaries' office downstairs, and an outside connection.

Also on this desk were his cigars, a candle for lighting them, his watch, a 'pink-coloured, mild form of sleeping pill called Soneryl, [and] a huge diary about a foot square, noting his engagements'.[21]

People always came to see him – another reason why he could get so much work done, and have so much time for leisure. And if the appointment was at any time before 12.30 [p.m.], Churchill remained in bed, though he was, of course, shaved by the time anyone arrived. Every important appointment was meticulously prepared for in advance by the secretarial staff. On a single sheet of paper were typed the points to be discussed.[22] Churchill valued his time so highly that even the barber came, once a week, to his bedroom to cut his hair in the few stray moments between bath and lunch. 'I'll give you five minutes and no more,' Churchill usually quipped on these occasions.[23]

If Churchill was in the country, he got his main exercise of the day by taking a walk with one or more of his guests. These walks, however, were not just aimless meanderings through the gardens [of Chartwell]; the time was spent examining the water levels in the various reservoirs, feeding the fish, throwing a ball for Rufie to chase, and perhaps declaiming on the state of the world.

He ... took half an hour around 6 o'clock to scan the afternoon papers, see a movie, read any letters his secretary thought would interest him, and read and sign his own letters and memos. After that he would sleep for an hour or two.

Around 10.30 or 11 [p.m.], well-fed, rested, happy and free of his guests, Churchill settled down for two or three hours of hard, concentrated work, during which he accomplished more than in any other period. Often, the last thing he did at night, when in London, was to scan the first edition of the *Daily Express* which his great and good friend, Lord Beaverbrook, rushed to him by despatch rider. Churchill seldom got to bed before 2 a.m.[24]

It was not ... solely the delight of eating and drinking that made lunch and dinner high points of his day. It was also the fact that these two occasions were often the only times for relaxation in a long and busy day; the only times when he could have his family and friends around him in carefree and informal conviviality.[25]

In most things Churchill was orderly, but at cards he was almost fussy. He liked the table to be entirely clear except for the decks. Smoking had to be allowed because he wanted his cigar, but the place for ashtrays was on little tables nearby. That was also the place for the whiskies. If anyone inadvertently disturbed the arrangements and set his glass or ashtray down on the playing table, Churchill was visibly uncomfortable until he could find an opportunity to put things back where they belonged. Cards had to be shuffled properly and chips stacked neatly; and he insisted on the most careful score-keeping – by someone other than himself.[26]

Every Sunday night, except on fine summer evenings, movies were shown at Chartwell in a little theatre at the back of the house. Churchill derived enormous pleasure from them. He paid the strictest attention every minute and demanded absolute silence from the rest of the audience, though he reserved the right to give a running commentary if he chose, and to ask questions whenever a part was not clear.[27]

Graebner describes how Winston, having watched 'Crusade in Europe', a documentary film of the Second World War in five episodes, 'characteristically … showed no feeling of triumph over his vanquished enemy,

'Poor fellows, poor, poor fellows,' he would say with generous pity, as towards the end he watched scenes of German prisoners-of-war huddling together in their camps.[28]

For Clementine, Graebner was full of admiration, pointing out that although she was not 'over-strong', nevertheless, she

had to keep several houses running smoothly for a husband who liked perfection in most things … , to entertain large numbers of people constantly [and] to keep calm and comfortable and happy a genius who was certainly not the easiest man in the world to cope with. All these things she did admirably.[29]

By late June 1946, said Moran, Winston had regained some of his old fighting spirit, which he had attributed to the fact that he had inherited his mother's 'Jerome blood'.[30] However, said Moran, on 6 July,

When I called on Winston today he seemed in poor heart – one of his black moods. 'I'm fed up,' he said. 'Victory has turned to sackcloth and ashes.'

Nonetheless, said Moran, Winston found happiness at Chartwell, where the walls of his studio were 'covered with his canvases'.[31]

In that summer of 1946 the Churchills renewed their acquaintanceship with Oswald Birley and his wife, Rhoda. Birley was a highly decorated former soldier who had served as a captain in the First World War, and 'valour was always a passport to Winston's esteem and affection'. It was Birley who, as already mentioned, had unknowingly awarded Winston First Prize in the amateur painting competition held in 1925. Now he had been commissioned by the Speaker of the House of Commons to paint Winston's portrait, which would hang in his [the Speaker's] residence at the Palace of Westminster. In addition, Birley offered to paint a portrait of the Churchills' youngest daughter, Mary.[32] Also in that summer, the Churchills holidayed at Lac Leman, Switzerland, where they were joined by Winston's friend of long standing, Field Marshal Smuts.

When, on 7 August 1946, Lord Camrose (William Berry, Chairman and Editor-in-Chief of *The Daily Telegraph* newspaper) learned that Winston intended to sell Chartwell owing to the high expense of its upkeep, he, and others, purchased the property and donated it to the National Trust 'with the proviso that Winston and Clementine could remain there for their lifetimes'.[33]

In a speech to the University of Zurich, Switzerland, on 19 September 1946, sixteen months after hostilities had ceased in continental Europe, Winston declared,

> I am now going to say something which will astonish you. The first step in the re-creation of the European family must be a partnership between France and Germany. There can be no revival of Europe without a spiritually great France and a spiritually great Germany. Let Europe arise![34]

And he went on to describe his vision of a future 'United States of Europe'.[35]

As Leader of the Opposition, Winston still had a part to play in the political life of the country. In late October 1946, for example, he warned the House of Commons about the danger of the Soviet army (Red Army) which had not been demobilized. 'They could march to the Atlantic in a few weeks, practically unopposed. Only the atomic bomb keeps the Russians back.'[36]

To Winston, after the long years of toil, his home, Chartwell, with its lakes, artist's studio, pets and farm animals, had now become a playground, and in late November 1946 Moran was pleased to say of his patient, 'He is very happy at Chartwell, farming and painting and dictating his book.* In short, it has been a year of recovery.'[37]

---

* *The Gathering Storm*

Winston's brother, Jack, died on 23 February 1947. Winston told Moran, 'I was with him a quarter of an hour before. Yes, he meant a lot to me.'[38] On 16 March Winston wrote to Conservative politician Lord Hugh Cecil to say,

I feel lonely now that he is not here, after 67 years of brotherly love. I remember my father coming in to my bedroom at the Vice Regal Lodge in Dublin & telling me (aged 5) 'you have a little brother'. We have always been attached to one another, & after his house was blown up in the war he lived [with] me at No. 10 or the annexe.[39]

At about this time, Winston developed a hernia which required surgery. He was therefore advised to stop smoking for fear that 'pulmonary complications' might ensue after his forthcoming anaesthetic. This he promised to do, but only for a period of a fortnight before the operation. However, said Moran, when the time came, he made only 'a feeble and abortive attempt to keep his word; then he decided to cut down the number of cigarettes to half!'[40]

Winston submitted two of his paintings to the Royal Academy Selection Committee under a pseudonym on 3 May 1947, and only when both were accepted did he reveal his true identity.[41] Six days later he journeyed to Paris to meet with French Prime Minister Georges Bidault. But before he left, Clementine told her husband, gently but firmly,

I would like to persuade you to wear Civilian clothes during your Paris visit. To me, air-force uniform except when worn by the Air Crews is rather bogus. And it is *not* as an Air Commodore that you conquered in the War but in your capacity & power as a Statesman. [Also] You do not need to wear your medals to shew your prowess. I feel the blue uniform is for you fancy-dress & *I* am proud of my plain Civilian Pig. Clemmie.[42]

Agreement was reached on 3 June 1947 to partition the Indian sub-continent into India and Pakistan, and at midnight on 14 August India became independent from Britain and a sovereign nation.

On 7 December that year Winston announced that he proposed to return to Marrakech for a holiday. 'Psychologically one needs change from time to time – different lights, different scenes, and especially different colours. Colour plays a great part in life.'[43] In this, he was undoubtedly thinking of his painting. Nonetheless, Moran observed that 'Winston is ageing, and it is perhaps inevitable that he is very gloomy about the future.'[44] However, to

Clementine, Winston presented a very different face (reflecting the fact that a person will sometimes confide more in his doctor than in his wife) when, writing from Marrakech on 18 December, he told her:

> Here I have been rather naughty; the hours of going to bed have been [in successive nights] one o'clock, two, three, three, three, two, but an immense amount has been done and Book II [of *The Second World War*] is practically finished. I am not going to sit up so late in the future.[45]

Did Clementine believe Winston's promise? Probably not! On Christmas Eve he indicated to her that he was combining frenetic work with pleasure – i.e. painting:

> Book I [of *The Second World War*] is practically finished and so is Book II. I believe they will cease to be burdens on me except for minor corrections by the end of the year. It would have been quite impossible for me to do this work if I had not buried myself here, where every prospect pleases, and only the twenty-four hours are too short.[46]

In 1948 Clementine became Chairman of the National Hostels Committee of the Young Women's Christian Association (YWCA), a position which she would hold until 1951. In that year Winston was elected Honorary Academician Extraordinary, after which time he became a regular exhibitor at the Royal Academy's Summer Exhibition. That May, he returned to one of his favourite themes, his vision of the future of Europe, when, on the 9th in the Dutch capital of Amsterdam, he declared, 'We hope to see a Europe where men of every country will think as much of being a European as of belonging to their native land.'[47]

According to Graebner, after a day's painting at Aix-en-Provence in the August of that year, 1948, Winston declared,

> 'I have had a wonderful life, full of many achievements. Every ambition I've ever had has been fulfilled – save one.' 'Oh, dear me, what is that?' said Mrs Churchill. 'I am not a *great* painter,' he said ... .[48]

That September Winston thanked Clementine 'for making my life & any work I have done possible, and for giving me so much happiness in the world of accident & storm'.[49]

On the last day of March 1949, in an address, delivered to the Massachusetts Institute of Technology, Boston, USA, Winston opined that the communist system would ultimately fail:

Laws just or unjust, may govern men's actions. Tyrannies may restrain or regulate their words. The machinery of propaganda may pack their minds with falsehood and deny them truth for many generations. But the soul of man thus held in trance or frozen in a long night can be awakened by a spark coming from God knows where, and in a moment the whole structure of lies and oppression is on trial for its life. Peoples in bondage need never despair.[50]

When Winston's painting 'The Blue Room at Trent' (Trent Park, home of Sir Philip Sassoon), which Clementine had persuaded him to part with, was sold in that same year, 1949, in aid of the YWCA, the artist was typically modest:

The price paid for 'The Blue Room' is, of course all humbug. It was made up with seventy-percent notoriety, twenty-percent charity and, I hope ten percent the actual performance.[51]

Even though Winston was now in his seventy-fourth year, his daughter Mary Soames declared, 'His energy was prodigious … he was going full tilt, at a rate which might well have daunted a younger man.'[52] However, on 24 August 1949, Winston suffered a slight stroke. In September, having read Volume III of *The Second World War*, Clementine pulled no punches when she told him,

I am glad you have … at last said something generous about the Admiralty. Reading the Chapter up to this point I feared the Admiralty and officers of the Navy might be offended and worse still, wounded. You do not print a single reply to your sharp strictures and the reader would conclude you were addressing inert and slothful men.[53]

In the general election of February 1950 Clement Attlee's Labour Party was again victorious, but won only narrowly. Clementine was not altogether surprised, for a year previously she had warned Winston that, as Leader of the Opposition, he had not been giving of his best:

In my humble way I have tried to help – the political luncheons here, visits to Woodford, attending to your Constituency correspondence – But now & then I have felt chilled & discouraged by the creeping knowledge that you do only just as much as will keep you in Power. But that much is not enough in these hard anxious times.[54]

From Marrakech, on Christmas Day 1950, Winston wrote to Clementine to say, 'I came here to Play, but so far it has only been *Work* under physically agreeable conditions.'[55] It was here, in January 1951, that Winston met French painter Jacques Majorelle, who instructed him how, by using tempera (paint, consisting of pigment mixed with egg to make an emulsion), 'a sky of wonderful blue, the intensity of which I have never before seen' could be created. (In fact, a special type of coloured paint, which Majorelle used, is named after him – 'Majorelle blue'.)[56]

In early August 1951 Winston complained to Clementine that he had spent 'a rotten day at Goodwood [Races]' where his horse, Colonist II, which he acquired in 1949, had cast a shoe.[57] Old habits die hard, or, in the case of Winston and gambling, not at all!

Notes

1. Moran, Lord, *Winston Churchill: The Struggle for Survival 1940-1965*, p. 295.
2. Soames, Mary, *Clementine Churchill*, Winston to Clementine, 3 September 1945, p. 392.
3. Ibid, pp. 392-3.
4. Moran, Lord, op cit, p. 297.
5. Ibid, p. 299.
6. Soames, Mary (ed.), *Speaking for Themselves: The Personal Letters of Winston and Clementine Churchill* [SP], p. 537.
7. Moran, Lord, op cit, p. 300.
8. Ibid, p. 301.
9. Churchill, Sarah, *A Thread in the Tapestry*, pp. 94-5.
10. Gilbert, Martin, *Never Despair: Winston S. Churchill 1945-1965*, p. 143.
11. Moran, Lord, op cit, p. 304.
12. Soames, Mary op cit, Winston to Clementine, 18 September 1945, p. 539.
13. Moran, Lord, op cit, p. 309.
14. Ibid, p. 310.
15. Ibid, p. 311.
16. Thompson, Walter H., *I was Churchill's Shadow*, p. 147.
17. Soames, Mary., *Winston Churchill: His Life as a Painter*, (*LP*) p. 149.
18. Gilbert, Martin, op cit, p. 225.
19. Graebner, Walter, *My Dear Mister Churchill*, p. 34.
20. *Churchill: The Greatest Briton of All Time*. A TW1/Carlton Production.
21. Graebner, Walter, op cit, pp. 48-9.
22. Ibid, p. 50.
23. Ibid, p. 51.
24. Ibid, pp. 48-53.
25. Ibid, p. 57.
26. Ibid, p. 36.

27. Ibid, p. 37.
28. Ibid.
29. Ibid, pp. 112-13.
30. Moran, Lord, op cit, p. 313.
31. Ibid, p. 313.
32. Soames, Mary, *LP* op cit, pp. 151-2.
33. Soames, Mary, *SP* op cit, p. 541.
34. **Churchill*. BBC Enterprises Ltd.
35. Cannadine, David (ed.), *The Speeches of Winston Churchill*, p. 313.
36. Moran, Lord, op cit, pp. 315-16.
37. Ibid, p. 317.
38. Ibid, Moran, Lord. *Winston Churchill: The Struggle for Survival 1940-1965*, p. 318.
39. Gilbert, Martin, op cit, Winston to Lord Hugh Cecil – later Lord Quickswood, 16 March 1947: Quickswood Papers, p. 317.
40. Moran, Lord, op cit, pp. 319-20.
41. Soames, Mary, *SP* op cit, p. 556.
42. Gilbert, Martin, op cit, note, undated, on Chartwell notepaper: Churchill Papers, 2/252, p. 329.
43. Moran, Lord, op cit, p. 321.
44. Ibid, p. 327.
45. Soames, Mary, *SP* op cit, Winston to Clementine, 18 December 1947, p. 547.
46. Ibid, Winston to Clementine, 24 December 1947, pp. 547-8.
47. *Daily Mail*, 10 May 1948.
48. Graebner, Walter, *My Dear Mister Churchill*, p. 92.
49. Soames, Mary, *SP* op cit, Winston to Clementine, 12 September 1948, p. 549.
50. Gilbert, Martin, op cit, p. 466.
51. Soames, Mary, *LP* op cit, p. 168.
52. Ibid, p. 169.
53. Gilbert, Martin, op cit, undated notes: Churchill Papers, 1/46, p. 489.
54. Soames, Mary, *SP* op cit, Clementine to Winston, 5 March 1949, p. 551.
55. Ibid, Winston to Clementine, 25 December 1950, p. 559.
56. Soames, Mary, *LP* op cit, p. 173.
57. Soames, Mary, *SP* op cit, Winston to Clementine, 3 August 1951, p. 559.

CHAPTER 25

How Winston's Workload and Lifestyle Took their Toll

On 10 May 1940, when Winston, then aged sixty-five, became Prime Minister of Britain's coalition government, Charles McMoran Wilson (who was Dean of St Mary's Hospital Medical School) became his personal physician, a capacity in which he served for the remainder of Winston's life. (Here, it should be mentioned that Wilson would accept no payment for his services, even though he suffered financially from having to wind down his private practice.) In the New Year Honours of 1943, Wilson was created 1st Baron Moran).[1]

In 1966 Lord Moran published *Winston Churchill: The Struggle for Survival 1940-1965*, the material for which was taken from his diaries. Whether it is ethical for a doctor to publish a book about his patient, even though that patient was by then deceased, is questionable. Nevertheless, as has already been demonstrated, the work gives a unique insight not only into Winston's health but also into his state of mind, for nobody, with the exception of Winston's wife, Clementine, was closer to Winston than his personal physician.

Winston arrived at the White House on 26 December 1941 as the guest of President Roosevelt. The following day he developed a pain in his chest which radiated down his left arm, leaving Moran in no doubt that 'his symptoms were those of coronary [artery] insufficiency'.[2]

While attending the Casablanca conference in February 1943 Winston developed a high temperature and, on the 16th, Moran diagnosed pneumonia at the base of his left lung.[3] However, said his personal detective Walter Thompson, within a day or two of his collapsing with pneumonia 'Mr Churchill, although confined to his bed, carried on his duties without ceasing. He would not rest his mind.'[4]

In May of that year Moran commented that 'for three years the Prime Minister has been doing everyone else's job, as well as his own, wallowing in detail; and there is no end to it in sight'. But was there 'something else sapping his strength', Moran wondered? It was his doctor's opinion that if Winston was to cope with the stresses and strains imposed upon him, he would have to change his nature, by cutting off

> those messages from the outer world that reach the brain at times like these and threaten its balance. As First Minister of the Crown in time of war he was bound to receive in the course of his lonely mission wounds deeper and more lasting than any weapon can inflict; it was vital to him that he should be able to shed the kind of thought that might distract or distress his mind; forget, if he could, for a short space at any rate, the anguish of the hour. [But, said Moran regretfully] He could not do it.[5]

At Teheran in November 1943 Moran examined Winston and discovered a raised pulse rate. This, he suggested, was 'due to all the stuff he drank and that he ought not to go on at this rate'. To which his patient replied, nonchalantly, 'It will soon fall.'[6] Moran diagnosed a recurrence of pneumonia, again at the base of Winston's left lung, on 13 December.[7]

At Marrakech, where Winston stayed from 27 December 1943 to 14 January 1944, when he was recovering, his pneumonia having been followed by a heart attack, Thompson declared,

> No more suitable place for Mr Churchill to be at his painting could be imagined for the whole scene was a riot of the colour from which he draws his inspiration.

However, according to Thompson, Winston had his own idea of the meaning of the word 'convalescence':

> He would start painting in the early morning and continue with the work until 7 o'clock in the evening with only a short break for lunch. At the end of the long day, I would take it upon myself to clean his palette which always looked like fifty rainbows.[8]

Meanwhile, Clementine expressed the following opinion to socialite and actress Diana Cooper:

> I think Winston will die when it's over [a reference to the war]. You see, he's seventy and I'm sixty and we're putting all we have into this war, and it will take all we have.[9]

How wrong Clementine was, on this occasion.

On 20 September 1944 Winston complained of being 'very tired. I have a very strong feeling that my work is done', he said.[10] But this time it was *he* who was very much mistaken.

Others commented on Winston's self-indulgence in respect of alcohol and tobacco. Sir Ian Jacob, for example, avowed that

> He smoked cigars from morning till night ... [however] he didn't really smoke at all. He used to light the cigar and hold it in his hand and occasionally put it to his mouth and suck it, and then when it went out he would relight it. Except when actually lighting the cigar he rarely drew in and puffed out smoke, and he did not inhale the smoke at any time.
>
> He drank a good deal at lunch, often champagne followed by brandy. He didn't have tea, but at about tea-time or later, according to when he had had his sleep, he would start drinking iced whisky and soda. He probably had two or three glasses, not very strong, before dinner, and then at dinner he always had champagne, followed by several doses of brandy. Then during the late evening and night he had more whisky and soda. He had obviously been accustomed to this kind of routine for years, and yet he was never the worse for drink in my experience.[11]

Winston's heavy drinking may be seen as another example of his propensity to indulge in risky activities, for he would undoubtedly have been aware of the possible consequences – principally alcoholism and cirrhosis of the liver. However, he chose to carry on regardless.

According to Graebner, when Winston was ill he became excessively demanding:

> colds generally struck three or four times a year. They were invariably accompanied by fever, and until they were gone there was no peace in the household. Churchill insisted on having his temperature taken every fifteen minutes. [However] He was not only interested in all details of his own state of health, but acted rather like a concerned mother hen about everyone else's.[12]

Winston's doctor, the long-suffering Lord Moran, would undoubtedly have concurred with these statements.

Whereas it is unlikely that Winston was adversely affected by his drinking habits, it is more than likely that smoking was responsible for his bouts of pneumonia, and also for his angina (there being a correlation between smoking and damage to the walls of the arteries with narrowing). Winston, however, was inclined to stress what he perceived as the positive aspects of smoking:

> How can I tell that the soothing effect of tobacco upon my nervous

system may not have enabled me to comport myself with calm and with courtesy in some awkward personal encounter or negotiation, or carried me serenely through some critical hours of anxious waiting? How can I tell that my temper would have been as sweet or my companionship as agreeable if I had abjured from my youth the goddess Nicotine?[13]

US Professor Stephen M. Stahl, who has made a study of the effects of smoking, states that 'The reward experienced by smokers' as a result of smoking, includes 'elevation of mood, enhancement of cognition and decrease of appetite'. (This latter epithet, however, can hardly be applied to Winston, who, in the words of Sir Ian Jacob, 'had a very good appetite at all meals and ate whatever he liked'.)[14] Conversely, nicotine withdrawal is

characterized by craving and agitation ... . The pleasure of nicotine is a desirable, but a small boost in the sensation of pleasure is followed by a slow decline until the nicotine receptors switch back on and the smoker takes the next puff or smokes the next cigarette.[15]

Not everyone would agree with Winston that his temper was always 'sweet' and 'agreeable', and from Stahl's findings, one would not expect it to be so. Therefore, woe betide those who were unfortunate enough to encounter him when he had been without a cigar for any length of time.

Notes

1. From 1941 to 1950 Charles McMoran Wilson was President of the Royal College of Physicians.
2. Moran, Lord, *Winston Churchill: The Struggle for Survival 1940-1965*, p. 16.
3. Ibid, p. 88.
4. Thompson, Walter H. *I was Churchill's Shadow*, p. 114.
5. Moran, Lord, op cit, pp. 99-100.
6. Ibid, p. 140.
7. Ibid, p. 150.
8. Thompson, Walter H, op cit, pp. 167-8.
9. Cooper, Diana. *Trumpets from the Steep*, p. 182.
10. Moran, Lord, op cit, p. 183.
11. Wheeler-Bennett, Sir John (ed.), *Action this Day: Working with Churchill*, pp. 182-3.
12. Graebner, Walter, *My Dear Mister Churchill*, p. 32.
13. Churchill, Winston S, *Thoughts and Adventures*, p. 5.
14. Wheeler-Bennett, Sir John, op cit, p. 182.
15. Stahl, Stephen M, *Essential Pharmacology*, pp. 518-19 & 522.

CHAPTER 26

Prime Minister Again

In the general election – held on 25 October 1951 – the Conservatives won with a majority of seventeen, and the following day Winston became Prime Minister for the second time. He was delighted, but not so his wife, as daughter Mary Soames reveals:

> Clementine's heart had never been in Winston's last lap as Prime Minister; although she showed a brave face in public, behind the scenes her morale was often desperately low (exacerbated by neuritis, which had increasingly afflicted her from the end of 1953); and she was immensely touchy and difficult. Winston himself could be maddening, and on occasions behave like a spoilt child; but now there were times when Clementine harried him too much, and could be unreasonable and unkind. [Nonetheless] Both were always eager to repair rifts.[1]

In the USA in January 1952, Winston observed ruefully that the Americans 'have become so great and we are now so small. Poor England! We threw away so much in 1945.'[2] However, of his meeting with President Truman he said, 'Oh, I enjoyed it so much; we talked as equals.'[3] A year later, on 20 January 1953, Harry S. Truman was succeeded by Dwight D. Eisenhower as President of the USA.

King George VI died on 6 February 1952 and his elder daughter, Elizabeth, acceded to the throne whereupon, according to Walter Graebner, Winston said, with tears in his eyes, 'She is a fine and lovely woman. She will be a great Queen. England can be proud of her.'[4]

In June 1952 Winston declared, 'I love Chartwell; somehow it is home to me.'[5] That autumn, Her Majesty Queen Elizabeth II commissioned Croatian-born Oscar Nemon 'to sculpt a bust of her Prime Minister for Windsor Castle'. (Two years later, in 1954, Nemon was called upon again: this time to sculpt a statue of Winston for the City of London's Guildhall. Not only that, but Nemon inspired Winston himself to try his own hand at sculpting.)

In January 1953 Winston visited actor, playwright and composer Noel

Coward at his home in Jamaica. He not only enjoyed Coward's songs, plays and films, but the two also shared a love of painting, and it was through Winston that Coward, formerly a watercolourist, 'became completely converted to oils'.[6] Relations between Winston and Coward had not always been easy for, in the autumn of 1942, the latter had breached wartime currency exchange regulations by spending £11,000 on a trip to the USA. This led Winston, on 29 December 1942, to write to the King to say 'the conferment of a knighthood on Mr Coward so soon afterwards [i.e. after Coward's misdemeanour] would give rise to unfavourable comment'. Coward was subsequently knighted, but not until 1970.

Stalin died from a cerebral haemorrhage in March 1953, and Georgi Malenkov became Soviet Premier. On 24 June Winston himself had a stroke whereupon he told Graebner, 'I must be sure that I can master the House of Commons. I'm not worried about anything else, but if I can't master the House I must not go on.'[7] He also confided to Moran that 'he had been wrong about India'[8] (i.e. in his vehement and prolonged opposition to the granting of independence by Britain to that country).

Following his stroke, Winston began to experience frequent bouts of impairment of speech, unsteadiness of gait, and forgetfulness. And, said Moran,

There were black moods, of course, especially at first, when the uncertainty played on his spirits. But not for a moment did he allow these moods to deflect his purpose. His mind was irrevocably set.[9]

However, his memory was as good as ever, as he demonstrated by quoting at length to his doctor extracts from Henry Wadsworth Longfellow's poem, 'The Sicilian's Tale: King Robert of Sicily'.[10]

In July and August, said Sir John Colville, it was Winston's hope that 'talks [between the USA, the Soviet Union, Britain, and possibly others] ... might lead to a relaxation of the Cold War'. He was 'looking into the mists of the future in search of a permanent cure for the antagonism between the East and West', his 'great objective' being to create 'a détente with the Soviet Union'.[11]

Despite his previous stroke Winston made few concessions, as far as his lifestyle was concerned. And when, in September 1953, he confessed to having 'talked with Harold Macmillan [Minister of Housing] and Anthony [Eden] till a quarter to two [in the morning]', Moran rebuked him, saying, 'It won't do!'[12]

In October 1953 Winston was to be found reading Thomas Hardy's *The Dynasts: A Drama of the Napoleonic Wars* ... .[13] This epic drama, written in verse, encompassed far more than its title suggests. In it, Hardy raises questions about the meaning of life itself, and suggests that, during their lives, on earth, human beings are continually being manipulated by some supernatural force, which he calls the 'Urging Immanence', or 'Will'. This 'Will' is both 'Loveless' and 'Hateless' at the same time, and of its influence human beings are completely unaware. It is likely that, for Winston, the fascination of *The Dynasts* was that it offered an alternative way of thinking to that proposed by conventional Christianity, whose message and rationale he had always found difficult to accept.

Early in that month of October Winston's mind was focused on the preparation of a speech, which he was due to deliver on the 10th of that month to the Conservative Party Conference, to be held at Margate in Kent. Said Moran:

> Sometimes his terrific concentration on his immediate purpose frightens me. He is like a gambler who doubles, then trebles his stake until all that he has depends on the turn of the dice. The PM has put his shirt on this speech.[14]

Yes, Moran was right: Winston was, by nature, a gambler. In the event, the speech was a triumph, and in the course of it Winston declared, in respect of his prime ministership:

> If I stay on, for the time being, bearing the burden at my age, it is not because of love for power, or of it. I have had an ample share of both. If I stay, it is because I have a feeling that I may, through things that have happened, have an influence in what I care about above all else: the building of a sure and lasting peace.[15]

On 15 October Winston was awarded the Nobel Prize for Literature.

From 4 to 8 December 1953, a Summit Conference was held on the island of Bermuda, a British overseas territory. It was attended by Winston, President Dwight D. Eisenhower, and French Prime Minister Joseph Laniel but not by Soviet Premier Georgi Malenkov, whom Winston planned to meet later. On the eve of the Summit Moran, who had accompanied Winston, said of the latter, 'It was one of his black days when his imagination conjures up what might happen to mankind if he fails with Malenkov ... .' This was a reference to the fact that, after the conclusion of the Summit, Winston hoped to meet with Malenkov and be able to report favourably to him, in the hope of breaking the stalemate of the Cold War. However, in the event, no such meeting took place, probably because, as a dejected Winston told Moran, 'Ike [Eisenhower] doesn't think any good can come from talks with the Russians.'[16]

While Clementine was in France in August 1954, recovering from neuritis in her arm and shoulder, Winston wrote to her from Chartwell:

My darling one I brood much about things, and all my moods are not equally gay. But it does cheer my heart to think of you in the sunlight and I *pray* that Peace & Happiness may rule y[ou]r soul.[17]

In late September, when Winston was preparing his speech for the annual Conservative Party Conference, to be held this time at Blackpool, he told Moran, 'I don't know why I get depressed as I do.'[18] On 30 November Winston celebrated his eightieth birthday.

Clearly, even Winston could not battle on indefinitely against old age and failing health but, as Sir Evelyn Shuckburgh[*] said,

He was really afraid of giving up because of the terrible depressions which always overtook him when he did cease to be busy and in the flood of activity. I think that Churchill found it impossible to give up, so long as he was capable, in his own opinion, of carrying on.[19]

In other words, if the target of Winston's 'goal-directed activity' was to be removed, then the 'Black Dog' spectre of depression would inevitably and immediately raise its ugly head once more. In a subsequent conversation with Moran, Brendan Bracken, 1st Viscount Bracken, who had been wartime Minister of Information, elaborated further:

Winston has always been moody; he used to call his fits of depression the 'Black Dog'. At other times, as you know, he goes off into a kind of trance. I have seen him sit silent for several hours, and when he is like that only a few people can make him talk.[20]

Cecily (Chips) Gemmell, who was Winston's secretary from 1949 to 1955, described how, quite innocently, she happened to touch upon a subject which, as already mentioned, even one as courageous as Winston was petrified of.

I found myself sitting, at mealtimes, with Mr Churchill and General Pownall (Lieutenant General Sir Henry Pownall) who was his adviser on the military side of the war memoirs, and General Pownall and I were having a light-hearted discussion on suicide – if such a thing is possible. And it seemed that Mr Churchill was deep in his own thoughts – wasn't listening – when suddenly, he jerked upright in his chair and shouted, 'Stop it! You mustn't talk like that. It's not right. Once I almost thought of throwing myself under a train.'[21]

---

[*] A British diplomat between 1933 and 1969.

The significance of this darker side of Winston's psyche will be discussed shortly.

Finally, on 5 April 1955, and at the age of eighty, Winston tendered his resignation as Prime Minister to Her Majesty The Queen and, on 6 April, he left Number 10 Downing Street for the last time. He was succeeded by Anthony Eden. On 26 May a general election was called; the Conservatives were re-elected and Eden continued as Prime Minister.

The question was how would Winston adapt now that his time in government had come to an end? Moran provided the answer. Said he, 'Whenever Winston is deeply stirred he instinctively turns to action.' His doctor was right, for Winston now busied himself with his correspondence and, on the lighter side, paid a visit to the Epsom Races, and holidayed with Clementine in Sicily, where he 'read the history of the island' and did some painting.[22]

Notes

1. Soames, Mary (ed.), *Speaking for Themselves: The Personal Letters of Winston and Clementine Churchill,* [*SP*] p. 588.
2. Moran, Lord, *Winston Churchill: The Struggle for Survival 1940-1965*, p. 353.
3. Ibid, p. 355.
4. Graebner, Walter, *My Dear Mister Churchill*, p.111.
5. Moran, Lord, op cit, p. 391.
6. Soames, Mary. *Winston Churchill: His Life as a Painter*, p. 186.
7. Graebner, Walter, op cit, p. 18.
8. Moran, Lord, op cit, p. 182.
9. Ibid, p. 477.
10. Ibid, p. 425.
11. Wheeler-Bennett, Sir John (ed.), *Action this Day: Working with Churchill*, p. 132.
12. Moran, Lord, op cit, p. 464.
13. Ibid, p. 484.
14. Ibid, p. 477.
15. *Churchill*. BBC Enterprises Ltd. Address to Conservative Party Conference, Margate, Kent, 10 October 1953.
16. Moran, Lord, op cit, p. 504.
17. Soames, Mary, *SP* op cit, Winston to Clementine, 10 August 1954, p. 585.
18. Moran, Lord, op cit, p. 600.
19. *Churchill*. BBC Enterprises Ltd.
20. Moran, Lord, op cit, p. 745.
21. *Churchill*. BBC Enterprises Ltd.
22. Moran, Lord, op cit, pp. 649 & 652-3.

CHAPTER 27

Winston's 'Highs' and 'Lows': An Explanation

Hitherto, an attempt has been made to highlight the various aspects of Winston's personality which may be regarded as aberrant. Now the time has come to draw the various strands together and attempt to make sense of them. They fall naturally into two categories: a Low state and a High state.

Winston on a Low

When Winston was on a Low he was depressed. Sometimes preoccupied with death, and experienced feelings of guilt and hopelessness, and even suicidal ideation. Also, he was apt to display irritability and aggressiveness, particularly towards those who failed to share his sentiments and endorse his plans. But this was but one side of the coin, for Winston, more often than not, was on a High.

Winston on a High

When Winston was on a High he was highly energetic, impulsive and agitated, indulged excessively in goal-directed activity, and exhibited a decreased need for sleep. He was prone to euphoria, with inflated ideas about himself and his abilities. He experienced 'flights of ideas', where his thoughts and speech raced from one topic to another, and his attention was drawn easily to unimportant or irrelevant matters. He produced plans which might be grandiose (grandiosity, in this context, meaning boastful, self-important, or perceived to be superior by the planner) but which were, in fact, unrealistic. He was likely to engage in risky activities, disregarding the fact that this might have painful consequences, not only for himself, but also for those who were in company with him, or dependent upon him. Such activities included, in wartime, getting as close to the scene of the 'action' as possible, and, at other times, gambling, heavy drinking and overspending. Also, he might behave in an uninhibited and unselfconscious manner.[1]

The Origin of Winston's Condition

From a conversation with Winston's doctor, Lord Moran, held in July 1958, it is clear that Brendan Bracken considered Winston's depressive condition to be an inherited one:

> Winston ... has had to struggle with a fearful handicap. Have you read Rowse on the Later Churchills? [a reference to historian A. L. Rowse, and his biography entitled, *The Later Churchills*]. He [Rowse] says that of the last seven Dukes of Marlborough, five suffered from melancholia.
>
> This strain of melancholy, a Churchill inheritance, is balanced in Winston by the physical and mental robustness of the Jeromes. [Winston's] healthy, bright red American blood [i.e. the blood of the Jeromes] cast out the Churchill melancholy. But not entirely.[2]

It has to be said, however, that the only compelling evidence produced by Rowse for his assertion that there was an inherited component to Winston's make-up was in respect of the latter's father, Lord Randolph, as will shortly be demonstrated.

In August 1944, however, Moran indicated that he concurred with Rowse when he said to Winston, 'Your trouble – I mean the Black Dog business – you got from your forebears. You have fought against it all your life.'[3] And fifteen years later, in June 1959, Moran 'taxed him [Winston] with giving way to the Churchill melancholia ... '.[4] In other words, Moran was also of the opinion that Winston's condition was a hereditary one.

It so happens that both Lord Moran and A. L. Rowse, a non-medical man, were on the right track as regards there being a hereditable component to Winston's depression, as will shortly be seen. But despite this fact, it is perfectly obvious that neither his doctor nor any of his family, friends or colleagues had the remotest inkling as to the origin of the High and Low states of mind which alternated within him.

How Winston Coped with the 'Black Dog'

Referring to Winston's 'Black Dog, Bracken stated that 'these attacks of depression might come on him without warning, and he avoided anyone or anything that might bring them on'.[5] And Moran made an almost identical statement when he related how Winston 'dreaded these bouts and instinctively kept away from anyone or anything that seemed to bring them on'.[6] In other words, Winston did have *some* control over this aspect of his life. As Moran wrote these words in September 1944 – when Winston was aged sixty-nine – this suggests that, for the latter, the 'Black Dog' was a lifelong problem. On the positive side, Moran said of Winston that he 'always liked buoyant people around him',[7] presumably not only for his pleasure but as an antidote to the 'Black Dog'.

Another 'coping mechanism' which Winston used to combat his depression and suicidal ideation is revealed in the following statement, vouchsafed by him to Moran: 'It helps to write down half a dozen things which are worrying me. Two of them, say, disappear; about two, nothing can be done so it's no use worrying; and two perhaps can be settled.'[8]

How Winston Coped with his Highs

Such questions as, 'Is much known about worry, Charles?' – addressed by Winston to his doctor, Lord Moran,[9] indicate that Winston was puzzled entirely by the 'Black Dog', and had not the remotest idea as to why he suffered from it, let alone what its origins were. Alternatively, when he was on a High, this aspect of his nature was so deeply ingrained in him that he regarded it as nothing abnormal. So, whereas it was *he himself* who suffered as a result of his depression, it was *those around him* who were obliged to endure the effects of his Highs, in particular the long-suffering Sir Alan Brooke and also Winston's wife, Clementine, who, although she made light of it, probably suffered more than anyone, reading between the lines.

A Diagnosis is Made

Even in Winston's time, a competent psychiatrist would have had no difficulty in making a diagnosis of his condition, which was a combination of depression alternating with mania – or what psychiatrists term 'manic depression' – a 'manic-depressive' being defined, according to the *Concise Oxford Dictionary of Current English*, as a person who is 'affected by ... a mental disorder with alternating periods of elation and depression'. However, caution is needed with the use of this term, for the full-blown manic-depressive may exhibit, in addition to the symptoms already described under the heading 'Winston on a High', symptoms of psychosis, including hallucinations, delusions, paranoia and episodes of severe depression. Furthermore, in such cases

> the mood disturbance [in a manic episode] is sufficiently severe to cause marked impairment in occupational functioning or in usual social activities or relationships with others, or to necessitate hospitalization to prevent harm to self or others.[10]

Clearly, it would be erroneous to describe Winston as a full-blown manic-depressive. Instead, the term Hypomania – this being defined as a mood state which is more moderate and less severe than mania, and without its more extreme features – is more appropriate in these circumstances. To conclude, Winston may therefore be described as a 'hypomanic-depressive' (rather than a manic-depressive).[11]

As to the origin of mania and hypomania, and manic depression and hypomanic depression, the fact that these conditions are known to run in families suggests that a genetic component is either wholly or partly responsible for the malady (possibly combined with environmental factors), but which gene or genes are involved has not yet been elucidated. This begs the question, is there any evidence that any of Winston's forebears suffered from hypomanic or manic depression? The answer is yes, for, as already mentioned, A. L. Rowse, who made a study of the Churchill family, describes Lord Randolph as having 'the defect of the … manic-depressive alternation …', and Lord Rosebery's account of how His Lordship 'would descend from the highest summit to a bottomless pit and up again, at the shortest notice' is a classic description of the manic-depressive.

At what time of his life, it may be asked, did Winston's condition first manifest itself? Research indicates that when hypomanic-depressive disorder is present in an individual, it commonly begins to show itself at about the age of twenty. However, it is not unknown for teenagers, or even younger children, to exhibit the symptoms. In January 1888, when Winston was aged thirteen, his grandmother Frances, invited him and his brother, Jack, to Blenheim Palace for a week. She subsequently informed her son, Lord Randolph, that Winston was 'so excitable' and 'certainly a handful'. However, 'Jack is a good little boy & not a bit of trouble'.[12] Was Lady Marlborough simply witnessing youthful high spirits on Winston's part, or was his rambunctiousness an early sign of the hypomanic component of 'hypomanic depression'?

Finally, was Winston's Emotional Deprivation Disorder and need for constant and continuing affirmation, which he experienced throughout his life, part of his 'hypomanic-depressive' syndrome? The answer is no, for he exhibited this as a young schoolboy, and perhaps even earlier, well before his symptoms of 'hypomanic depression' became apparent.

Notes

1. The criteria for Winston's 'Highs' and 'Lows' – known by psychiatrists as mania/hypomania and depression respectively are based on the chapter entitled 'Mood Disorders', contained in the American Psychiatric Association's publication, *Diagnostic and Statistical Manual of Mental Disorders. DSM-IV-TR.*

2. Moran, Lord, *Winston Churchill: The Struggle for Survival 1940-1965*, conversation between Brendan Bracken and Moran, 24 July 1958, p. 745.
3. Ibid, p. 167.
4. Ibid, pp. 753-4.
5. Ibid, p. 746.
6. Ibid, pp. 181-2.
7. Ibid, p. 746.
8. Ibid, p. 167.
9. Ibid, p. 167.
10. American Psychiatric Association, *Diagnostic and Statistical Manual of Mental Disorders. DSM-IV-TR*, p.362.
11. The term 'Manic Depression' has now become obsolete and has been replaced with the terms, 'Bipolar I Disorder', and the term 'Hypomanic Depression' has been replaced with the term 'Bipolar II Disorder'. However, in this narrative, the traditional nomenclature has been retained, this being considered to be more descriptive of the disorders to which it relates.
12. Churchill, Randolph S., *Winston S. Churchill, Youth, 1874-1900*. Duchess of Marlborough to Lord Randolph, 19 January 1888 and 23 January 1888, p. 104.

CHAPTER 28

Winston's Hypomania and its Dividend

W ith regard to Winston's depressive periods, when he was suffering from what he called the 'Black Dog', there was no positive dividend, either for his family and friends, or for the country and world at large. But what of his hypomanic periods?

Winston's bravery drew the highest admiration, but the reckless risk-taking aspect of his hypomania was a two-edged sword. His exploits in the military, both before and during the First World War (and in particular the armoured-train incident during the Boer War, and his capture by the enemy followed by his escape), established him as a national hero. However, there were occasions, throughout his life, when he risked that life, and those of others, unnecessarily. Nonetheless, the positive dividends of his hypomania far outweighed the negative.

As already mentioned, when Winston was on a High, he galvanized those around him by his example, dedication to the task in hand, and super-abundant energy. His fertile mind could be likened to a continuously active volcano, which spewed out one idea after another; and it was the duty of those around him who were strong enough in mind, and in a position to do so, to discard the worthless, and recognize and cherish the valuable. However, sometimes even Winston's genuine 'pearls of wisdom' were ignored. An example of this was Winston's awareness of the danger a resurgent Germany was likely to pose, as, during the 1930s, that country's military machine grew to such size and strength as to rival that of Britain. This was a theme to which Winston devoted himself, both inside and outside the House of Commons, only to find that he had virtually no support, and that his was a voice 'that crieth in the wilderness'.[1]

Another 'pearl of wisdom', which Winston vouchsafed to give to Franklin D. Roosevelt during the Second World War (and which the US President chose largely to ignore), was his fear of the danger of Soviet expansionism.

Had Roosevelt adopted the same attitude as his successor, President Harry S. Truman, in his negotiations with Stalin, then the story might have had a different ending. As it was, the Soviets having overrun Eastern Europe they were able to maintain their presence there unchallenged.

However, not all of Winston's good ideas were wasted for, had this been the case then it is highly unlikely that the Nazi jackboot would have been removed from the neck of the countries of Europe. For example, Winston had the foresight and breadth of vision to realize how vital it was for the Allied cause that the Soviet Union kept up the fight on the Eastern Front. To this end, numerous naval convoys sailed from Britain, taking military supplies to Northern Russia, and continued to do so, despite the dreadful war of attrition waged upon them by enemy U-boats.

Winston also realized, very early on, how vital it was, if victory was to be achieved, for the USA to enter the war, and he worked tirelessly to this end, crossing the Atlantic on several occasions, despite the risks involved, to meet with Roosevelt.

On a more practical level, what became known as 'Winston's Toyshop' (Ministry of Defence 1, or MD 1) was charged with the high-speed development of special weapons of war for all three of the armed services. This organization had begun life in late 1939 as the Military Intelligence Research Department (MIR) of the War Office. However, Winston saw its possibilities for, as Sir John Colville noted in his dairy, 'This was a war of science, a war that would be won with new weapons.'[2] The outcome was that when, in May 1940, Winston became Prime Minister and Minister of Defence, MD 1, which relocated from London to Whitchurch, Buckinghamshire, underwent a rapid expansion and produced such items as booby traps, naval mines and anti-tank weapons. According to Colonel Stuart Macrae, second-in-command of MD 1,

> By the end of the war, no fewer than twenty-six entirely new weapons designed by MD 1 had been accepted by the [armed] services and were in quantity production.[3]

As Whitchurch was only ten miles from the prime-ministerial residence at Chequers, it was convenient for Winston, usually accompanied by his Scientific Advisor, Professor Lindemann, to attend demonstrations of these new 'toys', which, at other times, were held at a rifle range at Princes Risborough, also in Buckinghamshire and a mere four miles from Chequers, and, on occasion, even in the garden at Chequers itself. At these times, said Macrae, Winston 'would be like a small boy on holiday'.

This is not to say that the best of Winston's ideas were the result of his having a hypomanic personality for he would probably have had these ideas in any event. But it was the hypomania which gave him the almost superhuman energy and determination to pursue these ideas, and see them through to a conclusion, and the free world is eternally grateful that he did.

Finally, the sheer volume of written works published by Winston in the course of his lifetime, and paintings executed by him, may also be regarded as a part of the 'hypomanic dividend'. This amounts to forty-three books in seventy-two volumes together with booklets, and newspaper and magazine articles, as well as many hundreds of works of art.

Notes

1. Holy Bible, Isaiah 40:3.
2. Sir John Colville, Diary.
3. Macrae, Stuart. *Winston Churchill's Toyshop*, Introduction.

CHAPTER 29

Winston's 'Dream'

One evening at Chartwell, when Winston was aged seventy-three, an extraordinary event occurred which he related to his daughter Sarah and to his son, Randolph:

One foggy afternoon in November 1947 I was painting in my studio at the cottage down the hill at Chartwell. Someone had sent me a portrait of my father which had been painted for one of the Belfast Conservative Clubs about the time of his visit to Ulster in the Home Rule crisis of 1886. The canvas had been badly torn, and though I am very shy of painting human faces I thought I would try to make a copy of it. I must have painted for an hour and a half, and was deeply concentrated on my subject. I was drawing my father's face, gazing at the portrait, and frequently turning round right-handed to check progress in the mirror. Thus I was intensely absorbed, and my mind was freed from all other thoughts except the impressions of that loved and honoured face now on the canvas, now on the picture, now in the mirror.

I was just trying to give the twirl to his moustache when I suddenly felt an odd sensation. I turned round with my palette in my hand, and there, sitting in my red leather upright armchair, was my father. He looked just as I had seen him in his prime ...

There followed a long conversation in which Lord Randolph asked Winston what had happened in the previous five decades since 1894. Winston now brought his father up to date with such matters as who was on the throne; whether the Carlton Club, the Turf Club and the Church of England were still in existence, which they were, and which political party was in power. He also apprised his father of the fact that women now had the vote and that home rule had been granted to the south of Ireland. Then Lord Randolph enquired as to whether Winston lived 'in this cottage' and was told 'No, I have a house up on the hill ... ' – i.e. Chartwell Manor. His Lordship also enquired as to how Winston earned his living. To which the reply came, 'I write books and articles for the Press.'

Had Winston's military career been a success, his father enquired? 'Yes', came the reply, 'I was a Major in the Yeomanry [Queen's Own Oxfordshire Hussars].' Winston also apprized his father of the fact that he was married with children and grandchildren, and that America was now the leading power in the world.

'I don't mind that,' said his father. 'You are half American yourself. Your mother was the most beautiful woman ever born. The Jeromes were a deep-rooted American family.'

'I have always worked for friendship with the United States, and indeed throughout the English-speaking world,' replied Winston.

'English-speaking world,' he repeated, weighing the phrase. 'You mean with Canada, Australia, and New Zealand and all that?'

'Yes, all that.

'Are they still loyal?'

'They are our brothers.'

'And India, is that all right? And Burma?'

'Alas! They have gone down the drain.'

He gave a groan. 'But perhaps they will come back and join the English-speaking world.' 'Is Russia still the danger?'

'We are all very worried about her.'

'Is there still a Tsar?'

'Yes, but he is not a Romanoff. It's another family. He is much more powerful, and much more despotic.'

'What of Germany? What of France?'

'They are both shattered. Their only hope is to rise together.'

Winston told his father that, after the latter's death, there had followed the South African War and two World Wars. 'What happened in the Boer War?' Randolph enquired, to which Winston replied, 'We conquered the Transvaal and the Orange Free State.' 'England should never have done that,' said his father. 'To strike down two independent republics must have lowered our whole position in the world.'

Finally, Lord Randolph declared:

Winston, you have told me a terrible tale. I would never have believed that such things could happen. I am glad I did not live to see them. As I listened to you unfolding these fearful facts you seemed to know a great deal about them. I never expected that you would develop so far and so fully. Of course you are too old now to think about such things, but when I hear you talk I really wonder you didn't go into politics. You might have done a lot to help. You might even have made a name for yourself.

Concluded Winston,

He gave me a benignant smile. He then took a match to light his cigarette and struck it. There was a tiny flash. He vanished. The chair was empty. The illusion had passed.[1]

It is not unusual for a bereaved person, even many years after the loss of a loved one, to imagine a further encounter with that loved one. However, whereas Winston describes the above episode, in which he saw his late father sitting in his [Winston's] red leather upright armchair, as an *illusion*, i.e. 'a misperception or misinterpretation of a real external stimulus',[2] it would seem more appropriate to describe it as a *hallucination*, a 'sensory perception that has the compelling sense of reality of a true perception but that occurs without external stimulation of the relevant sensory organ'.[3]

So if Winston was, in fact, hallucinating, how may this be explained? The symptoms of hypomanic depression, from which, as has been demonstrated, he was a chronic sufferer, are known to increase with age, and may progress from hypomania to mania itself, of which hallucinations are a feature. Is it possible, therefore, that Winston's hypomanic depression had advanced, to the extent that he was now beginning to show symptoms of manic depression?

Notes

1. Gilbert, Martin, *Never Despair: Winston S. Churchill 1945-1965*, pp. 364-72.
2. American Psychiatric Association, *Diagnostic and Statistical Manual of Mental Disorders. DSM-IV-TR*, p. 824.
3. Ibid, p. 823.

CHAPTER 30

Winston's Children and Grandchildren

Winston did his utmost to give his children the love and affection which, rightly or wrongly, he considered had been denied him by his parents during his childhood. But even he, despite his best efforts, could not ensure that their lives would be happy ones. His daughter Mary Soames described Winston 'greatly enjoying his children in the brief moments he could spend with them. His children, and later his grandchildren, were always conscious that he loved to have them around.'[1] And of family life at Chartwell she declared, 'There was so much laughter, activity, and high spirits, and, above all, the golden skein of warmly expressed love and loyalty gleams throughout, strong and unfailing.'[2] But later, said Mary, ominously, 'threads of anxiety, sorrow, disappointment and misunderstanding crept here and there into the tapestry of our family life'.[3] She might also have added the word *tragedy*.

Diana (born 1909)

On 16 September 1935 Diana married Conservative Cabinet Minister Duncan Sandys, by whom she had a son and two daughters. However, said Mary of her sister:

In 1953, Diana suffered a severe nervous breakdown, which continued to affect her over a considerable period of time … the root causes of which may well go back to adolescence and childhood.[4]

After she had parted from Duncan Sandys, some time in 1956-57, Diana had settled in a charming house in Chester Row, SW [London], where she lived with her daughters, Edwina and Celia. The misery her bouts of nervous ill-health had caused her had been accentuated by the break-up of her marriage.[5]

Both Winston and Clementine grieved deeply for her, and saw with dismay the great unhappiness this illness caused Diana, and the difficulties and anguish it brought into her life. [Nevertheless] Diana in her moments of distress ... found in him [Winston] tenderness and rock-like stability.[6]

In 1960, Diana and Duncan were divorced. They 'had known great happiness together in earlier days', Mary commented sadly.[7] On the night of 19 October 1963, Diana died from an overdose of sleeping pills.

Randolph (born 1911)

Winston's son, Randolph, described how, in 1917 when he was aged six, his father played a delightful game with him at Lullenden. It was called the 'Bear Game', and

> Father was the Bear. We had to turn our backs and close our eyes and he would climb a tree. All us children – six or seven perhaps [i.e. he, his siblings, and the children of family or friends] – had then to go and look for Bear. We were very much afraid but would advance courageously and say, 'Bear! Bear! Bear!' and then run away. Suddenly, he would drop from a tree and we would scatter in various directions. He would pursue us and the one he caught would be the loser.[8]

Having attended Eton College and Christ Church College, Oxford, Randolph became a journalist. On 4 October 1939 he married the Honourable Pamela Digby, by whom he had a son, Winston.

During the Second World War, Randolph served with the rank of major in Winston's former regiment, the 4th Hussars. On 25 September 1940 he was elected Conservative MP for Preston, Lancashire (in an uncontested, wartime by-election). Attached, for a time, to the newly-formed Special Air Service, he participated in several operations in the Libyan desert. In early February 1944, he was parachuted into Yugoslavia where he joined the British Military Mission headed by Brigadier Fitzroy Maclean. Here, 'he shared the life and vicissitudes of the partisans', led by Josip Tito.[9]

In December 1945 Randolph and Pamela were divorced. On 2 November 1948 Randolph married June Osborne, by whom he had a daughter, Arabella.

Evan Davies, a Special Branch Protection Officer from 1948 to 1950, described the fraught relationship which existed between Winston and his son, Randolph, and how the mere presence of the latter almost invariably affected Winston adversely, to the extent that

> he would go into an absolutely thunderous mood, at times. He would hardly speak to anybody, and perhaps his girls [a reference to

Winston's daughters, Diana, Sarah and Mary] would say, 'Don't bother, he's got a black dog,' as he used to call it himself, if he had a black mood on. I think the most disturbing factor, I'm afraid, was usually when Randolph came. He could not seem to stay away from upsetting his father, and the old boy [Winston] would be in a black mood for two days afterwards.[10]

Randolph clearly regretted this state of affairs, but nonetheless blamed Winston for the rift that had developed between them. So much is evident from a letter which he wrote to his father on 16 October 1952, in which he said,

In one thing I have never changed or faltered – my absolute love, devotion & loyalty to you. I don't think that anything you could say or do to me … could make more than a dent in the wholehearted admiration I have for you & which, despite everything, has grown with the years. Can't you understand the maladjustment, the frustration, yes even recently the jealousy that urges the bile of resentment when one's love is scorned as worthless & the person one loves scarcely troubles to hide from friend or foe the indifference or hostility which he feels?[11]

Matters did not improve, and it was the opinion of Anthony Montague Browne, Private Secretary to Winston from 1952 to 1965, that the fault for this lay with Randolph. For example in the summer of 1960, when Browne accompanied Winston and Randolph on a cruise on Greek shipping magnate Aristotle Onassis's yacht, he describes how,

Randolph … suddenly came out in one boiling rage at dinner, at which his father had been perfectly polite to him … . [Said Randolph] 'Well, why did you do this and that? Why wouldn't you speak to me?' It was terrible. Ari [Aristotle] and I had arranged for Randolph to leave the yacht from Corfu. I took him on shore; I kept him company. He [Randolph] was very silent and I saw him weeping. 'It's so difficult Anthony. I always loved that man. I can't get on with him.'[12]

Sir John Colville said of Winston and Randolph, 'It is a sad tale, for they loved each other; but they could never meet without quarrelling.'[13] In 1961 Randolph and June were divorced.

Randolph died suddenly of a heart attack on 6 June 1968, aged fifty-seven.

Sarah (born 1914)

From the age of fourteen onwards, said Sarah, 'my love for him [her father, Winston] grew and my hero-worship of him never lessened …'.[14]

From October 1941 Sarah served in the Women's Auxiliary Air Force (WAAF). On 18 October 1949 she married war artist and society photographer Antony Beauchamp. In 1955 the couple separated. 'From the mid-1950s,' said her sister Mary, 'Sarah had started having a drink problem.'[15] On 18 August 1957 Anthony Beauchamp committed suicide. In 1962, Sarah married Henry, 23rd Lord Audley of Heleigh, who died the following year.[16]

Towards the end of Winston's life, Sarah wrote, 'I thought of how much fun he had been. Come a grey day he managed somehow to change it.'[17] And she expressed her love for her father in this poignant poem entitled, 'Forgive Me'

Yet forgive me if I do not cry
The day you die
The simplest reason that I know
You said you'd rather have it so
And that I held my head serenely high
Remembering the love and glory that we knew.
Forgive me if I do not cry
The day you die …
Forgive me
If I do … [18]

Sarah died on 24 September 1982.

Mary (born 1922)

Winston's love for his children, and his concern for their happiness, is revealed by the following incident. When Mary's dog, a pug [named, appropriately, 'Pug'], became 'desperately ill' Winston, who was 'greatly upset' at the distress caused both to her and to her sister, Sarah composed the following poem:

Oh, what is the matter with poor Puggy-wug
Pet him and kiss him and give him a hug.
Run and fetch him a suitable drug,
Wrap him up tenderly all in a rug,
That is the way to cure Puggy-wug.[19]
July 1944 found Mary 'in charge of a plotting battery' at an anti-aircraft

gun-site somewhere in southern England.[20] She married Conservative politician Christopher Soames on 11 February 1947 and they had three sons and two daughters.

Mary's moving account of the last few days of Winston's life will be recounted shortly.

Some of Winston's Grandchildren

Winston Churchill (son of Randolph)

Winston's grandson and namesake, young Winston, describes the following delightful scene:

> I suppose I was about 3½ years old [i.e. it was the spring of 1944] and apparently I had been peremptorily demanding a model railway set, and it was in the room in what is known as the Annexe to No. 10 [Downing Street], immediately above what is today the Cabinet War Rooms, and this cardboard box was delivered. He and I got down on our knees on the carpet, and started setting up the track – which was a circle – and to my grandfather's huge delight he saw that there was not one, but two little clockwork-powered locomotives. He gave me one and said, 'Winston, you wind that one up and I'll wind this one up. We'll put them back to back; let's have a crash!' And, you know, this is a wonderful vignette on the man who actually had rather weightier responsibilities and was fighting the war against Hitler. But, you know, that was the side of him that I saw, inevitably, it was the loving grandfather.

Early in 1947 Winston presented young Winston, now aged six, with what the latter described as 'a box of very lovely paints, and some brushes' with instructions as to how the paints were to be mixed.[21] Said young Winston, 'He was the most approachable, adorable human being imaginable.'[22]

These sentiments were entirely reciprocated by Winston who, on 22 August 1961, in a letter to Clementine, described his grandson, then an undergraduate at Christ Church College, Oxford, as 'a wonderful boy. I am so glad I have got to know him.'[23]

Arthur, Emma, Jeremy, Charlotte and Rupert Soames (Mary's children)

On 19 August 1954 Winston wrote to Clementine to say, 'I lunched yesterday with Mary & the children. They are a wonderful brood. It is a lovely home circle and has lighted my evening years ....'[24]

Celia Sandys (Diana's daughter)

Said Winston's granddaughter Celia Sandys:

> I remember my grandfather [Winston] as a relaxed person, which seems strange in a way but I always saw him, on the whole, at home when he was enjoying himself either entertaining friends, or painting or visiting his animals. So, I saw him in a very benign mood and our life with him was one, really, of pleasure. Either we were watching films at Chartwell after dinner, or we were enjoying a lovely walk with him around the gardens. So, clearly, I think this, in a way, was lucky. We were able to grab him for moments when he was wanting to relax and not do anything of momentous note.[25]

On another occasion, Celia said of Winston, 'It's as though I'm looking at two different people. One whom I knew and loved, and the other whom I wonder at the extraordinary things that he did.'[26]

* * *

According to psychiatrists Anna Terruwe and Conrad Baars, if a person has not been adequately loved and cherished (affirmed) by the time that person reaches adulthood, then he or she will be incapable of affirming others, 'even their spouses and children'.[25] Winston, however, *was* an affirmed person, thanks principally to his nanny, Elizabeth Everest, and to his parents (even though his demands were often far in excess of what Lord and Lady Randolph could supply, though he himself would undoubtedly have denied this latter proposition). And therefore, as has been demonstrated above, he was in turn (and in conjunction with Clementine) able to affirm his children and also help to affirm his grandchildren.

Notes

1. Soames, Mary, *Clementine Churchill*, [CC] p. 237.
2. Ibid, p. 234.
3. Ibid, p. 234.
4. Ibid, p. 443.
5. Ibid, p. 480.
6. Ibid, pp. 443-4.
7. Ibid, p. 480.
8. Gilbert, Martin, *Churchill*, p. 62.
9. Soames, Mary, *CC* op cit, p. 352.

10. *Churchill: The Greatest Briton of All Time*. A TW1/Carlton Production.
11. Randolph to Winston, 16 October 1952: Churchill Papers, 1/51.
12. *Churchill: The Greatest Briton of All Time*. A TW1/Carlton Production.
13. Gilbert, Martin, *Never Despair: Winston S. Churchill 1945-1965*, (*ND*) Sir John Colville to Martin Gilbert, 12 May 1987, pp. 767-8.
14. Churchill, Sarah, *A Thread in the Tapestry*, p. 33.
15. Soames, Mary (ed.), *Speaking for Themselves: The Personal Letters of Winston and Clementine Churchill*, [*SP*] p. 621.
16. Ibid, Winston to Clementine.
17. Churchill, Sarah, op cit, p. 20.
18. Ibid, p. 102.
19. Ibid, p.28.
20. Thompson, Walter H., *I was Churchill's Shadow*, p.143.
21. Soames, Mary, *Winston Churchill: His Life as a Painter*, pp. 155-6.
22. *Churchill: The Greatest Briton of All Time*, 2002, A TW1/Carlton Production.
23. Gilbert, Martin, *ND* op cit, Winston to Clementine, 22 August 1961: Spencer-Churchill Papers. p. 1328.
24. Soames, Mary, *SP* op cit, Winston to Clementine, 19 August 1954, p. 586.
25. *Churchill: The Greatest Briton of All Time*. A TW1/Carlton Production.
26. *Churchill: The Greatest Briton of All Time*. A TW1/Carlton Production.
27. Baars, Conrad W. and Terruwe, Anna A., *Healing the Unaffirmed: Recognizing Emotional Deprivation Disorder*, p. 191.

CHAPTER 31

Declining Years

Winston rose to many challenges during his lifetime, and to some of them he rose superbly. However, the challenge of old age was one which he found impossible to overcome, though he did his utmost to keep it at bay. And one way in which he achieved this was through his painting, which he described as

> a friend who makes no undue demands, excites through no exhausting pursuits, keeps faithful pace even with feeble steps, and holds her canvas as a screen between us and the envious eyes of Time or the surly advance of Decrepitude ....[1]

In April 1955, said Mary Soames, far from being downcast,

> Winston's morale was quite high over the Easter weekend which followed his resignation. Forty-eight hours after laying down his office, Winston started work again on his *History of the English-Speaking Peoples*; and on 12 April he and Clementine flew off for a holiday in Sicily [accompanied by their] tried and trusted companions, ... 'the Prof' and Jock [John] Colville [together, needless to say, with Winston's precious painting equipment].[2]

Colville subsequently told Winston's doctor, Lord Moran, that, in Sicily, Winston 'had been in good spirits [with] no regrets [and] no looking back. He had played bezique every day for about eight hours and had painted for another four hours.' And Winston himself told Moran, 'I painted with great vigour. What mattered was that I found that I could concentrate for three hours – I got interested in it, and was always late for luncheon.'[3]

Winston continued to play a part in public life, said Mary. He received visits from foreign dignitaries, including German Chancellor Konrad Adenauer (1959) and French President Charles de Gaulle (1961). Also, the traditional concert of 'Songs', held by his former school, Harrow, was a firm fixture in his diary. Continued Mary

After the few sad months which succeeded his resignation his interest in life and all his 'toys' and occupations revived. But in these latter years he did tend, from time to time, to sink into periods of silence and gloom; from which he would often emerge with startling suddenness – rather like a sinking fire which suddenly burns up bright and clear.[4]

When, on 29 May 1955, Moran asked Lord Beaverbrook about Winston's fluctuating moods, the answer came:

Since his resignation he has sent me three letters … very revealing letters. Moods of exultation seem to alternate with moods of depression. One moment he talks as if he was still Prime Minister, the next as if he were no longer anyone at all.

However, Beaverbrook felt sure that Winston would 'fight his mood of despair inch by inch'.[5] Here, Beaverbrook, albeit unwittingly, is describing in Winston the typical symptoms of a 'hypomanic-depressive' who, nonetheless, is determined not to fall victim to his condition, even though he had no insight into the fact that he is a sufferer from it, nor any notion as to what its cause might be.

Following an 'arterial spasm' of the brain which occurred on 2 June 1955, Mary stated that 'although Winston made a quick recovery … he was deeply afflicted by depression and inertia'. But this did not prevent him from continuing to see his friends, and from working on his book *A History of the English-Speaking Peoples*.[6] On 6 June Winston told Moran that he would like to present him with one of his paintings, which he did. Said Moran, 'When I left him his eyes were filled with tears' as he told his devoted doctor, 'It is wonderful that you have kept me going for so long.'[7]

From his London home at Hyde Park Gate on 20 June Winston declared, 'I'd like to go to Chartwell, and stay there. But Clemmie doesn't like it, and her [ill] health will keep her here. Any fun I get now is from my book.[8] To Lady Lytton, formerly Pamela Plowden, 'Winston's first great love from the far-off days in India',[9] Winston wrote, on the 30th, 'I am getting much older, now the stimulus of responsibility & power has fallen from me, and I totter along in the shades of retirement.'[10] Winston's life was now punctuated by attacks, caused by spasm of his cerebral arteries, which affected his gait and also impaired his speech and memory.

It had been the ambition of Sir John Rothenstein, Director of the Tate Gallery, to acquire one of Winston's works for the Tate and, to this end, Winston invited him, in mid July 1955, to visit his studio at Chartwell 'to select a worthy picture'. Subsequently, Rothenstein, in an article entitled 'Mr Churchill the Artist', recorded his impressions of Winston at that time: 'If it weren't for painting,' Mr Churchill observed as we left the studio, 'I couldn't live; I couldn't bear the strain of things.' And of Winston's pictures, Rothenstein went on to say:

> There comes up bubbling irrepressibly his sheer enjoyment of the simple beauties of nature, water, whether still, bubbling, or agitated by wind; snow immaculate and crisp; trees, dark in their density or dappled by sunlight; fresh flowers and distant mountains, and above all sunlight at its most intense.[11]

Mary Soames confirmed that Winston's life had not entirely lost its sparkle:

> It is pleasing now to realize that at the time, despite moments of gloom and inertia, Winston still could and did feel life held interest and pleasure. Sir John [Rothenstein] records that Winston said to him: 'I look forward to a leisure hour with pleasurable agitation: it's so difficult to choose between writing, reading, painting, bricklaying and three or four other things I want to do.'[12] I think it was only as old age and increasing feebleness began to take their inevitable toll that my father came to experience boredom; I do not believe that before his eighth decade he would have known how to define the word. Oh happy man! [13]

In early August 1955 Clementine travelled to Switzerland for health reasons. Meanwhile, in her month of absence, Winston painted her portrait using an old photograph for the purpose.[14]

From mid January 1956 Winston spent six weeks at the 'Villa La Pausa' on France's Côte d'Azur as the guest of Emery Reves and Wendy Russell, a Texan and a former fashion model, and Reves's partner since 1948. Reves had acquired the villa three years previously and furnished it with a fine art collection, 'mostly by the Impressionists'.[15] Meanwhile, for health reasons, Clementine remained in London. Winston would revisit La Pausa another nine times between then and March 1959.[16]

On this first visit to La Pausa, Winston was joined by Conservative politician Richard Austen Butler ('RAB'), and the two men, said Mary, 'spent congenial hours painting together in the garden ...'.[17] On 30 January, Winston wrote to Clementine to say that he was

> being taken through a course of Manet, Monet, Cézanne & Co by my

hosts who are both versed in modern painting, and practise in the studio ... . I am in fact having an artistic education with [very] agreeable tutors.[18]

May 1956 found Winston visiting Germany where he met with Chancellor Konrad Adenauer. Mary Soames wrote:

The years from 1956 to 1958 also saw the completion and publication, in four volumes, of Churchill's last great work of history and literature, his panoramic *History of the English-Speaking Peoples*.[19]

As the years went by Winston and Clementine's affection for one another remained undiminished as the following incident, which took place on 16 September 1956, reveals. As she tried to persuade her husband to persevere with his hearing aid, Clementine teased him gently, saying, according to Moran,

'It's just a question of taking a little trouble, my dear. Quite stupid people learn to use it after a short time.' His eye twinkled as he put his hand affectionately on hers.[20]

Winston had a second stroke on 20 October 1956.

Nine days into the new year of 1957 Prime Minister Anthony Eden resigned, following the debacle of the invasion of the Suez Canal Zone by Britain, France and Israel. Eden was succeeded by his Chancellor of the Exchequer, Harold Macmillan.

In June Winston was once again at La Pausa, from where he wrote to Clementine to say that he was 'absorbed in *Wuthering Heights*', the novel by Emily Brontë, published in 1847. He wrote, 'It is a relief to find the shelter of Victorian literature, when the alternative [would] be to stare out at really bloody prospects from the windows ... .' He was referring to the weather, which was cloudy with only 'occasional gleams' of sunshine, an atmosphere which was hardly conducive to painting! 'My dearest one I love you from a gloomy background I fear.'[21]

Writing again from La Pausa in January 1958, Winston told Clementine:

I have started painting again: *indoors* for the snow is on the hills all round. Flowers arranged by Wendy [Russell] is the subject & she has painted for three days herself just from memory. The sun shines brightly & today I got up before luncheon and sat in the porch.[22]

On 19 February Moran diagnosed in Winston a recurrence of bronchial pneumonia. In that year a trust was established with Winston as its chairman, the purpose of which was to build and endow a new college at Cambridge. Called Churchill College, it would be a national and Commonwealth memorial to Winston.

In July Brendan Bracken had this to say to Moran about Winston:

It has not been easy for him. You see, Charles, Winston has always been a 'despairer'. Orpen [Sir William] who painted him [i.e. Winston's portrait, in 1916] after the Dardanelles, used to speak of the misery in his face. He called him the man of misery. Winston was so sure then that he would take no further part in public life. There seemed nothing left to live for, it made him very sad. Then in his years in the wilderness, before the Second War, he kept saying: 'I'm finished.' He said that about twice a day. He was quite certain that he would never get back to office, for everyone seemed to regard him as a wild man.[23]

Here, Bracken is describing Winston in the low or depressive phase of his hypomanic-depressive disorder, though it has to be said that, at the time in question, Winston was going through a particularly difficult time in his life. Bracken also stated that 'Winston has always been wretched unless he was occupied', and went on to say, 'You know what he has been like since he resigned? Why, he told me that he prays every day for death.'[24] Here again, Bracken is describing how the hypomanic Winston, unless he was furiously engaged in goal-directed activities, would relapse from a high state into a low state of depression, and become obsessed with morbid thoughts.

By autumn 1958 Winston and Clementine were to be found on the French Riviera at Lord Beaverbrook's villa, 'La Capponcina', at Cap d'Ail near Monte Carlo, where, on 12 September, they celebrated their Golden Wedding anniversary. Afterwards, they set forth, once more, on a cruise of the Mediterranean with Aristotle Onassis on his magnificent yacht, *Christina*, named after his daughter by his wife, Athina (known as 'Tina', née Livanos). Between then and June 1963, Winston 'sometimes accompanied by Clementine, and always by a harmonious group of family and friends' embarked on no fewer than seven further cruises with Onassis.[25] Winston loved the sea, and, as Thompson affirmed, he also enjoyed bathing:

Mr Churchill was a strong swimmer and he is fond of turning over and over like a porpoise in the water. He enjoys swimming and gets much benefit from it.[26]

Writing from La Pausa on 14 October 1958 Winston told Clementine, 'The closing days or years of life are grey and dull, but I am lucky to have you at my side.'[27] At the Matignon Place in Paris, Winston received the Croix de la Libération from President de Gaulle on 6 November.

Winston and Clementine revisited Marrakech where they stayed, once again, at the Mamounia Hotel, this time for a period of six weeks from 7 January 1959. In company with them were John (Jock) and Margaret (Meg) Colville and Bridget (Biddy) Monckton, wife of Conservative politician Sir Walter Monckton, who remained with them for the first part of the holiday.

On 28 January Clementine wrote to her daughter Mary, to say:

When Papa [Winston] heard that Biddy was coming without Walter, he was rather sulky … . But soon he took to her like a house on fire & kissed her tenderly on departure. As for Meg, she & Papa flirted outrageously & almost romped … . When they all went away poor Papa fell into the doldrums – He is better now & started a picture from the terrace outside his bed-room … . Thank God Papa is blooming in his health. His memory fails a little more day by day & he is getting deafer. But he is well.[28]

During this holiday Winston painted two pictures.

At Safi, in western Morocco, the Churchills joined Aristotle Onassis and his wife, Athina, on their yacht *Christina* on 19 February for a cruise to the Canary Islands. They arrived home on 2 March and, only four days later, Winston 'flew off to stay with Emery and Wendy [Reves] at La Pausa'.[29]

Winston wrote from La Pausa, where he was staying for a month, to Clementine to say, 'Yesterday [15 March] Paul Maze and his wife [Jessie] came to lunch. He talked a good deal about painting, and will come and paint with me.'[30] Maze, a Frenchman, was also a highly decorated soldier whom Winston had met on the Western Front in 1916. There was always room in Winston's life for a man of valour.

In April Clementine told Moran, 'Winston isn't a worrier. But he is profoundly depressed. The days are very long and dull. It was never like this in the past. He found a hundred things to do.'[31] In June Winston enquired of Moran:

Why do I get stuck down in the past? Why do I keep going over and over those years when I know I cannot change anything? You, Charles, have spent your life puzzling how the mind works. You must know the answer.

Alas, Winston's doctor did *not* know the answer. 'That I am so useless to him torments me,' said Moran sadly.[32]

On 22 July Winston set sail, once more, with Onassis, this time on a voyage to the eastern Mediterranean. However, prudently it was decided to avoid sailing through the Dardanelles strait until Winston had retired to bed, because, said Anthony Montague Browne's wife, Noel ('Nonie'), 'they knew it would upset him'.[33]

In the election of 8 October 1959 the Conservatives were returned with an increased majority and Harold Macmillan continued as Prime Minister. As for Winston, he held his seat at Woodford with ease. In November, on a car journey from London to Chartwell, Clementine observed, 'When we drove down last night Winston did not smoke at all. This is something new.'[34]

From 9 March to 14 April 1960 Winston went cruising once again with Onassis, after which, said Mary:

> Back at home Winston led a carefully structured life: he often attended debates in the House of Commons, and he made a few speeches in his constituency. He greatly enjoyed his sorties to the races with Christopher [Soames, Mary's husband] and was a faithful attender at the convivial dinners of the Other Club [a political dining society founded in 1911 by Winston and F. E. Smith, 1st Lord Birkenhead – said by Lord Moran to be Winston's closest friend].[35]

It was in that year, 1960, that Moran decided to discontinue writing his biographical diary of Winston's life.

On 27 July 1964 Winston visited the House of Commons for the last time, having decided not to contest his seat at the October 1964 general election. This decision was for him, said Mary, an 'infinitely depressing' one.[36] This was borne out by his private secretary, Anthony Montague Browne:

> I found him very unhappy and melancholy, sitting after dinner and brooding, and I asked him why he was so melancholy – this was after his retirement. And [I] pointed to his extraordinary achievements, both in politics, and in the armed forces, having won the war – if you can put it down to a single man it was he – but of course you can't. And, things like the Nobel Prize for Literature; a large family who all loved him. And apart from that he was popular. I said he'd had a life which was given to so few people, so why was he so gloomy? And he said this: 'Yes, you're right. I have worked very hard all my life and I have achieved a great deal. In the end, to achieve nothing.'

Browne interpreted Winston's latter remark to mean that although he had striven to create a strong and united British Empire and Commonwealth, in a totally peaceful world, this had not come to pass.[37]

Sir Norman Brook described how Winston declined in his latter years:

He could rise to the great occasion, by an effort of will and a modest use of the stimulants prescribed by his doctor. But in the daily round of his responsibilities he no longer had the necessary energy, mental or physical, to give to papers or to people the full attention which they deserved.[38]

Winston's daughter Sarah described how, in those latter years, 'a certain silence descended upon him and he spoke rarely'.[39] And his daughter Mary described how

barely a few years before my father died, when we'd had rather a silent evening ... I was alone with him, and I said to him, 'Is there something in your life which you feel you've missed or not had? And you know, I thought he would say, 'Yes I would like to have won the Victoria Cross,' which I'm sure he would have liked to have done. But he said to me, without much long delay of thought, 'Oh yes, I'd have liked my father to have lived long enough to have seen that I was going to be some good.'[40]

At least Mary could take comfort from the fact that Winston had been prepared to acknowledge that his life had been of 'some good'.

Notes

1. Churchill, Winston S., *Painting as a Pastime*, p. 13.
2. Soames, Mary, *Winston Churchill: His Life as a Painter*, [LP] p. 196.
3. Moran, Lord, *Winston Churchill: The Struggle for Survival 1940-1965*, p. 653.
4. Soames, Mary, *Clementine Churchill*, [CC] p. 464.
5. Moran, Lord, op cit, p. 658.
6. Soames, Mary, *LP* op cit, p. 197-8.
7. Moran, Lord, op cit, p. 665.
8. Ibid, p. 670.
9. Soames, Mary, *LP* op cit, p. 105.
10. Gilbert, Martin, *Never Despair: Winston S. Churchill 1945-1965*, Winston to Lady Lytton, 30 June 1955, p. 1148.
11. Soames, Mary, *LP* op cit, Churchill Papers, from a draft by Sir John Rothenstein of an article entitled 'Mr Churchill the Artist' later published in 'Churchill: A Tribute by Various Hands on his Eightieth Birthday', pp. 198-9.

12. Rothenstein, Sir John, *Time's Thievish Progress*, p. 144.
13. Soames, Mary, *LP* op cit, p. 199.
14. Moran, Lord, op cit, p. 684.
15. Soames, Mary, *LP* op cit, p. 201-2.
16. Wendy Russell and Emery Reves were married in 1964.
17. Soames, Mary, *LP* op cit, p. 202.
18. Soames, Mary (ed.), *Speaking for Themselves: The Personal Letters of Winston and Clementine Churchill*, [*SP*] Winston to Clementine, 30 January 1956, p. 603.
19. Soames, Mary, *LP* op cit, p. 203.
20. Moran, Lord, op cit, p. 706.
21. Soames, Mary, *SP* op cit, Winston to Clementine, 5 June 1957, p. 619.
22. Gilbert, Martin, op cit, Winston to Clementine, 23 January 1958, p. 1259.
23. Moran, Lord, op cit, Conversation between Brendan Bracken and Moran, 24 July 1958, p. 745.
24. Ibid.
25. Soames, Mary, *LP* op cit, p.203.
26. Thompson, Walter H., *I was Churchill's Shadow*, p. 83.
27. Soames, Mary, *SP* op cit, Winston to Clementine, 14 October 1958, p. 627.
28. Soames, Mary, *LP* op cit, Clementine to Mary, 28 January 1959, Mary Soames Papers, p. 206.
29. Ibid, p. 207.
30. Soames, Mary, *SP* op cit, Winston to Clementine, 16 March 1959, p. 631.
31. Moran, Lord, op cit, p. 749.
32. Ibid, pp. 753-4.
33. Gilbert, Martin, op cit, p. 1298.
34. Moran, Lord, op cit, p. 762.
35. Soames, Mary, *LP* op cit, p.203, and Moran, Lord, op cit, p. 746.
36. Soames, Mary, *CC* op cit, p. 484.
37. *Churchill*. BBC Enterprises Ltd.
38. Wheeler-Bennett, Sir John (ed.), *Action this Day: Working with Churchill*, pp. 44-5.
39. Churchill, Sarah, *A Thread in the Tapestry*, pp. 17-18.
40. *Churchill: The Greatest Briton of All Time*, 2002, A TW1/Carlton Production.

CHAPTER 32

Between 'Highs' and 'Lows': the 'Real' Winston

Whether there ever were times when Winston was neither on a High, or on a Low of depression is a matter of conjecture, but the following portrayals of him by his friends and colleagues suggest that, yes, perhaps there were.

His love of animals
It was at his beloved Chartwell that Winston was at his most contented and at one with his animals, birds and pets. The cows on the Chartwell Estate, said Walter Graebner

> invariably came lumbering up to receive a pat from their owner. He even had time for the lowly pig. He never passed the pens without saying a few words to the occupants and picking up the rake to give them a good back scratching.[1]

Graebner describes how, after one of his black New Zealand swans was killed by a fox, Winston, at luncheon

> hardly touched his food. He attempted to talk, first about politics, then about his books, but he always lapsed into gloomy silence, and if not that, talk always led to the black swan and fox. He was almost overcome with grief.[2]

In another tragedy, Rufie, Winston's miniature French poodle, ran into the path of a bus and was killed. He was buried at Chartwell with a headstone to mark his grave. He was succeeded by Rufie II who

> was allowed to sit on a chair very near the table at Mr Churchill's side. Every few minutes Churchill would turn and look at him affectionately. 'Poor darling, come and talk to me,' he would say tenderly three or four times during lunch or dinner.[3]

Walter Thompson describes how Winston relaxed by playing gramophone records on his radiogram. Marching tunes were a favourite of his, and he would 'march up and down the Great Hall' at Chequers to the strains of a military band. He also loved songs, including those sung by Scottish entertainer Sir Harry Lauder, such as 'Keep Right On to the End of the Road'.[4] Thompson also describes how two baths a day 'were essential to him as a form of relaxation'.[5] However, at bagatelle he 'played as if the game was of the utmost importance, and made careful note of every score on a piece of paper which was kept by the board'.[6] When Winston painted, it was with the same all-consuming intensity. However, perhaps when watching film shows, when his scope for hyperactivity would, of necessity, have been severely limited, he was able to relax.

A man of emotion and sensitivity

According to Sir John Martin, Winston

> was a great-hearted man with deep feelings, which he was never ashamed to show. Those of us who saw him in tears in the House of Commons after announcing the attack on the French fleet at Oran (3 July 1940), or the agony of reluctance before dismissing a loyal minister when Cabinet changes were necessary, will never think of him as hard or unsympathetic.[7]

Following the bombing of Britain's parliament buildings at Westminster on the night of 10 May 1941, Winston declared, with tears running down his cheeks, 'There I learnt my craft, and there it is now, a heap of rubble.'[8]

In early February 1943 Winston flew to North Africa to celebrate the defeat of Rommel by the British Eighth Army. Here, in Tripoli, as Brigadier Sir Edgar Williams, who served in Eighth Army Headquarters, recalled, he took the salute at the Victory Parade in which the New Zealanders and Scotland's 51st Highland Division participated. As the fighting men marched past 'absolutely superbly ... Churchill was very moved and he stood there with tears pouring down his cheeks as he watched'.[9]

Graebner opined that,

> By normal standards Churchill was rather a vain man. He thrived on praise and appreciation, and when they were not forthcoming he was miserable. He carefully noted whether his speeches and doings made front page news or not. If the newspaper attacked him, he felt it keenly. He would worry over the ill-starred passage for hours, and

keep referring to it in conversation, as if hoping for reassurance from those around him that he was not such a bad fellow after all.[10]

'Vain' is not a word which one normally associates with Winston, and what Graebner is actually describing is the former's constant need for 'affirmation', which in his case was a lifelong one.

A lover of poetry

Graebner commented of Winston's 'table conversation':

> Sometimes he would suddenly start to quote the poetry he loved. I remember one luncheon when, for a good ten minutes, he repeated passages from Siegfried Sassoon's war poems. At the end his eyes were filled with tears. Poetry moved him deeply, as did any stirring or tragic tale. And it was an extraordinary and deeply impressive sight to see the old man quietly weeping into his pudding while the guests looked on, somehow not a bit abashed, and Mrs Churchill, at her end of the table, quietly took up a new line of conversation.[11]

An appreciation of beauty

After the Casablanca Conference (14-24 January 1943), recalled Lord Moran, when Winston and President Roosevelt were driving to the Moroccan city of Marrakech, Winston insisted that they stop the car so that the President could see the sun setting over the snow-capped Atlas Mountains.[12] Also, said Thompson, 'Mr Churchill loves trees. He seems to find inspiration from just looking at them.'[13]

Winston could also be swept away by the beauty of the female form. For example, Lady Williams, who was Winston's secretary from 1950 to 1955, described how, when Laurence Olivier and his wife, Vivien Leigh, were invited to Chartwell in 1951,

> Vivien Leigh [was] sitting beside Churchill at the table and he was just looking at her, quite naturally, and he said to her, 'All I want is just to look at you.' And you realized that he was spellbound by her beauty.[14]

A sense of humour

Winston's sense of humour is illustrated by Sir John Peck, his Private Secretary from 1940 to 1945, who described how, in Tunis on 1 June 1943, German prisoners of war were paraded before Winston:

In this procession there was an immaculate German general, sitting rigidly in a German, open staff-car, and looking neither to the right nor to the left. [As there was no petrol] The car was being towed along by a mule. As it passed the place where Winston and his entourage was standing, the general, I suppose, in a form of salute, did an eyes right to Churchill, who looked straight at this man. Whereupon they both, for a moment, started to burst out laughing and then the moment had gone. It was just one of those little human touches, that both of these responsible men – the Prime Minister and an enemy general – saw the ludicrous aspect of the situation at the same time.[15]

At 'La Pausa', being thoroughly 'spoiled'

Anthony Montague Browne said of Wendy Reves, wife of Emery of the 'Villa La Pausa' on France's Côte d'Azur:

She had a wonderful sparkle. She would devote herself 100% to his needs. She was a charming conversationalist and she looked after him in a most delightful way. Her nickname at one time was the 'Champagne Kitten'. She was enormously bubbly and charming and terribly fond of him, and she did everything to make him happy.[16]

And Denis Kelly, Winston's literary researcher, said of Wendy:

She mothered him. I remember once he was upset about something or other – doesn't matter what it was – and she put his head in her arms and cradled him. He adored it – just being spoilt.[17]

As for Wendy herself, she declared of Winston:

I could call him 'Darling' or 'Monkey Pie' or 'You Bad Boy'. I could tease him you see, because I didn't very often call him 'Sir Winston' when he was here. I would say, 'Good morning darling. How are you this morning?' Or I would say, 'Are you hungry eh?' I could tease him. I could push him. I could pat him. I could shake him. He liked it, you see. No one ever did that. He felt terribly *loved* here.

He was so happy here that, as you know, he came back and came back and came back and came back. When he came the first time he was to stay 10 days. He stayed 3 weeks. Each time he prolonged and prolonged until finally [in] the last three or four years, he stayed here more than he stayed in England.[18]

Winston, for his part, described Wendy as being 'young, beautiful [and] kind'.[19]

God and the Afterlife

In times of quiet contemplation, Winston often returned to what, for him, was the vexed question of religion.

It had been his habit, during the Second World War, to make frequent references to God, and to affirm that it was with the assistance and blessing of The Almighty that the Allies eventually would emerge victorious from the conflict. For example, on 13 May 1940, in a speech to the House of Commons, he quoted from the *Holy Bible*, as follows,

> Arm yourselves, and be ye men of valour, and be in readiness for the conflict; for it is better for us to perish in battle than to look upon the outrage of our nation and our altar. As the Will of God is in Heaven, even so let it be.[20]

And in another speech to the House of Commons, made on 4 June 1940, he declared,

> Even if, which I do not for a moment believe, this island or a large part of it were subjugated and starving, then our Empire beyond the seas, armed and guarded by the British Fleet, would carry on the struggle, until, in God's good time, the New World, with all its power and might, steps forth to the rescue and the liberation of the old.[21]

However, in August 1944, Winston revealed just how uncertain he was about the validity of the Christian doctrine when he put the following question to Moran, 'I suppose you believe in another life when we die?' To which his doctor gave no reply, but was inwardly of the opinion that Winston 'desperately wanted to believe in something'.[22]

May 1955 found Winston again discussing with Moran the question of the immortality of the soul. 'I believe the spirit of man is immortal,' he said, but nevertheless, 'I do not know whether one is conscious or unconscious after death.'[23]

Notes

1. Graebner, Walter, *My Dear Mister Churchill*, p. 104.
2. Ibid, p. 98.
3. Ibid, p. 100-2

4.   Thompson, Walter H., *I was Churchill's Shadow*, p. 51.
5.   Ibid, p. 44.
6.   Ibid, p. 52.
7.   Wheeler-Bennett, Sir John (ed.), *Action this Day: Working with Churchill*, p. 142.
8.   Moran, Lord, *Winston Churchill: The Struggle for Survival 1940-1965*, p. 123.
9.   *Churchill*. BBC Enterprises Ltd.
10. Graebner, Walter, op cit, pp. 45-6.
11. Ibid, p. 26.
12. Moran, Lord, op cit, p. 82.
13. Thompson, Walter H., op cit, p. 166.
14. *Churchill*. BBC Enterprises Ltd.
15. Ibid.
16. Ibid.
17. Ibid.
18. Ibid.
19. Ibid.
20. Holy Bible, King James version, 1 Maccabees, Chapter 3, Verses 58 & 60. Gilbert, Martin, *Finest Hour: Winston S. Churchill 1939-1941*, speech to the House of Commons, 13 May 1940, p. 333.
21. Gilbert, Martin, *Finest Hour: Winston S. Churchill 1939-1941*, speech to the House of Commons, 4 June 1940, p. 468.
22. Moran, Lord, op cit, p. 170.
23. Ibid, p. 659.

CHAPTER 33

The Death of Winston

Winston died at 8.00am on 24 January 1965, in his ninety-first year. After a state funeral conducted at St Paul's Cathedral, and attended by Her Majesty The Queen, he was buried in the churchyard of the Parish Church of St Martin's, Bladon near Woodstock, next to his father, his mother, and his brother, Jack, his final resting place being within a mile of his birthplace at Blenheim Palace.

Winston's daughter Mary spoke lovingly and reverentially of her father's final few days and hours at Hyde Park Gate, holding back her tears as she did so:

> Clementine sat for hours by his bed, holding his hand. It was a peaceful scene, really. He had a dear orange kitten which was a fairly new acquisition that used to lie curled up on his bed. The grandchildren came up to say their goodbyes. My children were rather small, but I am glad they saw him looking so peaceful.[1]

A few weeks after Winston's death Clementine handed Chartwell over to the National Trust and, in early September 1965, she moved into a new home, 7 Princes Gate near London's Hyde Park.[2] She died on 12 December 1977, in her ninety-third year, and was laid to rest in Winston's grave.

Notes

1. *Churchill*. BBC Enterprises Ltd.
2. Soames, Mary, *Clementine Churchill*, p. 504.

Epilogue

Those close to Winston found him to be, on the one hand, exasperating, bombastic, tiresome, exhausting to be with, foolhardy, and inconsiderate in the extreme; and, on the other, caring, compassionate, endearing, and generous to a fault. But what his wife, family, friends and colleagues failed to comprehend was that he had a mental disorder, and that, because of this disorder, it would probably have been virtually impossible for him to have altered his behaviour, even if he had wanted to. Furthermore, on the occasions when he *was forced* to do so – say, by enduring obligatory inactivity, which was anathema to him – he became utterly miserable.

When Winston kept his long-suffering colleagues up for half the night, as his restless, peripatetic mind spewed out idea after idea – some good, and some bad – they regarded him as inconsiderate and often irrational, though no one would have been brave enough to tell him so. However, because he had little or no insight into the fact of his mental disorder, Winston would have seen nothing abnormal or untoward in his nocturnal activities and mental peregrinations.

Similarly, because he himself was obsessively goal-directed, it was incomprehensible to him that a colleague should take leave of absence during wartime, when, for him, the only way forward for himself and others was, in his own words to 'go on and on, like the gun horses, till we drop'.

People often complained that Winston ignored them, and thought him discourteous or impervious to the ideas of others. The truth was, however, that his feverish, hypomanic mind was so replete with its own ideas that there was precious little room in it for anyone else's.

For his exploits against the Boers, and in other theatres of war, Winston was justifiably accorded epithets such as 'heroic' and 'courageous'. However, although he delighted in the publicity that resulted from such exploits, Winston's hypomania meant that he would have viewed matters in a different light, and for the following reasons. When a 'normal' person finds him or herself in the presence of danger, the 'fight or flight' mechanism comes into play. In other words, that person makes an instant decision to do either one thing or the other. However, with Winston, although the 'fight' mechanism existed, because of his hypomania, the 'flight' mechanism did not. And, rather than flee, he behaved in quite the opposite way, by *actively seeking out danger*, and *positively revelling in its presence*. And, it probably never ever crossed his mind that others might see the situation differently.

When Winston was in the depressive phase of his hypomanic depression, his ability to contribute to life in general and to the affairs of the nation in particular was severely limited. As for the hypomanic phase, this too created problems, as has already been amply demonstrated. And yet, despite this, Winston's positive achievements were truly remarkable, and it is for the following that he will chiefly be remembered: his perception of the danger of Nazism in the 1930s, and his insistence that the nation must take heed of this fact and be prepared for the worst eventuality, namely war; his recognition that the Second World War could only be won with the help of the USA, and his untiring efforts to bring America into the war on the side of the Allies; his distrust of Stalin, and his warnings to President Roosevelt that, given the opportunity, the Soviets would overrun as much of Europe as they could; and, finally, his vision of a future United States of Europe. But there was more to it than that, for Winston's greatness also lay in the fact that he could inspire his countrymen and women – and others throughout the free world – touch their hearts, make them believe that they *could* win through, whatever the odds. And he achieved this, not by making idle or unrealistic promises but by 'levelling' with them, giving them an honest appraisal of the situation as he saw it – 'We have before us an ordeal of the most grievous kind' – and then, using his great powers of oratory and allusion, telling them precisely what he, and they, were going to do about it. And for this he was respected and revered as the torch-bearer; he who epitomized the soul of the nation and embodied the fighting spirit of Britain and her Allies.

However, it is not for a moment suggested that any of these positive qualities of Winston's were directly attributable to his hypomania. But the hypomanic component of his psyche meant that he was able to focus obsessively, and with almost superhuman energy, on the task in hand, and, by his example and exhortations, to galvanize others to join with him and do likewise. And the greatest task of all was, of course, to save the free world from tyranny.

Hypomanic (and manic) depressive disorders tend to run in families, and it is now known that their inheritance is governed, to a greater or lesser extent, by genes. It has been shown that this was almost certainly the case with Winston. However, this in no way explains what makes a person with, say, hypomania, behave differently to a 'normal' person, i.e. one who does not have this disorder. In fact, as far as the normal human mind is concerned, let alone the abnormal, the fundamental way in which it works is almost as much a mystery today as it ever was – despite the inventions of the X-ray, the electroencephalograph and the computerized tomography scanner. In this context, the words of scientist and mathematician Sir Isaac Newton are appropriate in respect of the modern-day scientist who endeavours to elucidate the workings of the human brain:

> To myself I seem to have been only like a boy playing on the sea-shore, and diverting myself now and then finding a smoother pebble or a prettier shell than ordinary, whilst the great ocean of truth lay all undiscovered before me.[1]

The continuation of the species depends not only upon genetic inheritance and genetic mutation, whereby, during cell division, the exact DNA sequence is not reproduced precisely, leading to variations in the species, but also on natural selection, whereby only those who are fittest, i.e. best adapted, to survive do so. In this context, the presence of hypomanic depression in an individual is a mixed blessing. In a worst case scenario, he or she may succumb, by committing suicide during an episode of what Winston described as the 'Black Dog', or be killed whilst engaged in some dangerous activity. Alternatively, that person, by virtue of his or her super-abundant energy and obsessional, goal-directed activity, may become a high achiever – which, in Winston's case, meant becoming a great leader, parliamentarian, man of letters, and an accomplished painter.

In *Winston Churchill: The Struggle for Survival 1940-1965*, Winston's personal physician, Lord Moran, never once suggested that Winston was suffering from a mental disorder. So is it possible that this highly qualified and experienced physician, who was not, however, a psychiatrist, did not recognize hypomanic depression in his patient? Alternatively, perhaps Moran *was* aware of Winston's condition, but feared that, were he to fall into the hands of a psychiatrist, his patient might be subjected to electro-convulsive therapy (ECT, the treatment of choice of the day, whereby an electric pulse is delivered to the brain in order to induce a fit).

But if Moran *had* sought a psychiatric opinion for Winston, and there is no evidence to suggest that he did, and had ECT been prescribed, then the likelihood is that the tiny candle flame which Winston embodied, and which would one day become a brightly burning beacon of hope to all who cherish freedom, would probably have been snuffed out, and what then would have been the fate of Britain and the free world? Thanks are therefore due to Moran, for, wittingly or unwittingly, sparing Winston from such a fate.

In fact, what Lord Moran *did* prescribe for Winston was, from 1940 onwards, Seconal (quinalbarbitone – a narcotic), to help him sleep; and from 1953 onwards, when Winston had what he described as a 'muzzy feeling in my head'[2] following his stroke, Drinamyl (containing d-amphetamine sulphate, a central nervous system stimulant, the side effects of which include excitability and irritability). He was also prescribed amylobarbitone, the side effects of which are similar to those of quinalbarbitone. Alternatively, if Winston's symptoms were less severe, Moran prescribed Edrisal, containing the analgesics, aspirin and phenacetin, together with a much weaker dose of amphetamine sulphate. As regards the effect of Seconal and Drinamyl on Winston's hypomania, it is probable that the narcotic effect of the barbiturates on the one hand and the stimulating effects of the amphetamines on the other would have cancelled one another out. As for the Edrisal, because the dose of amphetamine which it contained was small, its effect on Winston's hypomania was probably negligible.[3]

Thanks are also due to Sir Alan Brooke, Winston's loyal and long-suffering Chief of the Imperial General Staff, who, in 1946, became Lord Alanbrooke. He saw his role as being to filter out Winston's more grandiose and preposterous plans and ideas well before they could even reach the drawing board but he was, nonetheless, full of admiration for Winston:

> I wonder whether any historian of the future will ever be able to paint Winston in his true colours. It is a wonderful character, the most marvellous qualities and superhuman genius mixed with an astonishing lack of vision at times, and an impetuosity which, if not guided, must inevitably bring him into trouble again and again.
>
> Perhaps the most remarkable failing of his is that he can never see a whole strategic problem at once. His gaze always settles on some definite part of the canvas and the rest of the picture is lost.

However, although 'He is the most difficult man to work with that I have ever struck ...', said Alanbrooke, 'I would not have missed the chance of working with him for anything on earth.'[4]

The cynic might argue that Winston should have confined himself to his speechmaking, which inspired the nation and the free world alike. However, it would behove that same cynic to question who else but Winston foresaw, so clearly, the rise of Nazism and Bolshevism and strove so tirelessly to alert the world of this twin danger to freedom, whilst at the same time enlisting the support of Britain's allies, and in particular the USA, without whose intervention – as he recognized right from the very beginning – the Second World War could not have been won?

It is, perhaps, fitting that Winston's former personal bodyguard and detective, Walter Thompson, should have the final word:

> It is ironic that one who craved love and affection all his life was able to inspire love and affection in others, not only in those associated with him, but in millions throughout the world who had never seen him and never would see him face to face.[5]

Notes

1. More, L.T., *Isaac Newton*, p. 664.
2. Moran, Lord, *Winston Churchill: The Struggle for Survival 1940-1965*, p. 478.
3. Lovell, Richard, 'Lord Moran's prescriptions for Churchill'. London: *British Medical Journal*, Volume 310, Number 6993.
4. Bryant, Arthur, *The Turn of the Tide 1939-1943*, p. 723.
5. **Churchill's Bodyguard*. Nugus/Martin Productions Ltd.

Appendix

Opinion of Dr John H. Mather as to the cause of Lord Randolph Churchill's death and the author's response

An article may be viewed on the website of the Churchill Centre and Museum at the Churchill War Rooms, London, by John H Mather, MD, which is entitled, 'Lord Randolph Churchill: Maladies Et Mort'. Extracts from that article are given below, followed by the author's comments in italics (preceded by A.N.). The article begins as follows:

i It is impossible to say at this late date what killed Sir Winston Churchill's father. But it is no longer possible to say that he died of syphilis.

A.N. *Is this statement true? See below.*

ii Against their doctors' advice, Lord and Lady Randolph made a world tour in 1894 which was cut short by his rapidly deteriorating health. He returned to England in late 1894, 'as weak and helpless in mind and body as a little child,' according to his son and biographer, Winston.

A.N. *Correct.*

iii Lord Randolph was seriously ill in 1890, with palpitations associated with exhaustion. His family physician, Dr Robson Roose, prescribed belladonna, laudanum and digitalis. The following year, he experienced an episode of severe confusion, which suggests acute high blood pressure.

A.N. *Dr Mather's suggestion that Lord Randolph suffered from high blood pressure is pure speculation.*

iv Earlier, in 1882, he had had an extended illness which Lady Randolph's diary refers to as tiredness and fevers. Later, in mid 1893, Dr Roose told Jennie, who was distraught over her husband's illness, that Randolph's heart condition had, nonetheless, been cured. But, around this time, Randolph began to have speaking difficulties which were associated with hearing and balance problems.

Over the next two years until his death in 1895, Lord Randolph complained of dizziness, palpitations, and intermittent numbness in his hands and feet.

A.N. *The probable cause of this numbness of the extremities is syphilitic degeneration of those neurons in the spinal cord which carry sensory information to the brain (a condition known as tabes dorsalis), which occurs in tertiary (untreated), syphilis, and becomes manifest ten to twenty-five years after the primary infection. In addition, on 4 November 1894, Dr Keith described Lord Randolph's gait as 'staggering and uncertain',[1] this being another classic feature of tabes dorsalis.*

v His speech became more slurred, and during one of his last parliamentary speeches, he hesitated on the text. He eventually became quick-tempered and combative. Finally, he died in a coma, with pneumonia and, probably, kidney failure.

His biographers, including his son Winston, were divided on the nature of Lord Randolph's medical problems and the cause of his death. They have generally attributed his deterioration and death to syphilis (Winston in conversation, though not in print) and its late effects.

A.N. *This paragraph is ambiguous. Winston was not 'divided'. He was* in no doubt whatsoever *that his father had suffered from syphilis, viz: a) His letter to Lady Randolph of 2 November 1894, where he states, 'I asked Dr Roose and he told me everything and showed me the medical reports. I have told no one ....[2] b) The fact that, years later, Winston confirmed that he knew the truth about the illness which killed his father when he told his secretary Anthony Montague Browne, 'You know my father died of locomotor ataxia [inability to control one's body movements], the child of syphilis.*[3]

vi Some have suggested other neurological conditions, such as epilepsy, multiple sclerosis, amyotrophic lateral sclerosis (Lou Gehrig's disease), chronic alcoholism or a brain tumour.

A.N. *Why introduce 'red herrings' such as these when Lord Randolph's symptoms can be accounted for by the presence of syphilis?*

vii The dramatic deterioration in his health and the various descriptions of his behaviour in his last three years might support a diagnosis of dementia paralytica [a term which is synonymous with General Paralysis of the Insane] in late or tertiary syphilis, which affects the brain and appears ten to twenty years after the primary infection.

A.N. *Agreed.*

viii This would likely have affected Jennie and their two sons, Winston and Jack.

A.N. *No, because assuming, as all the evidence suggests, that Lord Randolph had contracted syphilis whilst at Oxford (1867-1870), by the time he married Jennie and his children were born, the disease would have progressed to a non-infectious phase. (The current view is that a patient infected with syphilis remains infectious for up to two years from the time he develops the 'primary lesions', or chancre – i.e., during the primary, secondary, and early latent phase of syphilis.)*

ix But if a diagnosis of advanced syphilis is to be accepted, there must have been an initial infection.

A.N. *Agreed and there was.*

x There has been considerable speculation about when Randolph might have become 'infected.' The most notorious account is by journalist Frank Harris in his 1924 autobiography, *My Life and Loves*, who recounts a story told by Louis Jennings, Randolph's friend and political colleague, who had published Randolph's 1880-88 speeches.

A.N. *The use by Dr Mather of the word 'notorious' suggests that he has closed his mind to the possibility that Harris may have been telling the truth.*

xi After a drunken party, Jennings said, fellow students put Randolph with an 'old hag.' The next morning he woke, discovered his situation, threw money at the woman and fled. He was immediately treated by a local doctor with disinfectant. Eventually, 'a little, round, very red pimple appeared ... on his peccant member.' (This is not the description of a primary syphilis chancre, but of herpes.)

238

APPENDIX

A.N. *Untrue, in that the primary chancre may have the appearance either of an ulcer, or of a pimple.*

xii A doctor supposedly treated him with mercury and warned him off alcohol.

Jennings's story is questionable for several reasons. First, the chance of contracting syphilis in one sexual encounter is less than one percent.

A.N. *According to the Sexually Transmitted Disease Surveillance 2007 Supplement: Syphilis Surveillance Report, Atlanta, US Department of Health and Human Services, 'The risk of being infected with syphilis from a single sexual encounter with an infected person is approximately 3-10%.' Dr Mather's assessment of the risk is therefore an underestimate.*

xiii Jennings's account as reported by Harris has never been corroborated.

A.N. *Untrue. It was corroborated by Julian Osgood Field, a contemporary of Lord Randolph at Oxford.*[4]

xiv Lord Randolph's nephew Shane Leslie, and Shane's daughter Anita, both concluded that Harris's 'old hag' story was incredible, and offered their own scenarios. Shane Leslie alleged that Randolph was infected by a chambermaid at Blenheim Palace around the time of Winston's birth.

Anita Leslie theorizes that Randolph had a French mistress who had syphilis.

A.N. *There is no reference by Shane Leslie in his book,* Men Were Different, *to Lord Randolph being infected by a chambermaid at Blenheim Palace. Neither is there any reference by Anita Leslie in the literature to a 'French mistress' in relation to Lord Randolph.*

xv Was this the year [1886] Randolph first became aware of a deterioration in his health?

A.N. *No. It was Dr Buzzard's recollection that Lord Randolph had first consulted him in October 1885.*

xvi Roose would also have inquired into any history of secondary syphilitic features such as a rash over much of the body. There is no record of any such problems.

A.N. *Simply because Dr Roose's medical notes have survived, this cannot be taken to mean that no rash occurred.*

xvii There is no indication that Lady Randolph or her sons were infected with syphilis.

There is likewise no evidence that Jennie's subsequent husbands, or the many lovers she is alleged to have had, ever contracted syphilis.

A.N. *How could Jennie or the children have contracted syphilis when, by the time Lord Randolph met her in August 1873, the disease would have long since progressed to its non-infectious phase?*

xviii In the late nineteenth century, there was a clear predisposition toward syphilis in clinical diagnosis. In 1889, Dr. William Gowers, a well-respected neurologist, emphasized this overdiagnosis of neurologic syphilis when he delivered the Lettsomian Lecture to the Medical Society of London. He chose as his topic 'Syphilis and the Nervous System.'

A.N. *There is no evidence whatsoever that Dr Buzzard, an acknowledged expert in the field, 'overdiagnosed' syphilis in his patients.*

Dr Mather quotes from a scientific paper, which Dr Roose had written in 1875, which reads as follows:

xix 'Chronic inflammation of the brain attacks persons of exhausted habits, brought on by excesses and irregular living. The patient has frequent headaches and gradual loss of health, and then gets a perversion of most of the senses, as of sight, taste, smell, etc., and in fact, all the symptoms of the incipient mania. The only treatment is to try and combat the various morbid symptoms as they arise and improve the general health in every way; but, in two or three years, general paralysis is almost sure to occur.'[5]

A.N. *From this, Dr Mather, ignores the fact that the terms 'General Paralysis' and 'Syphilis' were synonymous and instead concludes that the term 'General Paralysis' is associated, in the case of Lord Randolph, with exhaustion, not syphilis. Dr Mather also ignores the fact that Dr Roose was not an expert on syphilis.*

xx   Lady Randolph Churchill may have been apprised of her husband's condition during a secret visit to his doctors in 1892, which provoked a fearful row.

A.N. *Agreed.*

xxi Winston may have learned from the doctors about the seriousness of his father's illness in 1894.

A.N. *Not 'may have' – 'did'.*

xxii He wrote a distraught letter to his mother while her parents were on their world tour.

A.N. *Correct.*

xxiii But it is not certain whether he understood Randolph's illness to be syphilis.

A.N. Absolutely untrue – *see above.*

xxiv At the end, it was evident that Drs Roose and Buzzard were convinced that Randolph had 'general paralysis,' which many people have taken to be a code word for syphilis of the brain.

A.N. *Here, Dr Mather ignores the possibility that Dr Buzzard may have chosen to omit to write such words as 'syphilis' or 'General Paralysis of the Insane' in medical notes, for fear of the fact of Lord Randolph's syphilis becoming public knowledge. (See below.) Alternatively, Dr Buzzard may have expunged such words from his medical notes at a later date, for the same reason. Also 'General Paralysis', as already mentioned, was not a 'code word' but a synonym for syphilis of the brain.*

xxv Much of his [Lord Randolph's] behaviour during his last five years seems to be no more than an accentuation of his prior personality.

A.N. *Agreed, Lord Randolph did possess a manic-depressive type of personality, but again the question is asked: how can his concurrent physical symptoms be explained?*

xxvi Lord Randolph had always had a slight speech impediment, and as a youngster he had had hearing problems, so it is difficult to single out problems with his speech, once thought to be a clear and common symptom of syphilis in its late stage affecting the brain.

A.N. *Agreed, but the paralysis of Lord Randolph's lower lip and chin (as described by Dr Keith), and his tremulous tongue, which would undoubtedly have affected his speech, were not of long standing.*

xxvii In the same sense, the muddled thoughts, memory lapses and profound confusion, all features of syphilis's paralytica dementia, were absent from Randolph's writings until the end of 1894. He wrote more lengthily, and his script became shaky, but it was never unintelligible. Until the last, when he was in a coma, his thoughts expressed in writing were rational; they include a cogent letter to Winston while on the world tour in August 1894.

A.N. *Dr Mather's choice of the word 'cogent' is a strange one. Perhaps 'coherent' might have been a better choice. True, the letter to which Dr Mather refers, dated 21 August 1894,[6] is coherent.*

xxviii In a letter to his mother on 8 October 1894, Lord Randolph describes how he cured the numbness in his hands and feet by putting them in hot water. If he had been suffering from dementia, he would not have been able to write such a cohesive letter.

A.N. *The seven-page letter from Lord Randolph to his mother, the Duchess of Marlborough, to which Dr Mather refers, unlike his letter of 21 August, is rambling, and repetitive, being largely devoted to telling Lady Marlborough how he had assuaged the numbness in his hands and feet by immersing them in hot water.[7] There is also a distinct deterioration in Lord Randolph's handwriting. Further evidence to suggest that the latter was suffering from increasing dementia, in the latter part of 1894, is provided by Dr Keith, who, writing from Malacca on 30 October 1894, said of His Lordship, 'There is perhaps more loss of mental power' and also that His Lordship had 'a tendency to use wrong words'.[8]*

xxix A likely explanation for the longstanding problem with his circulation is his chain-smoking. Spasms in the arteries reduce circulation which causes numbness and pain due to lack of oxygen in the tissues.

A.N. *Lord Randolph was in his early forties when he experienced numbness in his extremities, which makes it unlikely (but not impossible) that this was due to arterial narrowing caused by smoking. The presence of tabes dorsalis is a far more plausible explanation (see above).*

xxx His speech problems caused Randolph great frustration. 'I know what I want to say but damn it, I can't say it,' he told his friend Wilfrid Blunt in May 1894.

A.N. *Here, Lord Randolph is describing dysarthria, which is one of the cardinal symptoms of General Paralysis of the Insane.*

xxxi At several times he expressed similar anxiety over the difficulty of articulating his words. These fugue states, or 'psychic seizures' are strongly suggestive of a variety of epilepsy found in the deep parts of the brain, close to the speech area. The progressive march of the disease process strongly suggests an expanding lesion or mass.

A.N. *Lord Randolph's symptoms, which led him to consult Dr Buzzard, commenced in October 1885, if not earlier. Is Dr Mather suggesting that this 'expanding lesion or mass' had been present since then – i.e. for more than a decade? Also, such an 'expanding lesion or mass' would lead to a rise in intracranial pressure, with consequent headaches and vomiting. Although Mrs Moreton Frewen stated (see Chapter 7) that, on one occasion, Lord Randolph did have a severe headache, there is no mention of vomiting in His Lordship's medical notes.*

xxxii Consistent with his right handedness is the possibility that Lord Randolph developed a left side brain tumour, for which no surgery was available. This would also be consistent with the circulation problems in his hands, which in turn would be related to his intermittent heart failure and arterial spasms from nicotine in cigarettes.

A.N. *As already stated, it is possible, though highly unlikely because of his comparatively young age, that Lord Randolph's heart problems were due to his cigarette smoking or that smoking caused him to have problems with his circulation. But what is far more likely is that syphilis, once again, is the culprit, for in patients with tertiary (untreated) syphilis, the heart is adversely affected by one or more of the following conditions: myocardial (heart muscle) degeneration, aortic incompetence, whereby the aortic valve is damaged, and narrowing or occlusion of the coronary arteries. All of these conditions increase the workload of the heart, causing it to fail.*

xxxiii Even Dr Buzzard might have agreed when he said '… intense pain in the head, when it is coupled with amaurosis [partial or total blindness] (or prostration) is very suggestive of the presence of an intra-cranial tumour … If instead of atrophy of the discs we had found optic neuritis, this condition, when taken in connection with the intense severity of the pain in the head, would have gone far towards enabling us to pronounce a somewhat confident diagnosis of intra-cranial tumour.'

A.N. *Here, Dr Mather has introduced a 'red herring'. The patient to whom Dr Buzzard was referring, in the above account, was a forty-nine-year-old whom he refers to as 'J.D.' This person had a medical history quite different from that of Lord Randolph,[9] and therefore the two cases are not in any way comparable.*

xxxiv If Dr Buzzard had been convinced that Lord Randolph Churchill had advanced syphilis, he would certainly have treated him with mercury and with potassium iodide, which he strongly espoused for all neurosyphilitic patients.

A.N. *This statement is true, and is borne out by Dr Buzzard in his booklet,* 'Clinical Aspects of Syphilitic Nervous Affectations'.

xxxv But Dr Buzzard makes no mention of such treatments in any of his papers during Randolph's illness – and, had Randolph taken these two, their toxic effects would have been evident.

Indeed, the only medications Lord Randolph received that can be documented were for pain (laudanum) and heart failure (belladonna and digitalis).

A.N. *Dr Mather is right to draw attention to this apparent inconsistency. So how can it be explained? There are several possibilities:*
a) Dr Buzzard did, in fact, treat Lord Randolph with mercury and potassium

iodide, but failed to record this in the notes for reasons of discretion (just as he had referred to 'General Paralysis of the Insane' simply as 'General Paralysis').

b) Lord Randolph was evidently in denial about his condition. For example, on 8 July 1893, in a letter to Dr Buzzard, he describes what he considers to be 'all this stupid gossip about my health', and states, '...if I am in bad health I assure you I have no knowledge of it.'[10]

c) It is also the case that Lord Randolph treated his doctors in a somewhat cavalier fashion. He refused to allow Dr Roose to consult with Dr Buzzard about his case;[11] he failed to keep his appointment with Dr Buzzard in June 1896[12] and he proceeded with his world tour, against the express advice of his doctors. In fact, on 11 September 1894, a despairing Dr Keith wrote from Yokohama, Japan, to Dr Buzzard to say, 'that for the time being I have lost all control over your patient.'[13]

It is therefore distinctly possible that Lord Randolph may have refused treatment with mercury and potassium iodide, just as (according to Osgood Field) he had refused to take the medication prescribed for him by the doctor whom he consulted in Paris all those years before.

xxxvi Dr Buzzard's reference to 'general paralysis' in Randolph's case is not diagnostic of syphilis, although it suggests this was his eventual conclusion. While syphilis may have been a reasonable diagnosis in the absence of modern techniques, the patient's temperament, combined with his main symptom of speech and articulation problems and absence of dementia, is more consistent with a tumour deep in the left side of his brain. It is not possible to be certain; but it is more likely to be the proper diagnosis.

A.N. *Disagree*

xxxvii His father's illness impressed Winston Churchill with a strong sense of impending mortality. He frequently remarked that he needed to accomplish his goals before his forties, and his resultant activity caused observers to refer to him as a 'young man in a hurry.' Presumably he was happily surprised at his longevity, but he long accepted the common rumours about his father's death. Late in life he told his private secretary, 'you know my father died of locomotion ataxia, the child of syphilis.'

When did Churchill pick up this story? The likely time seems to be 1924, when Frank Harris's book was published, precisely when Winston had left the Liberal Party and reverted to the Conservatives. The Tories were incensed and attempted to blacken his name, calling him a drunkard and saying that he was infected with syphilis. This same year, his eleven-year-old nephew was confronted by a classmate at Summer Field Preparatory School, Oxford, who charged, 'My daddy says all you Churchills have revolting diseases and are quite mad.'

A.N. *This is as may be, but Winston had, in fact, picked up what Dr Mather describes as 'this story' from Dr Roose in person, and was told 'everything' and shown the medical notes.*

xxxviii Now, his father's reputation can also be vindicated.

A.N. *Or can it? See below.*

Author's (A.N.'s) summary

1. Lord Randolph, having had sexual intercourse during his days as an undergraduate at Oxford (1867-1870), developed a pimple ('primary chancre') on his penis.

2. He consulted a doctor, who prescribed (appropriately) a course of mercury, the treatment of choice for a syphilitic infection.

3. The symptoms and signs which Lord Randolph exhibited from October 1885, when he first consulted with Dr Buzzard, until his death in January 1895, are entirely consistent with a diagnosis of syphilis, as is the pattern of their occurrence, and the overall time-frame in which they occurred. (This, in spite of the fact that the symptoms of syphilis are notoriously variable – which is why the disease is referred to as 'The Great Deceiver/Imposter'.) To quote Dr Buzzard, 'although the individual symptoms carry with them no conviction as to the specific origin of the disorder, the peculiar grouping of such symptoms may lead of itself to a probability but little short of certainty'.[14] There was, however, one clinical sign to which Dr Buzzard attached great importance, for he declared, in respect of General Paralysis of the Insane, that, whereas 'it is an alteration in the intellectual faculties which first attracts attention... succeeding to this, the tremor of the lips and mouth [which of course includes the tongue, as in the case of Lord Randolph] only too significantly betrays the fatal nature of the disorder'.[15]

4. When Dr Buzzard said, in his report of 25 December 1894, that Lord Randolph 'is well into the 2nd stage of G.P. [General Paralysis]', this, to any medically qualified person, is a clear and unambiguous indication that it was syphilis to which he was referring.[16]

5. Having diagnosed syphilis in his patient, Dr Buzzard was able to predict the outcome of the disease[17] *(see Chapter 7), as were the medical experts whom Lord Randolph consulted in Madras, which led Dr Keith to write to Dr Roose to say, 'Consultants confirm diagnosis – time [which His Lordship had left to live] about six months.'*[18]

6. An indication of the fact that Lord Randolph's family saw it as an absolute necessity that the truth about His Lordship's condition be concealed, is given by the following letter, written by Lady Randolph to her sister, Leonie, on 15 January 1895:

Up to now the General Public and even Society *does not know* the real truth & after *all* my sacrifice & the misery of these six months it would be hard if it got out. It would do incalculable harm to his [Lordship's] political reputation & memory & be a dreadful thing for all of us.[19]

Lady Randolph would hardy have written in such terms had her husband been suffering from, say, a tumour of the brain – the presence of which would have invoked no social stigma whatsoever.

For the same reason, when they alluded to Lord Randolph's illness in their correspondence, Dr Buzzard and others were scrupulously careful to avoid mentioning the word 'syphilis', preferring instead to employ the euphemistic phrase 'General Paralysis', or the abbreviation 'G.P.'.

7. The attempt made by Dr Mather to cast aspersions on Dr Buzzard's medical expertise[20] *(and, by implication, on that of Drs Roose and Keith, together with that of Sir J. Russell Reynolds*[21] *and Dr Gowers,*[22] *who were also consulted in regard to Lord Randolph's illness*[23]*)is simply not a credible one.*

8. Winston virtually worshipped his father. Is he, therefore, to be disbelieved, a) when he stated that he visited Dr Roose, was told 'everything' about his father's illness and shown the medical reports, and b) subsequently, when he told his secretary that his father had 'died of locomotor ataxia, the child of syphilis'? Such a notion, that Winston was not telling the truth, is patently absurd.

xxx

The above analysis proves beyond all reasonable doubt that Lord Randolph contracted syphilis as a young man, and that by middle age, the disease had progressed to its tertiary stage, and that this is what finally killed him, at the age of forty-five.

Because virtually all of Lord Randolph's symptoms and clinical signs, and the circumstances and the timeframe during which they developed, can be explained by the presence of syphilis, it is pure speculation on the part of Dr Mather (and others) to postulate that he may, instead, have been suffering from something entirely different, when there is little or no evidence to back up any such claims.

Notes

1. Churchill, Randolph S., *Winston S. Churchill, Youth*, 1874-1900. Companion Volume I, Dr G. Keith to Dr Roose, 4 November [1894]. p. 532.
2. Churchill, Randolph S., op cit, Winston to Lady Randolph, 2 November [1894], p. 237.
3. Browne, Anthony Montague. *Long Sunset: Memoirs of Winston Churchill's Last Private Secretary*, p. 122.
4. Julian Osgood Field, Matriculated from Merton College, Oxford 1869. Information kindly supplied by Oxford University Archives.
5. Roose, E. C. Robson 'Remarks Upon Some Diseases of the Nervous System', p. 12.
6. Churchill, Randolph S., op cit, pp. 515-16.
7. Lord Randolph Churchill to the Duchess of Marlborough, 8 October 1894. Papers of the 7th Duke of Marlborough. MARB 1/7, Churchill Archive Centre.
8. Royal College of Physicians of London MS.B.3626, RR:13:1. Correspondence between Thomas Buzzard, Robson Roose, G.E. Keith, Lord Randolph Churchill and Lady Randolph Churchill relating to Lord Randolph Churchill's state of health. Dr Keith to Dr Roose, 30 October 1894.
9. Buzzard, Dr Thomas. *Clinical Lectures on Diseases of the Nervous System*, p. 147.
10. Royal College of Physicians of London, op cit, Lord Randolph to Dr Buzzard, 8 July 1893.
11. Ibid, Dr Roose to Dr Buzzard, 4 May 1894.
12. Ibid, Lord Randolph to Dr Buzzard, 25 June 1896.
13. Ibid, Dr Keith to Dr Buzzard, 11 September 1894.

APPENDIX

14. Buzzard, Dr Thomas. 'Clinical Aspects of Syphilitic Nervous Affectations', p. 3.
15. Ibid, p. 11.
16. Royal College of Physicians of London, op cit, Report of Dr Buzzard and Dr Keith, 25 December 1894.
17. Churchill, Randolph S., op cit, Dr Thomas Buzzard to Sir Richard Quain, 1 January 1895, p. 544.
18. Royal College of Physicians of London, op cit, Dr Keith to Dr Robson Roose, Madras, 23 November 1894.
19. Lady Randolph to her sister, Leonie, 15 January 1895. Tara King Papers.
20. Dr Thomas Buzzard (1831-1919), MD, FRCP, consulting physician to the National Hospital for the Paralysed and Epileptic; Fellow of King's College, London; Vice-President of King's College Hospital; President of the Clinical, Neurological, and Harveian Societies, and corresponding member of the Société de Neurologie, Paris.
21. Sir J. Russell Reynolds (1828-1896), MRCS, FRCP, F.R.S. Professor of Medicine
at University College; President of the Royal College of Physicians.
22. Sir Richard William Gowers, MD, neurologist, clinical teacher, and author of *A Manual of Diseases of the Nervous System*.
23. *The Times*, 25 January 1895. 'Death of Lord R. Churchill'.

Bibliography

Baars, Conrad W. and Terruwe, Anna A., *Healing the Unaffirmed: Recognizing Emotional Deprivation Disorder* (New Rochelle, New York, 1972)

Balsan, Consuelo Vanderbilt, *The Glitter and the Gold* (George Mann, Maidstone, Kent, 1953)

Baron, Wendy, *Sickert* (Phaidon Press, London, 1973)

Beaverbrook, Lord, *Politicians and the War, 1914-1916* (Collins, London, 1960)

Berne, Eric, *Games People Play: The Psychology of Human Relationships* (Penguin Books, London, 1968)

Birkenhead, Earl of, *Churchill 1874-1922* (Harrap, London, 1989)

Blenheim Palace: World Heritage Site (Jarrold Publishing, Norwich, 2006)

Blunt, Wilfred S, *My Diaries* (Martin Sacker, London, 1919)

Bonham Carter, Violet, *Winston Churchill an Intimate Portrait* (Smithmark, New York, 1965)

Browne, Anthony Montague, *Long Sunset: Memoirs of Winston Churchill's Last Private Secretary* (Cassell, London, 1995)

Bryant, Arthur, *The Turn of the Tide 1939-1943.* (Grafton Books, London, 1986)

Buzzard, Dr Thomas, *Clinical Lectures on Diseases of the Nervous System* (J. & A. Churchill, London, 1882)

Cannadine, David (ed), *The Speeches of Winston Churchill* (Penguin Books, London, 1990)

Churchill, Randolph S (compiler), *Into Battle: Speeches by the Right Hon. Winston S. Churchill, CH, MP* (Cassell, London, 1941)

Churchill, Randolph S., *Winston S. Churchill*, Vol. I, *Youth, 1874-1900* and Companion Volumes in 2 parts (Heinemann, London, 1966)

Churchill, Randolph S., *Winston S. Churchill*, Vol. II, *Young Statesman*, 1900-1914, and Companion Volumes in 3 parts (Heinemann, London, 1967)

Churchill, Sarah, *A Thread in the Tapestry* (Andre Deutsch, London 1967)

Churchill, Winston S., *Great Contemporaries* (Thornton Butterworth, London, 1937)

Churchill, The Right Hon. Winston S., *The Great War* (George Newnes, London, 1933/4)

Churchill, Winston S., *Lord Randolph Churchill* (Odhams Press, London, 1905)

Churchill, Winston S., *My Early Life* (Collins, London, 1959. First published 1930)

BIBLIOGRAPHY

Churchill, Winston S., *Painting as a Pastime* (Odhams Press, London, 1949)

Churchill, Winston Spencer, (1902 Edition) *The River War* (The Echo Library, Teddington, Middlesex, 2007)

Churchill, Winston S., *Savrola* (Beacon Books, London, 1957)

Churchill, Winston S., *The Second World War, Vol. VI: Triumph and Tragedy* (Cassell, London, 1954)

Churchill, Winston S., *Thoughts and Adventures* (Odhams Press, London, 1932)

Cooper, Diana, *Trumpets from the Steep* (Hart-Davis, London, 1960)

Daintrey, Adrian, *I Must Say* (Chatto & Windus, London, 1963)

Diagnostic and Statistical Manual of Mental Disorders DSM-IV-TR. (American Psychiatric Association, Arlington, VA, USA, 2007)

Eade, Charles (ed.), *Churchill by his Contemporaries* (Hutchinson, London, 1953)

Eade, Charles (compiler), *The Unrelenting Struggle* (Cassell & Company, London, 1942)

Field, Julian Osgood, *Uncensored Recollections* (E. Nash, London, 1924)

Fieve, Ronald R., *Moodswing: The Third Revolution in Psychiatry* (Bantam Books, London, 1976)

Gelder, Michael, Harrison, Paul and Cowen, Philip, *Shorter Oxford Textbook of Psychiatry* (Oxford University Press, 2006)

Gilbert, Martin, *The Challenge of War: Winston S. Churchill 1914-1916* (Mandarin Paperbacks, London, 1990)

Gilbert, Martin, *Churchill* (Park Lane Press, London, 1979)

Gilbert, Martin, *World in Torment: Winston S. Churchill 1917-1922* (London, Mandarin Paperbacks, London, 1990)

Gilbert, Martin, *Prophet of Truth: Winston S. Churchill 1922-1939* (Mandarin Paperbacks, London, 1990)

Gilbert, Martin, *Finest Hour: Winston S. Churchill 1939-1941* (Heinemann–Mandarin, London, 1989)

Gilbert, Martin, *Road To Victory: Winston S. Churchill 1941-1945* (Mandarin Paperbacks, London, 1989)

Gilbert, Martin, *Never Despair: Winston S. Churchill 1945-1965* (Heinemann, London, 1988)

Graebner, Walter, *My Dear Mister Churchill* (Michael Joseph, London, 1965)

Harris, Frank, *My Life and Loves* (Grove Press, New York, 1963)

Hawkins, Desmond (compiler and ed), *War Report D-Day to VE-Day* (Ariel Books/British Broadcasting Corporation, London, 1985)

Hitler, Adolf, *Mein Kampf* (Jaico Publishing, Mumbai, India, 2009)

James, Robert Rhodes (ed.), *Victor Cazalet: A Portrait* (Hamish Hamilton, London, 1976)

Knight, Robert G. and Longmore, Barry E., *Clinical Neuropsychology of Alcoholism* (Lawrence Erlbaum Associates, Hove, UK and Hillsdale, USA, 1994)

Lavery, John, *The Life of a Painter* (Cassell, London, 1940)

Ledingham, John G. G., and Warrell, David A., (eds), *Concise Oxford Textbook of Medicine* (Oxford University Press, Oxford, 2000)

Lee, Celia and John, *The Churchills: A Family Portrait* (Palgrave Macmillan, New York, 2010)

Lee, Celia and John, *Winston & Jack: The Churchill Brothers* (Celia Lee, 2007)

Leslie, Anita, *Jennie: The Life of Lady Randolph Churchill* (Hutchinson, London, 1969)

Lloyd George, David, *War Memoirs of David Lloyd George* (Odhams Press, London, 1938)

Macrae, Stuart, *Winston Churchill's Toyshop* (Amberley, Chalford, Stroud, 2010)

Manchester, William, *The Last Lion: Winston Spencer Churchill* (Little, Brown & Co., Boston, 1983)

Marsh, Edward, *A Number of People* (William Heinemann, London, 1939)

Matthew, H. C. G. and Harrison, Brian (eds), *Oxford Dictionary of National Biography* (Oxford University Press, Oxford, 2004)

Meacham, Jon, *Franklin and Winston: A Portrait of a Friendship* (Granta Books, London, 2003)

Montague Browne, Anthony, *Long Sunset: Memoirs of Winston Churchill's Last Private Secretary* (Cassell, London, 1995)

Moran, Lord, *Winston Churchill: The Struggle for Survival 1940-1965* (Heron Books, London, 1966)

More, L. T., *Isaac Newton* (Charles Scribner's Sons, New York, 1934)

Nicholson, Andrew (ed.), *William Nicholson, Painter* (Giles de la Mare Publishers, London, 1996)

Pawle, Gerald, *The War and Colonel Warden* (George G Harrap, London, 1963)

Pease, Allan, *Body Language* (Sheldon Press, London, 1993)

Pottle, Mark (ed.), *Champion Redoubtable: the Diaries and Letters of Violet Bonham Carter 1914-1945* (Weidenfeld & Nicolson, London, 1998)

—, Bohhush

Roose, E. C. Robson, *Remarks Upon Some Diseases of the Nervous System,* (Brighton: Curtis Bros and Townes, 1875)

Rose, Norman, *Churchill an Unruly Life* (Simon & Schuster, London, 1994)

Rosebery, Lord, *Lord Randolph Churchill* (Arthur L. Humphreys, London, 1906)

BIBLIOGRAPHY

Rothenstein, Sir John, *Time's Thievish Progress* (Cassell, London, 1960)

Rowse, A. L., *The Churchills: The Story of a Family* (Book Club Associates, London, 1966)

Sebba, Anne, *Jennie Churchill: Winston's American Mother* (John Murray, London, 2007)

Smith, Dr Tony (medical ed.), *Complete Family Health Encyclopedia* (Dorling Kindersley, London, 1990)

Soames, Mary, *Clementine Churchill* (Cassell, London, 1979)

Soames, Mary (ed.), *Speaking for Themselves: The Personal Letters of Winston and Clementine Churchill* (Black Swan, London, 1999)

Soames, Mary, *Winston Churchill: His Life as a Painter* (Collins, London, 1990)

Spitz, René A., *Psychoanalytic Study of the Child*, 'Hospitalism: Genesis of Psychiatric Conditions in Early Childhood', 1: 53-74, 1945

Stahl, Stephen M., *Essential Pharmacology* (Cambridge University Press, Cambridge, 2000)

Storr, Anthony, *Churchill's Black Dog and Other Phenomena of the Human Mind* (Flaming, London, 1991)

Sturgis, Matthew, *Walter Sickert* (Harper Perennial, London, 2005)

Thompson, Walter H., *I was Churchill's Shadow* (Christopher Johnson, London, 1955)

Ward, Mrs E. M. (ed. Elliott O'Donnell), *Reminiscences* (Pitman Publishing, London, 1911)

Wheeler-Bennett, Sir John (ed.), *Action this Day: Working with Churchill* (Macmillan, London, 1969)

World Health Organization, *International Classification of Diseases*, 2007

*Film Documentaries

*Churchill, BBC Enterprises Ltd, 1993. A BBC-TV Production in association with The Arts and Entertainment Network and the Australian Broadcasting Corporation, © British Broadcasting Corporation and BBC Enterprises Limited, MCMXCIII.

*Churchill: The Greatest Briton of All Time, A TW1/Carlton Production, 2003, © TW1/Carlton Television.

*Churchill's Bodyguard, 2005, Nugus/Martin Productions Ltd., for BBC Worldwide Ltd and UKTV History, © Nugus/Martin Productions Ltd.

*Chasing Churchill: In Search of my Grandfather with Celia Sandys: To The Other Country, 2008, Discovery Knowledge.

Index